D0717364

THE
GLASGOW
BOOK
OF
DAYS

NORMAN FERGUSON

NOTE ON TEXT

For ease of reading, some of the older material has been edited for punctuation or meaning. The author is responsible for any mistranscription of older material, or for any other errors.

First published 2013

The History Press
The Mill, Brimscombe Port
Stroud, Gloucestershire, GL5 2QG
www.thehistorypress.co.uk

British Library Cataloguing in Publication Data.
A catalogue record for this book is available from the British Library.

ISBN 978 0 7524 7657 5

Typesetting and origination by The History Press
Printed in India

JANUARY 1ST

1784: 'Notice. The brewers in and about Glasgow having hitherto found much inconvenience from the practice of giving presents to their customers at New Year's Day are therefore resolved to discontinue that practice in future.' (*Old Glasgow and its Environs*)

———◆———

Late eighteenth century: 'Among the amusement of the lower classes in those days, perhaps the most reprehensible was the practice of shooting cocks at Govan on New Year's Day. On the morning of that day the road to this village might have been seen crowded with idle boys and half-tipsy operatives hurrying along armed with fowling pieces and guns of various forms and calibres in expectation of being able to bring home a cock to their dinner. The poor cock was tied to a stake and had no chance of escape. The price of a shot was one penny and whoever killed this noble bird received its carcass as the reward of his dexterity. On every New Year's Day Govan was the resort of a blackguard half-drunken mob who in addition to cock shooting passed the day at throwing the cudgel for gingerbread cakes and the like sports while there was free scope for all manner of thimblerigging.' (*Glasgow: Past and Present*)

JANUARY 2ND

1971: The New Year Old Firm game between Celtic and Rangers was drawing to a close at Ibrox Stadium. A crowd of around 75,000 had seen Celtic go ahead in the final minute. When fans started to make their way out, Rangers scored a dramatic equaliser to make it 1-1. On a stairway at the east end, a crush started. It was commonly thought that the accident was caused by fans trying to return back up the stairway, following the late Rangers goal, but the official enquiry stated the reason was that one or more of the fans had lost their footing. Sixty-six fans died and 145 were injured on Stairway Thirteen. Of those who died, the youngest was eight years old, attending his first football match. Five boys from the Fife town of Markinch were also killed. Celtic manager Jock Stein, who had helped give assistance to the victims, said afterwards: 'When human life is at stake, as it was after the barriers crashed, then bigotry and bitterness seem sordid little things. Fans of both sides will never forget this disaster.' It was the worst disaster in Scottish football and led to a major renovation of Ibrox to prevent it happening again. Legislation was subsequently brought in to ensure improved safety at football grounds.

JANUARY 3RD

1746: On this day, Jacobite forces under the Young Pretender, Charles Edward Stuart, left Glasgow, where they had spent time after retreating northwards from Derby. Many years later, a Dr Thom wrote of a witness's recollections of the Highlanders being in the town:

> I have conversed with only two other individuals who remembered anything personally concerning the affairs of 1745-6. One was Mr William Walker, who died, I think, in 1820. Well do I remember his taking me, in 1815, to a spot in the Saltmarket, two or three doors from my father's shop, and mentioning that under the then piazza, close to where we were, he had stood and seen the rebel army pass up from the review on the Green. The Pretender rode at their head. He was pale and, in Mr. Walker's apprehension, looked dejected. He said that he had a distinct recollection of Bonnie Prince Charlie after the lapse of 70 years. He saw the rebel forces, when they had reached the Cross, turn to the left, and march along the Trongate, on their way to Shawfield House, at the bottom of the present Glassford Street, then the residence and head-quarters of the Chevalier. Mr Walker was then, he told me, about ten years of age.

(*Glasgow: Past and Present*)

January 4th

1640: George Anderson was the first printer in Glasgow. He printed the reports of the famous General Assembly held in 1638. The Town Council records on this recorded his remuneration:

> This said day ordains the tresaurer to pay to George Anderson, printer, one hundred pounds, in satisfaction to him, of the surplus he disbursed in transporting of his gear to the burgh, by the ten dollars he gave him of before to that effect and also in satisfaction to him of his previous service from Whitsunday in 1638 to Martinmas last.

(Town Council records)

———— ◆ ————

1690: 'The freedom bestowed by the Revolution extended to the city of Glasgow. William and Mary, by their charter of this day, declared the town free and in the confirmation of this charter by act of parliament in 14 June 1690, it is inserted that they shall have power and privilege to elect their own magistrates, provost, baillies, and other officers within the burgh, as fully, and as freely, in all respects, as the city of Edinburgh, or any other royal burgh within the kingdom; and this freedom of election continues to this day.' (*The History of Glasgow*)

January 5th

1764: 'To the lovers of real curiosities. The brother of the famous Mr Zucker is just come to town, and will perform at the White Hart, in the Gallowgate. He had the honour to perform his surprising feats of arts, with general approbation, before the Royal family, nobility, and gentry in London. He has brought with him the most amazing learned little horse from Courland, whose wonderful knowledge is not to be paralleled by any animal in this kingdom, or perhaps in the whole world. As a specimen of his abilities, we shall mention the following particulars: He makes a polite and curious compliment to the company; tells the value of anything which is shown to him; he plays at cards, and finds the place where the card is hid; shows by a watch the hour of the day, and understands arithmetic; he distinguishes ladies from gentlemen; he plays at dice and is always sure to win; he drinks the company's health like a human person; his master borrows a piece of money of one of the company, and throws it on the floor; the horse takes it up, and returns it to the person that lent it.' (*Glasgow Journal*)

JANUARY 6TH

1876: 'Slander Case. The pursuer resides at 122 Cumberland Street, and he sues the defender, who is his nephew, for £1,000 in damages in respect of an alleged slander contained in a letter written by defender to pursuer. The allegation is that the defender called the pursuer "a low, sneaking fellow" and threatened to "kick him within an inch of his dishonoured life". It is further alleged that the defender accused the pursuer of having been hired by an Australian Jew to bring home a woman of bad fame, whom he introduced to his family as a respectable lady, and that whenever the Jew's purpose was served he had "dropped him (the pursuer) like a hot potato".' (*Glasgow Herald*)

———— • ◆ • ————

1931: 'Sentence of three months' imprisonment was imposed at Glasgow Sheriff Court on Joan Williamson (19) who pleaded guilty to a charge of culpable homicide. The Depute Fiscal remarked that the case, while distressing, was not uncommon nowadays. The girl, he said, started work in October last as a domestic servant in a house in Paisley. On December 16th she complained of feeling ill and her mistress had her sent home. Later a charwoman discovered the body of a child in a cupboard, and a post-mortem examination revealed that the child had been born alive and had been strangled.' (*Glasgow Herald*)

JANUARY 7TH

1450: The University of Glasgow was founded by a papal bull issued on this day by Pope Nicholas V:

> Amongst other blessings which mortal man is able in this transient life to obtain, it is to be reckoned that by assiduous study he may win the pearl of knowledge, which shows him the way to live well and happily, and by the preciousness thereof makes the man of learning far to surpass the unlearned, and opens the door for him clearly to understand the mysteries of the Universe, helps the ignorant, and raises to distinction those that were born in the lowest place. It was lately shown to us on behalf of James, the illustrious King of Scots, that the King was very desirous that a university should be set up in Glasgow, as being a place of reknown and particularly well fitted therefore, where the air is mild, victuals are plentiful, and great store of other things pertaining to the use of man is found, to the end that there the Catholic faith may be spread, the simple instructed, equity in judgement upheld, reason flourish, the minds of men illuminated, and their understandings enlightened.

(University of Glasgow Archive Services)

JANUARY 8TH

1798: 'Just arrived, and to be seen for a few days at the head of Miller Street, in four large broad-wheeled magnificent caravans, drawn by twenty horses, the largest assemblage of chosen Living Rarities that ever travelled this kingdom in the age of memory of man – consisting of a most stupendous Male Elephant, the largest ever seen in England. The sagacity and knowledge of this animal is absolutely beyond any thing that human imagination can possibly suggest. It will lie down and rise again at the word of command. Also, a real Bengal-striped Royal Male Tiger. The whole animal is streaked in this admirable manner, so as to appear to the distant beholder as if curiously covered with ribbons. A South American Vulture or Condor Minor, from the Brasils. Its wings, when extended, measure eight feet, and in a wild state will carry away a lamb with ease. A most beautiful Horned Horse. The wonderful Heifer with two heads. Four horns, four eyes, four ears and four nostrils, through each of which it breathes. One of the heads, together with the horns, represents that of a bull, the other, a cow. Is universally allowed to be the most astonishing phenomenon in nature. Admittance, one shilling each.'
(*Glasgow Advertiser*)

JANUARY 9TH

1801: This notice was printed in the *Glasgow Advertiser* on this day:

A Coal Work. Three miles east from Glasgow. To be sold, by roup, near the Exchange on Wednesday 19th February. That tack of coal, now wrought by the Eastmuir Coal Work Company, at Eastmuir near Shettleston. Along with the tack there will be sold, a good steam engine, two gins with ropes and tubs, several horses and cars and an excellent weighing machine. Also the benefit of a piece of land, with several brick houses and a stable, and counting house built thereon by the company. The exposers claim to the service of the colliers will be included in the sale. This field of coal consists of about 20 acres containing five workable seams and a part only of the upper seam has been wrought. Three pits have been sunk to this coal. Many superior advantages attend this work, among others the coal is of the best quality and the work is conveniently situated close to that spacious new road leading from Glasgow to Edinburgh, by Airdrie, whence there is scarcely any expense incurred in maintaining a road to the Hill and from the quality of the coals this work has always had a great command of sale.

JANUARY 10TH

1787: A series of reports appeared in the *Glasgow Mercury* beginning on this date recounting a street robbery:

> Late on Friday night a gentleman (Mr Wilsone) on his way home was knocked down by two fellows, at the west end of Argyle Street, and robbed of between six and seven pounds in notes and silver, with a case containing a number of surgeon's instruments and other articles. Besides robbing him, they gave him several severe blows when lying on the ground. The case with the instruments was found in a stair-case in the Saltmarket, on Monday night but the robbers have not been discovered, though diligent search has been made for them.

A week later:

> Friday last, Thomas Veitch, shoemaker, and John M'Aulay, stockingmaker, were apprehended on suspicion of knocking down and robbing Mr Charles Wilsone, surgeon. Mr Wilsone's gloves were found upon one of them, and on the other, one of his small silver cases for holding matter for inoculating for the small-pox. Veitch is about 22 years of age, and was lately whipped out of the 63rd Regiment. M'Aulay is about 19 years old. It is said they belong to a gang of twenty.

16th April:

> John M'Aulay and Thomas Veitch are to be hanged on the 23rd of May next.

JANUARY 11TH

1781: In the *Glasgow Mercury* on this day, the following advertisement appeared:

> By Permission. Just arrived in this City, and to be seen at Mr Heron's, at the Bull, the surprising Irish Giant. Only twenty years old, yet measures eight feet high, who is allowed to be the most extraordinary man for size and proportion that ever appeared in Europe. Admission, 1s each. Hours of admittance, from eleven in the forenoon till three in the afternoon, and from four till nine o'clock at night. To continue one week only.

The giant seems to have been very well pleased with his reception in Glasgow for, in the same newspaper a week later, we find the following intimation:

> The Irish Giant presents his most respectful compliments to the ladies and gentlemen of Glasgow, and desires to inform them that (by permission) he intends to remain at his lodgings, at the Bull, one week from the date hereof.

(*Old Glasgow and its Environs*)

January 12th

1790: A now well-known area of the city was offered for sale in the *Glasgow Mercury* on this day:

Sale of land in Lanarkshire. To be sold, by auction, in the Tontine Tavern, on Wednesday, 27th January, 1790. The villa and lands of Kelvingrove, beautifully situated upon the banks of the river Kelvin, and perfectly retired, although within one mile of the city of Glasgow. The house, which overlooks the river, is built upon a very comfortable plan, containing a dining room, drawing room, eight bed rooms, two lumber rooms, a kitchen, larder, and three cellars under ground. The offices consist of a stable, with stalls for four horses, a cow house, milk house, chaise and cart house, a hay loft, pigeon house, poultry houses, all in the most complete order. The garden (which, as well as the offices, is hid from the dwelling house by trees and shrubbery), is well stocked with fruit trees and small fruit, and is surrounded by a brick wall, and the whole of it is at present covered on both sides with a great variety of fruit trees of the best kinds. The lands of Kelvingrove and the grounds under lease for near half-a-mile are bounded by the river Kelvin, and being surrounded on all hands by beautiful landscapes, form such a situation as is rarely to be met with.

January 13th

614: St Kentigern died on this day. He is also known as St Mungo, the name stemming from the Welsh language term Mwyn-gu (dear friend). It is said that his mother Thenew was cast from the top of Traprain Law in East Lothian when her father, the King of Lothian, discovered she was pregnant. She boarded a small boat which found land across the Forth at what is now Culross in Fife, where St Mungo was born. He lived a frugal and spiritual life and was a contemporary of St Columba. St Mungo set up a church on the site of what is now Glasgow Cathedral. It is believed he is buried within the cathedral. Mungo's legacy is the city of Glasgow – his missionary work inspired a community to grow in the 'dear green place'. His work also gave rise to Glasgow's famous verse that inspired the city's coat of arms, with each line referring to a miracle he reputedly performed:

Here is the bird that never flew.
Here is the tree that never grew.
Here is the bell that never rang.
Here is the fish that never swam.

The city's motto, 'Let Glasgow flourish', also derives from a sermon delivered by St Mungo.

JANUARY 14TH

1909: 'Distress in Glasgow. Investigations Criticised. The Glasgow Distress Committee met yesterday in the City Chambers. A letter was read from Mr JT Howden on behalf of the Glasgow Unemployed Workers' Committee, drawing attention to the number of applicants rejected, the reason given being "No dependants". The printed regulations of the Local Government Board said that a preference might be given in certain circumstances and it appeared to them that the Distress Committee was interpreting "may" as "shall". In many cases, men without dependants were in as bad a position as those with dependants. They therefore appealed to the committee to relax this interpretation so that at least a chance to live would be given their unfortunate brethren. They also asked them to give full effect to the principle to the right of every human being to earn his or her bread by honest work by passing all applicants and thus give even the so-called bad characters a chance of redemption.' (*Glasgow Herald*)

JANUARY 15TH

1784: 'By letters from Edinburgh, we are informed that Mr Breslaw closes his Exhibition there on Saturday next: and we are to assure the Public, that those Variety of New Entertainments will be displayed at Mr Heron's great room in the Black Bull Inn, Glasgow, as follows: Several select pieces of Music; the First Violin by a foreign Young Lady, and Whistling the Notes by Sieur Arcalani. A variety of Deceptions, quite new, by Mr Breslaw, the particulars of which are expressed in the Bills. A Solo on the Violin by Miss Florella, who has had the honour lately of performing before their Majesties and the Royal Family and several Magical Card Deceptions by Sieur Andrea. The imitation of various Birds, by the New Venetian Rosignole, lately arrived from Naples. The whole to conclude with a New Invented Silver Cup, and more than Fifty other Deceptions too numerous to insert. The Room will be elegantly illuminated, warm, and commodiously prepared. Admittance two shillings each person. Any Person inclined to learn some deceptions, they may be taught in a few minutes, on reasonable terms, by applying to Mr Breslaw at the place above-mentioned.' (*Glasgow Mercury*)

JANUARY 16TH

1872: 'Yesterday at the Sheriff Small Debt Court, James Rhind Gibson, Elderslie Street, sued William Glover, Theatre Royal, for *2s 6d*, being the balance of a week's wage due. Charles Webb, who appeared for the defender, stated that the pursuer had been late in attending a rehearsal, and that, according to the rules of the Theatre, he was fined in the sum of *2s 6d*. The pursuer denied ever having seen the rules and said it was an unusual thing to fine a principal actor. On the day in question he was late, by leave granted by Mr Webb. Mr Webb said he had given the pursuer half an hour's leave, but instead of appearing at the proper time, he was an hour late. The pursuer denied this statement, and said that he was in attendance half an hour after the others had been called and was therefore only half an hour late. The Sheriff was of opinion that certain rules must be observed and fines imposed for actors being late. He did not think that in the present case the fine was heavy but as there had been faults on both sides he would punish them both and decern for *1s 3d* and half costs. (Laughter.) Parties then left the bar apparently quite satisfied with the decision.' (*Glasgow Herald*)

January 17th

1928: On this day Matt McGinn was born in Ross Street, Calton. He was one of nine children and was sent to approved school when aged twelve. He received a trade union scholarship to attend Ruskin College in Oxford. He returned to Scotland and became a teacher. After a few years he left teaching to devote all his time to writing and performing, whether it was songs, books, poems or plays. He played a large part in the folk revival of the 1960s. As a prolific writer he is said to have written over 1,000 songs, amongst them 'Red Yo Yo', 'The Wee Kirkcudbright Centipede', 'If It Wasn't For The Union' and 'Magic Shadow Show'. Matt McGinn had strong socialist beliefs which underpinned his view of the world, and when he died in 1977, his ashes were scattered over the grave of John MacLean – McGinn's hero. He once was asked to sign a visitors' book and seeing a name in the book of a member of the landed gentry decided to adopt the format. He signed it 'McGinn of the Calton'.

JANUARY 18TH

1790: This advertisement was printed in the *Glasgow Advertiser* dated this day:

Mercantile Diligence. Between Glasgow and Greenock, to hold Three Passengers. At the particular desire of a number of Gentlemen, a new Diligence is now begun to run every lawful day, at eleven o'clock forenoon, from Colin MacFarlane's Buck's Head Inn and at the same hour, from Mr Gibson's Rue End, Greenock. Tickets 6s, to be had at the Buck's Head Inn and at William Cockburn's Iron Rail Stair, Trongate. Parcels entered in the way-bill with the strictest attention, as well as carefully delivered at each place immediately on the arrival of the Diligence, a person being appointed for that purpose. The Diligence to stop each day at Crosshill (where the company may dine if agreeable) and will also call at Mr Buchanan's, Port Glasgow. Each passenger to be allowed one stone of luggage. NB – The proprietors will not be accountable for any parcel or package above One Guinea value.

JANUARY 19TH

1932: 'Employment in 1931. Though there had been a slight improvement in employment during the early months of 1931, a further decline began in June which continued until the end of September, when the highest number of unemployment ever recorded in Great Britain was reached. The estimated number of insured work people in employment in Great Britain rose from 9,215,000 in January 1931 to 9,516,000 in May but after some fluctuation fell to 9,326,000 in September. By December however it had risen to 9,593,000 as compared with 9,475,000 in December of the previous year. There was substantial improvement in most of the textile industries and some improvement also in the clothing trades, and in iron and steel manufacturing (except pig iron). The industries mostly contributing to the increase in unemployment were building and public works contracting, coal mining, engineering, motor vehicle manufacture, shipbuilding, and the distributive trades. The average percentage rates during 1931 of unemployment among insured persons were 12.8 in London, 12.0 in the South East, and 26.6 in Scotland. The average in Great Britain and Northern Ireland was 21.3 per cent. Figures for those registered at Glasgow Job Exchanges in December: Men – 96,793; Women –17,531; Juveniles – 6,124. Difference from November 4.6 per cent.' (*Glasgow Herald*)

JANUARY 20TH

1883: 'Terrible Explosions in Glasgow. Gasometer destroyed at Tradeston. Eleven persons injured. Shortly after ten o'clock, the inhabitants of Pollokshields and the neighbourhood were startled by an explosion the nature of which could not at the moment be surmised, although the impression instantaneously conveyed to the mind was that some terrible calamity had occurred. The air was first disturbed by a profound, concentrated shock, succeeded by a rumbling noise which continued for a second or two, and affected the nerves not less painfully. Glancing northward in the direction of the city it seemed as if a fire were raging in the neighbourhood of the harbour, scanning the sky to the east, the upward glow was seen to be much more vivid in that quarter, and with a sickening dread the mind reverted to Tradeston Gasworks. When the gas in dwelling houses became perceptibly lower, and for a little time appeared likely to go out altogether, there was no longer any doubt as to the source of the disturbance.' (*Glasgow Herald*)

The explosion was part of a bombing campaign orchestrated by Irish republicans, who also set off explosives at Buchanan Street station.

JANUARY 21ST

1919: 'Glasgow Street Fighting. Unprecedented scenes of violence and bloodshed took place in Glasgow in connection with the present strike movement. A huge crowd had assembled in George Square to hear the reply on behalf of the Government to the request for intervention made through the Lord Provost. Owing to a section of the strikers persisting in refusing to allow the tramcars to proceed the police made a baton charge on the crowd, and this was later repeated. In the course of the struggle which occurred, William Gallacher, who had been addressing the crowd outside the City Chambers, and David Kirkwood, who had formed one of the deputation to the Lord Provost, were injured and were subsequently placed under arrest, and will, it is understood, be charged with inciting to riot. Two other men were also arrested. Owing to the serious aspect of affairs Sheriff Mackenzie, after consultation, proceeded to the front of the City Chambers for the purpose of reading the Riot Act. After representation, Gallacher and Kirkwood were allowed to address the crowd. They advised the crowd to leave for the Green, where further conflicts with the police took place.' (*Glasgow Herald*)

JANUARY 22ND

1610: 'George Smyth, winder of the prison clock, is bound to the town to wind up the tolbooth clock, for all the days of his lifetime, for the sum of twenty pounds yearly, during his thankful service. And suchlike obliges him to wind up the high kirk clock, and keep the same in working order, and visit there two days of the week.' (Town Council records)

———— • ◆ • ————

1726: 'The Magistrates represented that they had met with the proprietors of the sugar houses, and had received from them some proposals: That, upon the town's exempting their servants from keeping of the town guard, they agree that the sugar boiler of each of their sugar houses, with their servants, shall be ready at all times when fire happens in the city, to give their best help and assistance, the town providing each sugar house with four slings, and stands and buckets, so that, upon the first occasion of fire, they shall come to the place with them filled with water.' (*Glasgow and its Clubs*)

———— • ◆ • ————

1787: 'A pickpocket being detected last week in the practice of his profession at Glasgow, was sentenced by the mob to lose an ear in the public marketplace, and the sentence was immediately carried into execution.' (*The Times*)

JANUARY 23RD

1778: 'On this day, about eleven o'clock, the adjutant of the Glasgow Volunteers arrived here and brought recruiting orders. In consequence of which, the magistrates and inhabitants, actuated by that zeal for the honour and prosperity of their country, which has on many former occasions distinguished this loyal city, eminently exerted themselves in promoting the present business. On Monday, at noon, the bells were set a ringing; the magistrates and town council, the deacons of the fourteen incorporated trades, and a great number of gentlemen, convened in the council chamber, from whence the following procession began:

1 The city sergeants to clear the way.
2 The magistrates.
3 The adjutant of the regiment.
4 The colours, borne by two young gentlemen, supported by two others with guns and fixed bayonets.
5 The sergeants of the regiment.
6 Two young gentlemen playing on fifes.
7 Two young gentlemen beating drums.
8 A gentleman playing on the bagpipes.
9 The members of the town council, the late deacon convener, the present convener and the deacons of the fourteen corporations.
10 The sovereign of the Cape Club, supported by two of the members.
11 A great number of gentlemen with cocades in their hats.'
(*Glasgow Mercury*)

January 24th

1898: 'The People's Palace on Glasgow Green was formally opened on the afternoon of Saturday by the Right Hon the Earl of Rosebery. The ceremony took place in the winter garden, which was specially fitted up for the purpose. The entire extent of the spacious interior was provided with seats, giving accommodation for between 3,000 and 4,000 persons. The Lord Provost said: "In some cases the wheels of the municipal machine move slowly, and the structure in which we are now assembled is a case in point. This erection was first spoken of so far back as 1839 but not until 1895 was it possible to make a practicable beginning. As your Lordship knows, the building is situated in the manufacturing and industrial portion of Glasgow where the residenters are largely composed of the working classes. The corporation felt that while erecting handsome and commodious premises in the West End for the adequate housing of their treasures, they should not neglect the claims of the inhabitants of the East End to some consideration in the direction of affording them similar facilities for intellectual and artistic culture.' (*Glasgow Herald*)

January 25th

1612: 'Richard Herbertson is accused of a most barbarous attack by him against James Watson, elder, flesher, and his son Jon Watson, in the house of Archibald Schelis, merchant, and on the next morning for striking James Watson's great dog, most necessary and profitable for him, worth to him the sum of 40 pounds, and that upon the complaint made by James Watson and his son Jon, craving to be freed of his oppression, threats and attacks in future and to make James satisfactory recompense for his dog. The said Richard, personally present and accused, confessed the undeserved malicious striking of the dog. Thereafter Jon Watson gave his oath that he feared Herbertson for bodily harm and for his life. All things considered the provost, baillies, and council said that Richard is of dissolute life and disparate in himself and ordained the said Richard to be imprisoned until Monday next, and that day be placed in the stocks at the cross, and the dog to be laid before him and thereafter to be put in prison until he finds securities for the said J Watson, that he shall be harmless and uninjuring of him in body, goods, and possessions.' (*Memorabilia of the City of Glasgow*)

January 26th

1889: This letter appeared in the *Glasgow Herald* on this day:

Sir, Within the past few weeks, a considerable amount of publicity has been given to certain remarks made by an East End clergyman of our city to his congregation on the subject of coughing in church. While admitting that the rebuke of the reverend gentleman might have been couched in milder terms, I am inclined to take the opinion that it was not wholly uncalled for. Many of his brethren, I doubt not, feel as keenly on the matter as he does, but hesitate to express their objections in the open and fearless manner adopted by the minister of St Luke's. That excessive coughing in church is objectionable, no one will deny. In the first place, it interferes with the comfort of the cougher's fellow worshippers and prevents them giving close attention to the preacher. It also distracts the mind of the preachers, especially if he, as in the case of the above-named minister, delivers his discourse without the aid of either notes or manuscript. One cougher sets a dozen a-going and so the epidemic spreads until it becomes almost universal. Of course I do not include persons suffering from severe colds as their good sense will teach them to remain at home. I am, etc. Respect.

JANUARY 27TH

1638: 'This day it is ordained that the wall at the cross to be taken down and made equal at the paving, in the best form that can be devised by craftsmen, and that the provost, bailies, dean of guild and deacon convenor, speak and deal with James Colquhoun, to draw and convey down the spouts of the tolbooth in most comely form that can be for directing of the drop to fall upon the flagstones, and that upon as cheap a price as they can.' (*Memorabilia of the City of Glasgow*)

———◆———

2004: On this day the well-loved entertainer Rikki Fulton died aged seventy-nine. He had been suffering from Alzheimer's disease. Rikki Fulton had started his entertainment career in radio and amateur theatre work. He went on to form a memorable double act with Jack Milroy where they played Francie and Josie. Fulton starred in the BBC TV comedy show *Scotch and Wry* playing characters such as the dour Church of Scotland minister Reverend I.M. Jolly and Supercop, the hapless motorcycle traffic policeman. The most memorable sketch saw Fulton as the Rangers manager, signing a young player who had scored seven goals in the first half but none in the second, as he had to go to Mass.

January 28th

1967: Rangers went out of the Scottish Cup at the hands of another football team bearing their name: Berwick Rangers. Only one goal separated the two clubs, although a wider gulf existed. Rangers were one of the biggest teams in the land, the current cup holders, while Berwick were a part-time club in the Scottish Second Division. Berwick, who although located in England played in the Scottish leagues, were given little chance of success in the run-up to the first-round game. Berwick's Sammy Reid scored in the thirty-second minute to create one of the biggest upsets in Scottish football history. Rangers captain John Greig described the defeat as 'probably the worst result in the history of our club'. Berwick's player-manager, Jock Wallace, later became Rangers manager and was coach at the Ibrox club when they won the European Cup Winners' Cup in 1972. After their win over the Gers, Berwick lost in the next round to Hibs.

January 29th

1736: The chimes from the Tolbooth's bells were not deemed to be satisfying. A minute in the Town Council's records described moves to improve the situation:

> This day, considering that the Town is under contract with Andrew Dick, Clockmaker in Stirling, to put up a new chime of bells, and that the magistrates have written to London for casting the said bells, which are expected here shortly, but that by the agreement they are not to be played upon by the hand, so that, unless a new bell be cast B flat, which will not be much cost, and cannot be done in a more proper time than now, in regard both the ways can be carried up at a time, and would be chargeable to do thereafter, the magistrates and council agree to the above, and remit to the magistrates to write to London for the said odd bell.

However, the resulting work was not to prove long-lasting, as three years later the council ordered new bells from Edinburgh. (*Sketch of the History of Glasgow*)

JANUARY 30TH

1915: On this day the *Glasgow Herald* published responses to 600,000 recruiting circulars sent in the West of Scotland:

A widow whose only son went to the front and was wounded at Mons writes: 'He is my only son. I have given him willingly, knowing the great need.' Another writes: 'I am a widow and could have done well with my boy (a splendid boy of 27 years) at home. Still, I am proud he is fighting for his country. My only other son is a boy of 11 years, just wishing he was 19 and had he been I would have been proud to let him go.' A lady whose three sons have enlisted says: 'That is them all. If every British mother gives all the sons she has got the war will soon be finished and Germany put down, never to rise again.'

The suggestion formerly made of an Amazon's Battalion is received with increasing favour and if the Corporation get Lord Kitchener's permission to form one there will be no difficulty filling it. A young lady of 20 says: 'I can promise you my two sisters also. We are all members of the Glasgow Women's Rifle Club and crack shots. We guarantee to lay out any Germans at 200 yards with great pleasure.'

JANUARY 31ST

1589: 'John Neill, cordiner, was made burgess without fee for furnishing yearly during his lifetime upon Fastern's E'en (Shrove Tuesday) of six good and sufficient footballs, or else twenty shillings as the price thereof.' (*Extracts from the Records of the Burgh of Glasgow*, 1881)

1638: 'Robert Fleming and his partners made offer to the Town Council to set up a manufactory in the City wherein a number of the poorer sort of people may be employed provided they met with sufficient countenance. On considering which offer the Council resolved in consideration of the great good utility and profit which will redound to the City to give the said company a lease of their great lodging and backyard in the Drygate excepting the two front vaults free of rent for the space of seventeen years. On 8th May thereafter the Deacon Convener reported that the freemen weavers were afraid that the erecting of the manufactory would prove hurtful to them. On which Patrick Bell one of the partners agreed that the Company should not employ any unfree weavers of the town.' (*Enumeration of the inhabitants of the city of Glasgow and county of Lanark, for the government census of 1831: with population and statistical tables relative to England and Scotland* by James Cleland, 1832)

FEBRUARY 1ST

1816: This report appeared in the *Caledonian Mercury* on this day:

Monday night, at eleven o'clock, a party of men collected at the burying ground of the High Church and fired a shot, while a party in the inside were employed watching a grave. A party of the police patrol were called and the men went away. About one o'clock the assistance of the patrol was again called for by the people watching the grave, who had a young man, a student, in custody. It is said that he, along with others, had entered the church-yard, and intended, the watchers supposed, to violate a grave only a short distance from the spot where they were stationed. The patrol had to be reinforced on account of the vast number of men collected round the ground. A large bag was found in the church-yard, probably intended to receive some corpse. The prisoner was on Tuesday sent to the Council Chambers.

FEBRUARY 2ND

1781: The *Glasgow Mercury* on this day printed the following notice regarding the statue of King William:

> Yesterday se'ennight, a young man, disordered in his mind by intemperance, got upon the pedestal on which the equestrian statue of King William stands, and mounted the horse, when his frenzy led him to cut off the laurel with which the statue was crowned, and otherwise maltreat it. What is surprising, he got up and down without receiving any hurt. He is since confined in the cells.

———◆———

1872: 'The Cotton Spinner and the Short-Time Movement. The hand mule cotton spinners of Scotland have issued a circular to their employers, requesting a reduction of the working hours from 60 to 55 per week, the new arrangement to commence on the 1st of March 1872. An increase of 5 per cent on the present price list, to be added to the piecers' wages, is also requested.' (*Glasgow Herald*)

FEBRUARY 3RD

1921: The Scottish Motor Show was taking place on this day at the Kelvin Hall and the *Glasgow Herald* printed some appropriate adverts:

The invincible Chevrolet. Stand 139 – Light delivery van £365. Stand 43-5 Passenger touring £450. H Prosser, Hope St.

Stand 22. First to lead and still leading. The new Panhard – 'Lasts for ever'. Immediate delivery. Any type of body supplied. Sole Scottish Agents – The Glasgow Automobile Co Ltd, West George St.

The most popular Light Car – The Albert, all weather model. Price £786 complete. Including two spare wheels, complete with tyres and free insurance for 12 months. Equipment: CAV lighting and self starter, five CAV lamps, day clock, speedometer, powerful electric horn, complete set of tools. Has all the advantages of a completely enclosed body and an open touring body. Call at Stand 11. See it and get full particulars from the sole Glasgow agent: the Botanic Gardens Garage, Vincombe Street.

Visitors to the show will find much to interest them at the Western Motor Company's stands 32 and 142 where a varied selection of the world's best pleasured and commercial cars are on view: Beardmore, Belsize, Buick, Cadillac, Delaunay-Belleville, Garford, Guy, Hampton, Karrier, Oldsmobile, Oveland, Ruston-Hornsby, Sizaire-Berwick, Talbot.

FEBRUARY 4TH

1842: 'Edinburgh and Glasgow Railway. On Monday the Directors of this splendid undertaking made the first complete trip along the line from end to end, with the view of inspecting the state of the works previous to the public opening. Shortly after nine o'clock in the morning a train left this city and after proceeding up the inclined plane and spending some time in the inspection of the workshops and other works at the Cowlairs station, the party made a fair start for Edinburgh about ten o'clock, which city they reached in about two hours and a quarter, it being deemed necessary to proceed at a moderate rate in consequence of the state of the weather. The length of the line is 40 miles. On their arrival at the Edinburgh terminus, the Glasgow party joined the portion of the directors belonging to that locality and the whole set out westwards on their trip of inspection of the stations and other works on their way, and reached Glasgow after a pleasant run of about three hours' duration.' (*Glasgow Herald*)

The railway line was officially opened two weeks later.

FEBRUARY 5TH

1901: 'The Lord Provost was perfectly right in deprecating any undue discussion of the present outbreak of smallpox. There is no occasion for panic, and everything likely to create excitement and alarm in the public mind should be avoided. The city showed an excellent example of philosophic calm during the brief incursion of bubonic plague a few months ago and one may hope that its reputation for cool commonsense will not suffer on the present occasion. Dr Chalmers expressed the belief that "the free movement of mild and unrecognised cases among a population largely susceptible to the disease from inefficient vaccination" is one of the chief factors in the rapid extension of smallpox. Mr Watson wanted to know whether persons whom the sanitary authorities look upon as in a manner under suspicion either through having been in contact with a patient or through having shown certain symptoms, are allowed to travel in the public conveyances and visit their friends on the way to the reception house. The answer was to the effect that while infirm people and children are conveyed in the ambulance, "in other cases they are instructed to proceed on foot direct to the reception house." We note these possibilities merely to call attention to what seems a weak point in the sanitary cordon.' (*Glasgow Herald*)

FEBRUARY 6TH

1885: These short articles appeared in the *Glasgow Herald* on this day:

Extension of hours in a Clyde Yard. Messrs A & J Inglis, Pointhouse, have intimated an extension of the working week. At present Messrs Inglis's employees work 39 hours a week but on and after the 13th instant the time will be extended to 48 hours.

Emigration from the Clyde. During the month of January, 785 emigrants of whom 503 were British and 282 foreigners, sailed from the Clyde. Of that number 747 went to the United States, 33 to Canada and 5 to Australia and New Zealand.

An Intoxicated Youth. In the Western Police Court a boy named James Belfort, 14 years of age, residing at 63 Alain Street, pleaded guilty to having been found in an intoxicated state in North Street. It was stated that he was brought to the police in a cab, and laid in the waiting room, where he was attended by Dr Johnston, district surgeon, for upwards of five hours, waiting for signs of returning consciousness. It was not until about seven o'clock yesterday morning that the lad was able to give his name and he stated that he got the whisky from a boy who was employed in a grocer's shop. He was fined 7s 6d with the option of five days' imprisonment.

FEBRUARY 7TH

1694: 'On this day Robert Park was elected town clerk. Later that year Park was involved in a dispute with an army major over some men suspected of being deserters. During the investigation Park, having made use of some expressions which incensed Major Menzies, the Major drew his sword and ran Park through the body. The Major immediately absconded and was pursued. He was overtaken in Renfield Garden where he was shot by one of the three pursuers.' (*Annals of Glasgow*)

1803: The following is an excerpt from the petition, sent to Parliament by the Corporation, for a patent for the Queen Street theatre:

> That the City of Glasgow has of late been much extended and enlarged and beautified, whereby the number of wealthy and opulent inhabitants has much increased and it has become expedient to provide for their amusement and that of the nobility and gentry of the neighbourhood, a public theatre or playhouse, for acting tragedies, comedies, operas, and other performances of the stage, under proper rules and regulations; therefore pray that leave may be given to his Majesty to issue letters patent.

(*Glasgow and its Clubs*)

The Theatre Royal was opened in 1804 but destroyed in a fire twenty-five years later.

FEBRUARY 8TH

1814: 'Disease and death made uncommon ravages among the inhabitants, especially the aged. Up until this day, from the 1st of January, the number of burials in the different churchyards of the city and suburbs amounted to 658, being nearly one-fourth of what had taken place in the preceding year.' (*The Picture of Glasgow*)

———•◆•———

1845: 'On Saturday last, James Beaumont Neilson, the inventor of the Hot Blast, was entertained at dinner, in testimony of their high respect for his character, and to mark their grateful sense of the merits of an invention which has exercised such a beneficial influence on the great staple production of Lanarkshire. Many gentlemen of the city and neighbourhood were invited to the banquet, which took place in the hall of the Tontine Hotel. The health of Mr Neilson, as a citizen of whom Glasgow might well feel proud, was then given with every demonstration of enthusiasm and respect. He replied in modest and becoming terms and observed that, but for this invention, it would have been impossible for the Iron masters of Scotland to compete with those of Wales and that the influence of the Hot Blast had been the means of reducing, in a ratio of about 3 to 1, the expense of production from our own mineral resources.' (*Glasgow Herald*)

FEBRUARY 9TH

1815: 'For some time, previous to 1801, the streets of the city were so much infested with idle boys, and women of dissolute characters, as to become offensive to every moral feeling. To remedy this evil as far as possible, a number of gentlemen formed themselves into a society, for the benevolent purpose of apprenticing, and taking charge of vagrant boys, from Bridewell, and others deprived of the protection of guardians and for providing an asylum for dissolute women, who might have a desire to return to the paths of virtue. The Society have built a spacious and very commodious asylum (Magdalene Asylum), which was opened on this day. At present, there are 30 penitents in the asylum. After having used the hot or cold bath, at admission, they receive a uniform dress, and are then employed in making clothes for the institution, sewing, tambouring, knitting, etc. Several of the women, at their admission, had every thing to learn, and had not only been idle, but ignorant of useful employment, and they were often in a state of health which rendered them incapable of much exertion. Such of them as cannot read, have a portion of every day assigned for their instruction.' (*Annals of Glasgow*)

FEBRUARY 10TH

1789: 'At a Court held in the Upper Storey of the Tolbooth of Glasgow, the rules and regulations to be observed by the debtors confined in the upper storey were agreed by the members (prisoners). Here are some of them:

Rule 7—No person incarcerated for any thing but a civil debt can be admitted into these apartments without paying a garnish of 6*s*, and he must be a person of good character.

Rule 8—Every member taking the benefit of the Act of Grace, shall treat his fellow-prisoners with the amount of the first day's aliment, in whatever liquor they think proper.

Rule 10—The smoke of tobacco being very disagreeable to many people, no member of these rooms shall smoke, provided three or more members object to it.

Rule 11—If any member shall have any of his property stolen, he is at free liberty to search any of the members he may suspect, without giving offence. And if any member is convicted of having robbed his fellow-prisoner, he shall instantly be expelled, and never again be admitted a member.

Rule 23—Seeing that debtors suffer sufficient punishment by being imprisoned, it is unanimously agreed, that if any creditor or creditors shall presume to come into these apartments, and insult any of the members, it shall be made a common cause, and every one shall aid and assist to turn such creditor down stairs with sufficient marks of indignity.'
(*Sketch of the History of Glasgow*)

February 11th

1889: This article was printed in the *Glasgow Herald* on the Scottish Cup final played at the weekend. The game was a replay following a protest by Celtic over the snowy conditions at the first game:

> The interest taken in the protested final tie played between the 3rd Lanarkshire Rifle Volunteers and the Celtic at Hampden Park on Saturday was as great as on the previous week. It is estimated that there were fully 18,000 persons within the enclosure and the money taken at the gates and the stands is believed to have slightly exceeded the previous Saturday, where £920 was realised. It was one of the finest displays of football witnessed for many years. During the first half, the 3rd LRV had most of the play but only succeeded in scoring one goal and that out of a scrimmage. In the second period the Celts early put on the pressure and equalised after 22 minutes. After this the Irishmen looked the winners all over. Towards the close, the Volunteers, by fine combined passing, got down the length of the field and scored the winning point. The Celtic are a young club and are to be congratulated upon having entered the final in the first year of their existence.

February 12th

1832: 'On this day the first decided case of cholera made its appearance in the vicinity of the suburbs of this City. The dread of the pestilence made a deep impression on this community. Every known preventive was therefore resorted to. The theatre, and other places of amusement, were shut, visiting and dinner parties suspended, and Sunday evening congregations for sermon postponed. Prayer meetings were held in almost every place of worship on the mornings or afternoons of week days, when fervent supplications were offered up to the Almighty, for mitigating disease, and averting the pestilence. Although the mortality was chiefly confined to the intemperate, the dissolute, the ill-fed and ill-clothed part of the population, there were instances where temperate individuals, moving in the higher walks of life, were in a few hours hurried into eternity by the pestilence. The victims were interred soon after death, without ceremony, being attended only by persons appointed by the Board of Health for that purpose.' (*Enumeration of the inhabitants of the city of Glasgow and county of Lanark, for the government census of 1831* by James Cleland, 1832)

Over 3,000 died in the epidemic, which lasted until November.

FEBRUARY 13TH

1817: 'On this day, the new silver coinage of sixpences, shillings, and half crowns, was first issued in this city. The civility, regularity, and readiness, which accompanied its exchange at the different banking offices, obtained the approbation and gratitude of all classes of society.' (*The Picture of Glasgow*)

1829: 'The Grand Fancy Ball. The list of subscribers to this superb and unequalled festive meeting continues to increase. The ladies of the leading fashionable sphere of Glasgow have inserted their names as patronesses of the evening and the Duke of Montrose, and many noblemen and gentlemen, have been added to the roll of patrons. On the whole, expectation is excited in an unparalleled degree, far exceeding any thing that we can ever recollect. Mr Seymour may justly be proud of the distinction thus paid to him by the very first families, both for rank and wealth, in the west of Scotland and it is at the same time grateful to see that the exertions he has hitherto made to bring the first performers of the age before the Glasgow public have not been fogotten.' (*Glasgow Herald*)

FEBRUARY 14TH

1689: 'Bailie Gibson, an adherent of episcopacy, having hired a party of reckless ruffians, proceeded with a minister to the High Church to make a forcible ingress. They found the door guarded by a party of forty women. A conflict was the consequence which, after a stout resistance on the part of the "weaker vessels", ended in their complete discomfiture: thirty-two of them being wounded in a most barbarous manner. But such a victory was not to be so easily gained. The yells, the cries, and the terrible ejaculations, for which even in those days the women of Glasgow were distinguished, aroused the mountain-men who were within hearing. The whole body of the covenanters were soon on the scene. The affray having been ended, it was found that even with all the assistance which had flocked to their standard, the women had the worst of it.' (*Chronicles of Saint Mungo: or, Antiquities and Traditions of Glasgow*, 1843)

1954: On this day Hollywood horse star Trigger arrived in Glasgow. Accompanied by co-stars Roy Rogers and Dale Evans, he posed for photographs and signed the Central Hotel register. He was then led up the staircase to his room, although opinion differs as to whether he spent the night in the hotel or at some railway stables. The film stars were in town for a number of shows at the Glasgow Empire.

FEBRUARY 15TH

1975: On this day Billy Connolly made his first appearance on *Parkinson*. His performance, which included the telling of a joke about a man's dead wife's bum, brought him to national attention. Connolly had started his working life as a welder in the shipyards, which he gave up in order to concentrate on his music career. He performed with Gerry Rafferty in *The Humblebums* before going solo. Finding the gaps between songs were getting longer and longer as his funny stories took over, he was advised to devote his time to performing more of his unique style of stand-up comedy. He became a household name with appearances in Amnesty International's fund-raising concert *The Secret Policeman's Ball* and ITV's *An Audience With....* He was able to combine his comedy with appearances in films, notably in *Mrs Brown* with Judi Dench. Billy Connolly married Pamela Stephenson in 1989, who he had met while appearing on the comedy show *Not the Nine O'Clock News*. He holds the record for having made the most appearances on Michael Parkinson's show and was a guest on the final show in 2007. Connolly later said about his 1975 appearance: 'That programme changed my life.'

FEBRUARY 16TH

1747: A barber in the city was forced to take action against clients who weren't settling their accounts. He published this appeal for fair dealings:

> To the citizens of Glasgow. Gentlemen, I take the liberty of addressing you in this manner. I make no doubt but you will be disposed to ease me of these hardships I complain of. At the end of some years I found my affairs going backwards; and I having met with considerable losses, I began to examine from whence this misfortune might arise. I plainly discovered it to be the effects of being under-paid in these articles of shaving and dressing. To remedy which, I humbly propose that every gentleman that is waited on at his own house, would pay yearly at so low a rate as a halfpenny for every wig dressing, and a penny for each shave, which is really little more than porter's wages, and yet it is considerably more than I am generally paid, I know well no gentleman will allow me to be a loser to his knowledge; but this is undoubtedly my case. I expect you will consider my reasonable and modest request.

(*Sketch of the History of Glasgow*)

FEBRUARY 17TH

1822: 'On the afternoon of this day a most extraordinary riot took place in the city. It was directed against George Provand, who then occupied the handsome house in Clyde Street. The house had the reputation of being haunted and in addition, the mob had become possessed with the idea that its then occupant, Mr Provand, a bold, tall, and vigorous man, was that obnoxious character, a resurrectionist and it might be even worse, a burker! The house was broken into and entered by a riotous and tumultuous assemblage of persons, who, besides breaking the windows, and destroying many articles of furniture in the house, were guilty of stealing and carrying away a number of gold, silver, and copper coins, silver plate, etc. The police of the city were overpowered, pelted with stones, and forced to run for their lives. The Riot Act was read. The dragoons charged with drawn sabres and the infantry advanced with fixed bayonets on which the mob, innocent and guilty, took to their heels and fled. Five persons were convicted and one, Richard Campbell, an ex-policeman, in addition to the sentence of transportation beyond seas, was further adjudged to be scourged through the city by the hangman, on the 8th day of May.' (*The Anecdotage of Glasgow* by Robert Alison, 1892)

FEBRUARY 18TH

1667: 'A merchant ship of Glasgow, laden with wines from Spain, was attempted by a Dutch man-of-war, for which encounter finding herself too weak, though sufficiently manned, the master commanded his men to conceal themselves. They immediately struck sail in token of submission which the man-of-war perceiving sent twenty-two of his men aboard, but at the close of the evening, the concealed men set so vigorously upon the Dutchmen that, making them prisoners, they regained the possession of their vessel, and returned safe to Glasgow.' (*London Gazette*)

———◆———

1822: This letter was printed in the *Glasgow Herald* on this day:

Mr Editor,

I beg to call the attention of the farmers etc around Glasgow, to an evil I have observed prevail for several years, in the competition for the premiums at Ploughing Matches. It often happens that the relations and servants of the person appointed as judges are amongst the competitors for prizes, and actually receive them, and although the judges themselves do not appear on the field on the day of trial, they have, through the means of their relations, servants etc, a sufficient opportunity of knowing where the plot ploughed by them lies, and consequently might as well be on the field on the day of competitions. This is the evil and one which in my opinion ought to be immediately remedied.

Yours, Filius Agricole

FEBRUARY 19TH

1798: 'Patent Medicines. A fresh supply of the Asthmatic Candy is just come to the hands of the agents. This justly celebrated medicine, by the experience of many thousands, is particularly recommended to the afflicted in this inclement season. It is of a warm and stimulating nature, affords great relief in all Asthmatic Complaints and Shortness of Breathing; and has been found of the greatest benefit to those exposed to cold and damp air, diffusing a glowing warmth over the whole system; particularly beneficial to those subject to violent coughs in time of frost. The above may be had in boxes at 1s, 1½d each of J Mennons, Tontine Close and John Buchanan, Sun Fire Office.' (*Glasgow Advertiser*)

———◆———

2005: On this day a special concert took place at the Scottish Exhibition and Conference Centre. The Concert for Tsunami Relief was held to raise funds for those affected by the Indian Ocean tsunami the previous Boxing Day. Among the Scottish acts that took to the stage to play fifteen-minute-only sets were Franz Ferdinand, Texas, Eddi Reader, Travis, Eugene Kelly, Idlewild and Deacon Blue. The sold-out event was watched by an audience of 10,000 and raised £300,000.

FEBRUARY 20TH

1893: 'Fatal Fight in Glasgow. A Duel with Knives. On Saturday night two young men quarrelled in a public house and fought a duel with knives with the result that one of them was killed in the encounter. The fight thus desperately conducted and ended so tragically, was of short duration and had few witnesses. The combatants were James Monaghan, 21, an iron dresser, and John Coyle, a foundry labourer. Monaghan and Coyle were drinking in the public house of James Maitland, Maitland Street, between six and seven o'clock on Saturday evening. Football was the subject of their conversation and there was considerable diversity of opinion among the young men as to the points under discussion. Eventually a dispute arose and they became greatly excited. The shopkeeper ordered the men out. In the meantime they had resolved to settle their differences by means of a duel with knives. They were turned into the street where the fight continued for a few minutes, when Monaghan fell heavily upon the roadway. He was found to be unconscious and it was at once evident that he had been seriously injured. Monaghan was taken to the police station where it was ascertained that he was dead. Coyle was apprehended and taken to the police office.' (*Glasgow Herald*)

FEBRUARY 21ST

1800: 'Proclamation. Whereas on Saturday, a mob of riotous and disorderly persons did, in an illegal and unwarrantable manner, assemble on the streets and (under the illegal pretext of searching for meal, potatoes, and other articles of provisions, falsely alleged by them to be concealed) did commit many acts of outrage and depredation on the property and persons of the peaceable inhabitants. The Lord Provost and Magistrates do therefore hereby intimate their determined resolution to use every legal means in their powers (by the most exemplary punishment of offenders) to prevent and suppress all tumults and riots and all persons are strictly prohibited from assembling in crowds in the streets and lanes in the evenings and night time as they shall answer at their highest peril. Parents, heads of families and masters are enjoined to keep their children, apprentices and servants within doors after it is dark as they will be considered accountable for their conduct, and liable for the consequences that may ensue. Finally, the Lord Provost and Magistrates do hereby declare their determined resolution to support, protect and encourage all persons who shall contribute to the supply of provisions and they do most earnestly entreat the farmers and dealers in corn to bring their grain to market as speedily as they possibly can.' (*Glasgow Advertiser*)

FEBRUARY 22ND

1913: 'The annual general meeting of the Glasgow and West of Scotland Aerated Water Manufacturer's and Bottler's Defence Association was held in Glasgow. There was a large attendance of members. Mr William Sillar, vice-president, in the absence of the president, Mr Robert F Barr, occupied the chair. Reference was made to the proposed by-laws, which were considered extreme and oppressive and a serious menace to the trade. The members felt the curtailment of the hours of trading on weekdays and total closing on Sunday was uncalled for.' (*Glasgow Herald*)

———◆———

1917: 'Glasgow Tramways. A Story of Success. In celebration of the extinction of the debt on the Glasgow Corporation Tramways, a company of about 150 gentlemen attended a luncheon in the Banqueting Hall of the City Chambers today, on the invitation of Councillor Montgomery, the convenor, and members of the Tramways Committee. The Lord Provost (Sir Thomas Dunlop, Bart) presided. Sir James Bell, Bart, who was Lord Provost when the tramways were taken over by the Municipality in 1894 recalled the vicissitudes of the early days and sketched the steady progress made by the undertaking up to the present time. The tramways, he said, provided a service which had not been surpassed or equalled in the world.' (*Glasgow Herald*)

FEBRUARY 23RD

1801: This advertisement appeared in the *Glasgow Advertiser* on this day:

Monday next, The British State Lottery begins drawing. The Original Tickets and Shares in halves, quarters, eighths and sixteenths, are sold and registered at the London prices in a variety of numbers by Thomsons and Co, at their State Lottery Office at J & J Scrymgeors, No 1 Glassford St, and at their old Licensed Office, No 8 South Bridge Street, Edinburgh, where the largest prize that ever came to Scotland was sold – No 13831, a prize of twenty five thousand pounds, divided into two fourths, two eighths and four sixteenths. And where No 2201, a prize of ten thousand pounds, divided into one half and eight sixteenths, and No 8447 a prize of ten thousand pounds in a whole ticket, in the Irish Lottery, were sold with a number of other capital prizes of inferior value. Present prices – Half £8 18s, Quarter £4 10s. Eight £2 5s 6d, Sixteenth £1 3s. Registering sixpence each number. Letters, post-paid, duly answered. Schemes gratis. Insurances on shipping, merchandise and lives done as usual.

FEBRUARY 24TH

1788: The poet and songwriter Robert Burns spent time in the city. On this day he wrote a letter to his friend Richard Brown, with whom Burns had recently met up with at the Black Bull Inn in Argyle Street:

My dear friend, I arrived here, at my brother's, only yesterday, after fighting my way through Paisley and Kilmarnock against those old powerful foes of mine, the Devil, the World, and the Flesh, so terrible in the fields of Dissipation. I have met with few incidents in my life which gave me so much pleasure as meeting you in Glasgow. There is a time of life beyond which, we cannot form a tie worth the name of Friendship. Life is a fairy scene, almost all that deserves the name of enjoyment or pleasure, is only charming delusion, and in comes ripening Age, in all the gravity of hoary wisdom, and wickedly chases away the dear, bewitching Phantoms. When I think of life, I resolve to keep a strict look out in the course of Economy, for the sake of wordly convenience and independence of mind, to cultivate intimacy with a few of the companions of youth, that they may be the friends of Age. My dear Sir, your most truly. Robert Burns.

(*The complete works of Robert Burns:containing his poems, songs, and correspondence,* Volume 1, 1853)

FEBRUARY 25TH

1869: On this day the acclaimed Victorian writer Charles Dickens gave the last of his public readings in the city. He had also given the inaugural address for the Glasgow Athenaeum, twenty-two years previously. On the day of his final performance this announcement was made in the *Glasgow Herald*:

City Hall, Glasgow. Mr Charles Dickens's Farewell. Tonight (Thursday). The Poor Traveller, Sikes and Nancy (from Oliver Twist) and Mr Bob Sawyer's Party (from Pickwick), being the last reading Mr Dickens will ever give in Glasgow. Doors will be open at seven. Admission – 5s, 4s, 3s, 2s, and 1s.

The following day, a report of the reading was published:

Last night Mr Dickens gave the last reading he is ever to give in this city to a brilliant and highly appreciative audience, which literally packed the City Hall in every part. The distinguished novelist acquitted himself with all his great and well-known dramatic power, and was repeatedly applauded in the most enthusiastic manner.

FEBRUARY 26TH

1573: 'Thomas Downy, paid for making a drum to the common minstral to play with.' (*Memorabilia of the City of Glasgow*)

---◆---

1642: 'The council ordains a letter to be sent to Patrick Bell, at London, to show him how the town is abused with thieves, without punishment, and to entreat him to do his best endeavour to get the same remedied, and that so soon as can be.' (*Memorabilia of the City of Glasgow*)

---◆---

1659: 'This said day ordains a proclamation to be sent through the town, to discharge all manner of persons from uttering rude or incivil speeches to the soldiers, under the pain of most severe punishment, according to the quality of the offence and the offender. As also that no person be found vagrant on the streets after the taptow be striking.' (*Extracts from the Records of the Burgh of Glasgow*, 1881)

FEBRUARY 27TH

1888: 'Dr JB Russell, the city's Medical Officer of Health, gave a talk entitled 'The city in which we live.' He dealt at length with the physical circumstances of the poor. In Glasgow the population density was 84 persons per acre. There was only one city in Great Britain which exceeded Glasgow in density and that was Liverpool. Of the inhabitants of Glasgow 25 per cent lived in houses of one apartment, 45 per cent in houses of two. It was these small houses which produced the high death-rate of Glasgow. It was these small houses which gave to that death-rate the striking characteristics of an enormous proportion of deaths in childhood, and of deaths from diseases of the lungs at all ages. Of all the children who died in Glasgow before they completed their fifth year, 32½ per cent died in houses of one apartment. There they died and their little bodies were laid on a table or on the dresser, so as to be somewhat out of the way of their brothers and sisters, who played, and slept, and ate in their ghastly company. From beginning to rapid ending, the lives of these children were short parts in a continuous tragedy.'
(*Glasgow Herald*)

FEBRUARY 28TH

1640: 'This said day ordains the treasurer to pay to John Corss twenty marks, to help to pay for the curing of his son's leg that was cut from him.' (*Memorabilia of the City of Glasgow*)

———◆———

1800: 'Early on Wednesday morning the warehouse in Trongate belonging to Messrs Lindsay, Smith and Co, which had been twice broken into of late, was observed by the watchman to be again broken open. After alarming the family of a gentleman in the neighbourhood who, with his two sons, got up and stood watch over the passage, the watchman proceeded to the house of one of the owners, who accompanied by some friends, hastened immediately to the warehouse and after some search found a man concealed in a dark corner of one of the rooms, who, on being brought to the light, proved to be one of their own warpers lately discharged. On being questioned as to the motives which could induce him to often to injure his masters, he handed one of the gentlemen a pocket book and told them it would explain the case. It was found to contain a certificate of the ban of his marriage. He wanted a little money to put it over decently. He was committed to prison.' (*Glasgow Advertiser*)

MARCH 1ST

1764: 'By order of the Magistrates of Glasgow. Whereas, there are several middens or quantities of dung laid down, and presently lying on the streets and avenues leading into the city of Glasgow, to the great nuisance of all persons coming in, or going out of the city, or taking the benefit of the air around the city. These are, therefore, requiring all persons interested in said dung, that they carry the same from off the streets and avenues, or lanes, leading into the city, betwixt this day and the 15th day of March next to come. Certifying all and every person who shall refuse or delay so to do, that the magistrates will confiscate all dung lying on the streets, avenues, or lanes, leading into the said city after the said day, and grant a warrant for carrying away and applying the same to other uses, and fine the persons who laid down the same, in ten pounds Scots each. And these are strictly prohibiting and discharging all and every person or persons whomever, from laying down any dung on any of the streets, avenues, or lanes leading into the city, under the penalty of ten pounds Scots, for each transgression.' (*Old Glasgow and its Environs*)

MARCH 2ND

1778: 'Prior to 1800, the affairs of police was under the sole management of the Magistrates and Council, and supported from the Corporation funds. The increasing population of the town, and other considerations, made it very desirable that a separate establishment of Police should take place; accordingly, on this day, the Magistrates and Council appointed an Inspector of Police, with a salary of £100 per annum. This Officer acted till 5th September 1781, when he resigned, and the office was abolished on 26th November thereafter. In 1788, the Magistrates and Council becoming still more anxious for such an establishment, appointed another gentleman to the office of Intendent of Police, and applied for an Act of Parliament to assess the inhabitants to defray the necessary expenses. As the public were not to have a voice in the election of the Ward Commissioners, nor any control over the expenditure, a powerful and successful opposition was set on foot, by which the bill was lost.' (*Annals of Glasgow*)

MARCH 3RD

1960: Despite being 32 miles from Glasgow city centre the airport at Ayrshire's Prestwick has a connection to Glasgow. It is called 'Glasgow Prestwick Airport'. The airfield had been the site for the Scottish Aviation Ltd aircraft factory and during the Second World War had seen the arrival of thousands of US aircraft to be used in the Allied attacks on occupied Europe. It was this role as a staging point for transatlantic crossings that gave Prestwick its unique claim to history, being the only place that Elvis Aaron Presley – the King of Rock 'n' Roll – made an appearance on British soil. Presley was returning to America from service in the US Army in Germany when his aircraft landed to refuel. Word had gotten around that the star was coming and a crowd gathered to meet him. He disappointed some by refusing to remove his peaked cap, but delighted others who could hardly believe 'Elvis the Pelvis' (a nickname he loathed) was there in front of them. He was only there a few hours and is reported to have asked a colleague: 'Where am I?' Presley never returned to Britain. It was rumoured his manager, 'Colonel' Tom Parker, was an illegal immigrant to America and would not have been able to return to America had he left.

MARCH 4TH

1848: 'On this day a very large number of the unemployed again assembled on the Green, and in the afternoon proceeded in a strong body to the City Hall. Here the Relief Committee and the Magistrates were assembled and received a deputation from the unemployed who urged upon the authorities their destitute condition and at the same time expressed their repugnance to accept employment at stone breaking. Many of them followed indoor occupations, at which they desired to be employed, or failing this, in earth work, viz delving and wheeling. The authorities represented their total inability to provide work of the kind required by the people, but after a deputation retired a discussion ensued, the result of which was a resolution to afford a gratuitous supply of meal the same evening and to open the soup kitchen on Monday for the temporary succour of the really destitute and at the same time to endeavour to provide work at least at stone breaking, to as many as possible. The remnant of the Relief Fund is already much reduced, and in the present state of the city it is difficult to see how this indiscriminate charity could be renewed. And again, were doles of this kind continued, the Committee would soon have 20,000 applicants on their hands.' (*Glasgow Herald*)

MARCH 5TH

1880: On this day an accident took place at the Glasgow Ironworks which was reported by the *Glasgow Herald*:

Terrible Boiler Explosion at Glasgow Ironworks. A terrible disaster occurred at the Glasgow Ironworks by which three men were killed on the spot, five died very shortly afterwards and upwards of thirty received such injuries that it is to be feared many of them will ultimately succumb. Indeed the probability is that the calamity will exceed in the loss of life any similar catastrophe which has occurred in the city in recent years. So far as can be learned there was no indication that anything was wrong with the furnace and everything was going on as usual when suddenly the boiler exploded with a terrific noise, shaking the ground with a force as if of an earthquake and carrying death and destruction around. The force of the explosion was unhappily to the eastward and the fragments of the broken boiler and of the roof of the shed were cast right into the centre of the work where the majority of the workmen were engaged. One immense fragment of the boiler, measuring some 15 feet in length was blown eastward for a distance of 35 feet.

MARCH 6TH

1754: 'Letters from Glasgow on this day bear that people were greatly surprised with the sinking of the walk along the river side, near the head of the Green, in breadth in some parts near twenty, and in length about eighty yards. The sinking, which appeared at first to be about five feet, continued gradually for some days, and then it was above ten. It is remarkable that though the distance from the walk to the river is about fifty or sixty yards, with a considerable descent, yet it is only the highest ground that is sunk. No alteration appears near the water edge, excepting a few small chinks or openings. Various are the conjectures about the cause. Some will have it that there are springs below ground which communicate with the river, and (as the soil is sandy) have formed a cavity by washing away the sand, and there being nothing to support the weight above, the earth has fallen in. Others suspect that the river which, at this part, forms a curve or crook, and is very deep, has, by degrees, washed away the foundation. They apprehend that if proper care is not speedily taken the river will cut out a new channel for itself.' (*Scots Magazine*)

MARCH 7TH

1780: 'On this day the Gaelic Club was established. The original qualification for becoming a member of the club was that the individual should be a Highlander, either by birth or connection. Another requisite was that he should be able to speak the Erse [Gaelic, from old Scots 'Erische'/Irish], or be the descendant of Highland parents, the possessor of landed property in the Highlands, or an officer in a Scots or Highland regiment. These conditions were perhaps very necessary, when it is mentioned, that among the standing rules of the fraternity, it was a law that the Club should meet on the first Tuesday of every month, in Mrs Scheid's tavern – then a first-rate house in the Trongate – and that the members were "to converse in Gaelic, according to their abilities, from seven till nine." In the progress of time, it may be easily supposed that those original regulations were departed from, and that, although the claim for membership was restricted to the applicant's ability to count kin with some Highland relative, the chance of his admission into what soon became a most aristocratic brotherhood, would depend more on his position in society, and on his connection with the leading members who governed it, than on anything peculiarly Celtic in himself.' (*Glasgow and its Clubs*)

MARCH 8TH

1793: This advertisement was printed in the *Glasgow Advertiser* on this day:

The last night of the Representation of La Foret Noire, or The Natural Son, as on Monday a change of performance will take place. By Permission of the Lord Provost. New Circus, Glasgow. Tomorrow evening will be presented, an incomparable variety of unparalleled Amusements. (Particulars expressed in the Bills.) The whole to conclude (for the fifth time) with a grand serious comic pantomimic entertainment called: La Foret Noire or The Natural Son. Books descriptive of the Entertainment will be delivered gratis at the Circus. Boxes 3*s*. Pit 2*s*. Gallery 1*s*. Doors will open at six and the amusements to begin at seven o'clock. No persons can be admitted behind the scenes on any account. Tickets to be had at J Aird's music shop, New Wynd, and at Mrs Wright's grocery, Argyle Street, where places for the boxes may be taken, from 9 till 2 o'clock and of Mrs Smith at the Circus from 12 till 2. Mr Jones has the honour of acquainting the ladies and gentlemen that the circus is thoroughly aired and warmed by stoves distributed in various parts of the building.

MARCH 9TH

1898: 'A Bad Boy. At Glasgow Sheriff Summary Court yesterday William Drover, a lad of 12 years, was sentenced to five years' detention in a reformatory for the theft of a cash-box containing £7 10s in money and two deposit receipts, the property of his grandfather, in their house at Westmuir Street, Parkhead. Accused had been previously convicted on which occasion he was given the benefit of the first Offenders' Act, sentence being delayed until 31st March.' (*Glasgow Herald*)

1898: 'Furious Driving in Glasgow. Matthew Tinley was charged with furious driving in Crown Street on Saturday, 26th February, whereby Patrick McKenna was knocked down, and several of his ribs were broken. It appeared that the accused was driving a brake up Crown Street in order to meet and take up the crowd coming from the football match at Cathkin Park between the Rangers and Third Lanarkshire Rifle Volunteers. He stated that he did not see McKenna and could not avoid running him down. The Sheriff said he was sorry he could not see his way to impose a fine. This was a very serious offence in a city like Glasgow. Sentence of 14 days imprisonment was pronounced.' (*Glasgow Herald*)

MARCH 10TH

1914: 'Mrs Pankhurst, who attended a women's suffrage demonstration in St Andrew's Hall last night, was arrested amid scenes of violence unparalleled in the history of the city's principal meeting place. While the leader of the militant suffrage movement was addressing the audience, a large body of Glasgow police suddenly entered the hall and proceeded to storm the platform. Tumultuous scenes followed. The suffragists on the platform met the attack of the police with a fusillade of pot plants which had been used for decorative purposes, and chairs were also hurled at the constables. Despite the strenuous defence set up the officers swarmed on to the platform with drawn batons and several violent free fights were in progress simultaneously in the midst of a surging mass of humanity. Meantime the audience were on their feet wildly shouting and gesticulating, and the tumult was intensified by the discharge by one of the suffragists of a number of shots of blank cartridge from a blank revolver. Several suffragists and policemen were injured. The meeting was arranged by the Women's Social and Political Union and there was an attendance of fully 4,000 persons, principally ladies.' (*Glasgow Herald*)

MARCH 11TH

1779: 'Notice. The magistrates of the city of Glasgow hereby intimate that every beggar found begging in the city will be sent to the workhouse and as all the poor who are entitled to charity are either in the Town's Hospital, or provided with meal, it is requested the inhabitants will serve none of them at their doors.' (*Glasgow Mercury*)

———◆———

1935: 'Big Order for Glasgow. The North British Locomotive Company has secured an order for 20 locomotives for service in Egypt. The order may be increased to 50 locomotives, which would bring the total value of the contract to £250,000 sterling. It is anticipated that other railway orders totalling £150,000 will be placed with British firms. An upward tendency has developed of late in the locomotive building industry. The North British Locomotive Company recently obtained an order for 14 superheated duplicated boilers for the Assam Bengal Railway and 28 boilers of a similar design for the East India Railway. In addition to 20 locomotives for the London and North Eastern Railway Company the firm have on hand several locomotives for home and overseas accounts.' (*Glasgow Herald*)

MARCH 12TH

1698: 'The magistrates of Glasgow granted an allowance to the jailor for keeping witches and warlocks, imprisoned in the Tolbooth, by order of the Commissioners of Justiciary.' (*Annals of Glasgow*)

───◆───

1782: 'The most memorable flood is that of this day which is still remembered by some living in the light of a "judgment". After long and heavy rains the Clyde rose to an alarming extent. It covered all the lower parts of the Green and laid the Bridgegate under water to the depth of several feet. As the inhabitants were accustomed to floods, many of them went to bed in the hope that the waters would have subsided by the morning, but they continued to rise during the night until the fires on the ground floors were extinguished, and then the flood entered the beds, from which the inmates hastily retreated to the upper stories. The then village of Gorbals was so completely surrounded, that it seemed like an island rising up in the midst of an estuary. A young woman was drowned there, which was the only loss of life occasioned by the flood: but a great many horses and cows were drowned in their stables.' (*Glasgow: Past and Present*)

March 13th

1805: 'An Act of Parliament passed on this day stipulated the rates of postage to be charged for letters mailed in the United Kingdom. Selected Rates of Postage of a single Letter from the Post-Towns in Scotland to Glasgow (in pennies): Aberdeen 11, Bo'ness 7, Brechin 10, Dundee 9, Edinburgh 7, Fort-William 10, Inverness 15, Kirkwall 14, Leith 7, Inverness 12, Oban 9, Paisley 4, Perth 9, Porto-Bello 7, Portree 13, Stornoway 13, Stromness 14, Tranent 7. Postage was also set for mail to and from England: London 14 pennies. The Mail is carried from Glasgow to London, a distance of 405 miles, in the space of sixty-three hours, being at the rate of seven miles in sixty-five minutes and one-third, including stoppages. It leaves London on the evening of every lawful day at eight o'clock, and at six o'clock on Sundays; and Glasgow every lawful day at three o'clock in the afternoon, and on Sundays at two o'clock.' (*Annals of Glasgow*)

MARCH 14TH

1785: 'On this day the ice on the Clyde broke up after four months. It was the longest continuation of frost ever remembered. During this period booths and dramshops with fires in them were erected on the river.' (*Annals of Glasgow; Enumeration of the inhabitants of the city of Glasgow and county of Lanark, for the government census of 1831* by James Cleland, 1832)

1794: 'About seven months ago, Mary McQueen, a girl about 13 years of age, suddenly left her service in Glasgow and has never since been heard of. She is of a fair complexion, black eyed, and has the mark of a cut on the side of her right eye. She had on, when she went away, a blue short gown and petticoat, and a white and green shawl about her neck. It would very much oblige her poor disconsolate mother if any person would inform where she is by writing to the publisher of this paper. If she will return home her mistress will receive her kindly.' (*Glasgow Advertiser*)

MARCH 15TH

1921: 'Women Jurors. Glasgow's First Seven. For the first time in the history of Glasgow Sheriff Criminal Court women served on the jury at trials in the Justiciary buildings in Jail Square today. So far as the attendance of the general public could be taken as a guide, the event did not seem to create a great deal of interest. Twenty four woman had been cited, eight as special jurors and sixteen as ordinary jurors. Of these, seven were balloted to serve. They were: Mrs Margaret Muirhead, Mrs Helen Clark, Mrs Annie Hay, Miss Agnes McKay, Miss Julia McNair, Miss Martha Anderson and Miss Bertha Paterson. No incident marked the empanelling of the jury. The ordinary procedure was followed by the Clerk of Court. As the required fifteen were called each rose and entered the well of the court, and took his or her seat in the jury box. The women must have found their first experience in the jury box somewhat fatiguing. The Court sat from ten in the morning till five in the afternoon, with only a brief adjournment for lunch and there was little in any of the cases to sustain interest.' (*Glasgow Herald*)

MARCH 16TH

1798: 'This day is published, in two volumes, price 5s. With the Doctor's Portrait, dedicated to the King's Most Excellent Majesty, the Ninth Edition, with considerable additions and alterations, new cases, etc of an entire new work, entitled: *Guide to Old Age Or A Cure for the Indiscretions of Youth*. Attention to the rules laid down will prevent the horrors attendant, and neither young persons, nor those of maturer years, should be a moment without having it in their possession, particularly sea-faring men on long voyages; in which the various disorders incident to mankind, and particularly those occasioned by irregular propensities in both sexes with the proper mode of relief, etc, are treated of under the following heads: Nervous disorders, headache, epilepsy, madness, deafness, diseases of the eye, consumptions, atrophy or nervous consumption, jaundice, bilious complaints, complaints of the female sex, diseases of the head, diseases of the liver, asthma, dropsy, gout, rheumatism, palsy, menstruation, chlorosis, scrofula, excess of libidinous indulgence, baneful effects of such indiscretions, especially among youth, venereal disease, on sea and hot-bathing, etc. By William Brodum, MD. Printed for the author and sold by J Mennons, printer, Glasgow. For an excellent character of this book see the different reviews.' (*Glasgow Advertiser*)

MARCH 17TH

1806: 'Died, on this day, was David Dale, one of the fathers of the cotton manufacture in Scotland. He was the model of a self-raised, upright, successful man of business. Sprung from humble parents at Stewarton in Ayrshire, he early entered on a commercial career at Glasgow. In company with Sir Richard Arkwright, he commenced the celebrated New Lanark Cotton Mills in 1783, and in the course of a few years he had become a rich man. He took his full share of public duty as a magistrate. The poor recognised him as the most princely of philanthropists. Though unostentatious to a remarkable degree, it was impossible to conceal that David Dale was one of those rare mortals who hold all wealth as a trust for a general working of good in the world, and who cannot truly enjoy anything in which others are not participators. His great object was to furnish a profitable employment for the poor, and train to habits of industry those whom he saw ruined by a semi-idleness. He aimed at correcting evils already existing, evils broad and palpable; and it never occurred to him to imagine that good, well-paid work would sooner or later harm anybody.' (*The book of days: A miscellany of popular antiquities in connection with the calendar, including anecdote, biography, and history, curiosities of literature and oddities of human life and character,* Volume 1 edited by Robert Chambers, 1863)

MARCH 18TH

1990: 'Tracey Patrick and her friend David Carracher, had been walking in Sauchiehall Street and had decided to cross Renfield Street in the early hours of the morning. They stepped from between parked vehicles and walked into the path of the Land Rover driven by Alan Parkhill, who braked and swerved. Young David was able to jump clear, but the Land Rover struck Tracey Patrick. As she lay unconscious, my young constituent Thomas McIntyre, a good Samaritan, ran to her assistance. As Thomas approached to assist Tracey, Alan Parkhill got out of the Land Rover and drew a 9mm Browning pistol. As Thomas McIntyre ran across the road to help Tracey Patrick, the gunman of almost impeccable character stood with both arms stretched in front of him and with his feet apart fired his pistol at Thomas. The first shot struck Thomas above the right wrist. As Thomas turned to run from the gunman, Parkhill fired four further shots into his back. He died immediately. One bullet went through his body and struck a taxi driver. Parkhill fired further shots, injuring several others, before placing the pistol close to his right temple, firing the gun and penetrating his brain.' (John Reid MP, *House of Commons debate on Firearms Control*, 1997. Licensed under the Open Parliament Licence v1.0)

MARCH 19TH

1851: 'A large and influential meeting of the inhabitants of Glasgow assembled in the City Hall and passed resolutions against the Papal Aggression in England. It was resolved to petition Parliament to withdraw from the Church of Rome the national encouragement she now receives from the public funds and otherwise; to place all convents and nunneries, and similar establishments of the Roman Catholic Church, under regular public inspection; to amend the laws of mortmain, and generally repress the aggressive spirit of Popery.' (*The Household Narrative of Current Events*, edited by Charles Dickens, 1851)

———•◆•———

1765: 'On this day Humphrey Ewing and Matthew Jack were tried before the High Court of Justiciary, for abstracting the king's weights in the scale of weighing tobaccos for exportation, thereby defrauding the revenue in the debentures to be granted on exportation. An unanimous verdict was returned, finding them guilty, and they were adjudged to stand, attended with the town-drummer and the hangman, at the Market Cross, for half-an-hour at mid-day, with their hands tied behind their backs, and a label on their breasts with these words "Convict of withdrawing his Majesties' weights, and substituting false weights in place thereof" and to receive fifteen stripes from the hangman, on their naked backs.' (*Glasgow: Past and Present*)

MARCH 20TH

1872: 'Can a Man Clean Tripe in his Own Premises? At the Western Police Court, James McAustin, eating-house keeper, 85 Main Street, was charged with a contravention of the Glasgow Slaughter Houses Act, by having cleaned tripe within his own premises. Accused pleaded not guilty and Mr Macfarlane appeared for the defence. Witnesses for the prosecution stated that there was abundant accommodation for the cleaning of tripe in the slaughter houses, while the witnesses for the defence said the accommodation was insufficient, especially in Moore Street, and that fleshers were often put to great inconvenience. Mr Macfarlane then contended that the Act made it compulsory for the Market Trustees to provide all the necessary space required and if they failed to do that, then he maintained that his client was justified in taking the course he did. He also stated that in the event of an adverse decision he intended to raise an action of declarator in the Court of Session. Mr Gordon Smith (assessor) did not think the construction put on the Act would justify contravention of it. It was then decided to delay giving judgment till Monday, in order that the opinion of all the assessors might be got on the point.' (*Glasgow Herald*)

MARCH 21ST

1921: These clothes were advertised in the *Glasgow Herald* on this day:

> For their return to School. Pettigrew and Stephens. Parents can fit out the Girls and Boys for return to school at greatly lessened prices now if they select here, without detracting one whit from the usual quality and smartness. Youth's Long Trouser suits in strong wearing tweeds, cheviots and worsteds, specially selected for hard school wear. Youth's 'Raintex' double-breasted belted raincoat, lined throughout, wool check to fit 12 to 17 years. 'Wooltex' underwear, pure wool, Scotch made. Vests, Knee Drawers, Combinations, Long Sleeves. Washing frock, with French knickers to match in Tootal print. Grey and blue checks, white pique collar and cuffs, stitched with contrasting colour. Ideal for washing.

———— • ◆ • ————

1955: Billy Graham began his All-Scotland Crusade in the Kelvin Hall on this day. The American evangelist spoke to a capacity audience of 15,000, the first full-house in a six-week-long run. During his time in Scotland he spoke to around 800,000 people, including 90,000 at Hampden Park. Graham's sermon on Good Friday was broadcast to the whole of Britain and received a large audience, second only to the Coronation. When he arrived in Scotland, he said: 'We have prayed for Glasgow all the way across the Atlantic.'

MARCH 22ND

1781: 'The magistrates hereby give notice, recommend, and enjoin what follows: That no mason or slater, or any person working on the roofs of the houses in this city, shall throw over rubbish of any kind without keeping a person as a watch to prevent danger to the inhabitants. That no person shall shake carpets, or throw water or nastiness over any of the windows of this city. That all boys, or others, who shall be detected, at any time, throwing stones, making bonfires, crying for illuminations, or attempting to make any disturbance on the streets of this city, calculated to endanger the public peace, shall be punished with the utmost severity. On all such occasions parents and masters are to be accountable for their children or apprentices, and a reward is hereby offered of Five Pounds sterling to any person who shall detect or discover boys, or others, guilty of these practices, to be paid on conviction of the offenders. That all horses going to water shall on no pretence be rode hard, nor shall any person be permitted to gallop through the streets or avenues of this city.' (*Glasgow Mercury*)

MARCH 23RD

1639: 'Proclamation. This said day it is ordained that a proclamation be sent through the town by sound of drum, that no more persons lend his arms to one other, under the punishment of 40 pounds, and that all men be ready to give his oath at the wapinschaw [weapon showing], that the arms he carries are his own, under the same punishment.' (*Memorabilia of the City of Glasgow*)

———— ◆ ————

1931: This advert appeared in the *Glasgow Herald*:

> Another Fall in Fur Prices. Sale of 190 Fur Coats and 150 Fur Ties Begins Today. At the most sensational prices in modern times. Buy Now! Prices definitely hardened at the recent Skin Sales. The garments offered were made up this year and all are in the latest and most up-to-date styles: Natural Antelope – 94/6, Real Hungarian Broadtail Lamb – 5 guineas, Natural Silver Fox – 8 guineas, Natural Musquash – 12 guineas, Mink Marmot – 11 guineas, Broadtail Lamb – 9 ½ guineas, Real Squirrel – 9 ½ guineas, Black Pony Skin – 8 guineas. Pettigrew & Stephens Ltd, Sauchiehall Street, Glasgow.

MARCH 24TH

1655: 'This said day, for as much as a motion being made by Patrick Bryce, weaver, and James Anderson in Gorbals, for the winning again of the heath land there, and the said Magistrates and Council being most willing to entertain the same for the good of this city and all inhabitants thereof, it is agreed to pay out for advancement of the said work two thousand marks Scots, and to draw up a contract with the said persons, in this manner: The said Patrick Bryce and James Anderson are to be obliged to keep the work on for a full thirteen years and to have the first year free but payment of any duty and to pay in yearly to the town for each year thereafter, six hundred marks and at no time to exceed four shillings for the price of the hutch of coals and to make the hutch of the quantity of nine gallons and they are to be limited only for eight hewers, and are to employ no more. And the foresaid two thousand marks is to be paid at these terms, the equal half thereof at the beginning of the work, and the other half thereof at the next Lammas.' (*Memorabilia of the City of Glasgow*)

MARCH 25TH

1982: On this day a by-election for the Westminster parliament was held in the Glasgow Hillhead constituency. It was caused by the death in January of the sitting MP, the Conservative Sir Thomas Galbraith. He had been Scotland's longest-serving Member of Parliament, holding the seat for over thirty years. In a close, highly publicised contest, the winner was Roy Jenkins, one of the Gang of Four – a group of four senior Labour politicians who had broken away to form their own party, the Social Democratic Party. The other three were David Owen, William Rodgers, and Shirley Williams. The SDP had formed an alliance with the Liberals, who didn't stand in the by-election. The results were:

Roy Harris Jenkins (SDP-Liberal Alliance) – 10,106
Gerald Malone (Conservative) – 8,068
David Wiseman (Labour) – 7,846
George Leslie (SNP) – 3,416
John Glass (Protestant against Papal Visit) – 388
Roy Harold Jenkins (Social Democratic Party) – 282
Nicolette Carlaw (Ecology Party) – 178
William Boaks (Democratic Monarchist) – 5 (The lowest votes ever polled by a candidate for a Westminster election.)

Jenkins' majority was 2,038. He held onto the seat in the 1983 General Election but lost out to George Galloway in 1987.

MARCH 26TH

1573: 'On this day William Glen, son to John Glen, is found in the wrong for casting of a stone at Robert Rank and hitting him sorely above the eye to the effusion of his blood. And also John Glen the younger and John Glen brother to the said William are found in the wrong, for striking of the said Robert and casting him down violently to the ground. And also Laurence Hoge for disorderly behaviour done to John Glen the younger in throwing of his fist and hitting him on his head with an iron file. And the said John Glen for attacking of the said Laurence with a drawn short sword after the first disturbance ceasing. And also George Laing for attacking John Glen with a drawn sword.' (*Memorabilia of the City of Glasgow*)

———— ◆ ————

1677: 'On this day there was seen by some inhabitants betwixt 11 and 12 at night great fires, as if it had been the burning of three corn stacks, on the south side of the Clyde, beside Little Govan, which flamed exceedingly. But there was no burning of houses, or stalks, as was found after search but before that time was a dreadful voice heard in the Blackfriar Church for several nights.' (*Memorials, or the memorable things that fell out within this island of Britain from 1638 – 1684* by Robert Law, Charles K. Sharpe, 1832)

MARCH 27TH

1848: 'On Friday night a Chartist meeting was held in the City Hall. The first resolution passed was to the effect that the time had now arrived when the People's Charter must become the law of the land. Mr James Adams, in moving this resolution, gave utterance to the usual amount of invective and by a logic peculiar to himself proved that the Central Government in communication with the Town Council were the originators of the late riots, which were got up and allowed by the Police to proceed a certain length, for the purpose of furnishing a pretext for getting up a force to attack and abuse the Chartists.' (*Glasgow Herald*)

———— ◆ ————

'A man named James Sweenie, a labourer on the quay, was charged with having on Friday, while in a state of intoxication, wantonly and recklessly, thrown himself into the river for the purpose of creating an alarm among the persons employed or passing along the wharfs, and with being in the practice of so doing. The case being proved against him, the Baillie found him guilty, and sentenced him to thirty days imprisonment. It came out that on this occasion, as on former ones, he was rescued by the life-hook.' (*Glasgow Herald*)

MARCH 28TH

1960: On this day a fire broke out in a bonded warehouse in Cheapside Street in the Anderston area of the city. The warehouse held over a million gallons of whisky and rum. The blaze took hold and was tackled by 450 fire-fighters from around the city. The heat from the fire caused the alcohol-filled barrels to explode, the blast of which collapsed some of the warehouse's walls. Nineteen men from the Glasgow Fire Service and Glasgow Salvage Corps were killed. Six men received bravery awards in fighting the fire and attempting to rescue their colleagues. A public fund was set up to provide money for the dependents which raised over £180,000. On the day of the funerals, thousands lined the streets in tribute, as the men were buried together in the Necropolis. The Cheapside Street Disaster is the worst peacetime disaster for the fire services in the whole of Britain. Glasgow earned the name 'Tinderbox City' because of the frequency of serious fires.

MARCH 29TH

1781: 'The subscription for the Tontine Coffee House will continue open till the 13th of May next and no longer. Those who choose to subscribe may apply to John Maxwell junior, writer, who is empowered to receive the subscriptions of all who may wish to promote the scheme. In consequence of a resolution of the subscribers at their general meeting, held on the 20th of March current, all persons interested in the Tontine scheme are requested, on or before the 15th of May next, to lodge with Mr Maxwell a note specifying the name of the person on the duration of whose life their interest in the scheme is to depend. If this is not complied with, the subscriber's own life, or the person's already named, where that is the case, will be considered as the life to be engrossed in the deeds.' (*Glasgow Mercury*)

The Tontine Coffee House was part of the Tontine Hotel, that stood beside the Tolbooth. There was also an assembly hall. The coffee house was the place where much of the town's business was done for half a century, until the main centre of business activity moved westwards. The Tontine Hotel was gutted by fire in 1911.

MARCH 30TH

1780: 'Notice. Whereas several persons take the liberty to walk and make roads through John King's grass in the High Green of Glasgow, the said John King begs of the inhabitants and others that they will refrain that practice, seeing there is a sufficient road and very pleasant walks without injuring his property, for which he pays a high rent. And (in order to prevent his grass being treaded and abused in time coming) he hereby certifies all trespassers, that they will be prosecuted as law directs, and further offers a handsome reward to any person who will inform upon trespassers, so as he or they may be convicted.' (*Glasgow Mercury*)

———◆———

1798: On this day, these adverts appeared in the *Glasgow Advertiser*:

Perfumery, sold by John Buchanan at the Sun Fire Office opposite to the Tron Steeple. JB has it in his power to furnish genuine articles, on as low terms as any in town.

Plain Starch Hair Powder 9d per lb. The following articles equally cheap: Violet Scented and Windsor Soaps - Wash Balls - Shaving Powder - Milk of Roses - Bergamot - Rose Water - Lavender Water - Hard and Soft Pomatums - Bears' Grease - Silk and Swandown Puffs Powder Bags - Tooth Brushes - Tooth Powder, etc.

MARCH 31ST

1820: Trouble had been brewing for several years and revolution seemed possible around this time. The *Glasgow Herald* reported some of the lawlessness:

On Wednesday morning, about day light, between 30 and 40 Radicals, armed with guns, pistols, pikes etc apparently from Glasgow, marched through the village of Condorrat, in military order. It is probable they are the same party who had the action with the cavalry at Bonnybridge. The smiths' shops in said village were taken possession of by the Radicals, who, after stuffing the windows with turf, etc, so as to prevent the sound of their hammers being heard, fell to work making pikes and such infernal instruments. They took two guns from feuars in the village. Wednesday afternoon, while one of the Ayrshire Cavalry was standing in an entry in Gallowgate, one of those abominable instruments called a cleg (horse-fly) was thrown at him, which cut him in the cheek. The villain who threw it made his escape. This instrument is somewhat of the nature of a shuttle-cock, has a steel point three inches long, is loaded with lead at the head, and dressed with feathers so as to guide it when thrown. It gets its name from being intended principally against cavalry.

APRIL 1st

1793: These adverts and notices were printed in the *Glasgow Advertiser* dated this day:

A Convenient Mangle. Mrs Whyte begs leave to inform her friends and the public that she has fitted up her Mangle (formerly Mrs Blair's) in the sixth close from the Cross, on the west side of the High Street and to solicit the favour of their employment.

Notice to Debtors of the deceased George Ferris. All persons indebted to the defunct will please settle the sums they owe with his executors, and for that purpose will call at the office of Peter Peterson, writer in Glasgow, otherwise, after this notice they will have themselves to blame if they are prosecuted.

Superb, the property of Alexander Govan, will cover this season at Kenniehill, two miles east of Glasgow. Superb is six years old, well marked, seventeen hands high, for strength and figure he is allowed by the best judges to be as true a horse as this country has produced, and proper to get a breed for any purpose, except the turf. He has covered three years and proves a sure foal-getter. Terms, a guinea and a half to Gentlemen, and a guinea to Farmers, with 2s 6d, to the groom to be paid at covering. Grass for mares at 3d per night.

APRIL 2ND

1798: 'Saturday night or Sunday morning some would-be wag stuck up on several public places of the town a bill purporting "That there was to be a sermon preached in the Green on Sunday afternoon by one of the Missionaries intended for Africa and that after service two negroes were to be baptized into the Christian faith, who were afterwards to act as auxilliaries in the conversion of their brethren in that country." In consequence of which, immediately after the dismission of the Churches, a great number of credulous persons repaired to the place mentioned, but waiting for a considerable time without any appearance either of the preacher or the converts, they began to recollect that they had been sent upon a fool's errand and that it was the first of April! When the crowd understood that they had been duped, the more disorderly fixed their attention on an old man, who they (notwithstanding every asseveration to the contrary) suspected to be the worthy missionary. In the rage which the disappointment had occasioned, they had recourse to the Jewish punishment, by pelting him with stones and otherwise maltreating him, so that it was with difficulty he escaped out of their hands.' (*Glasgow Advertiser*)

APRIL 3RD

1881: On the evening of this date the Census was taken. The results stated the population of the city was 511,415. One in seven of the people who lived in Scotland, lived in Glasgow. The population had more than doubled in forty years and it would continue to rise, increasing by over 50 per cent by 1921. This rapid rise in population resulted in overcrowding and with it associated adverse health issues. The Census also provided information on the most popular surnames in Glasgow. They were: Smith, Campbell, Brown, Wilson, Thomson, Stewart, Anderson, Robertson, Murray and Miller. (1881 Census)

1881: 'Mitchell Library. Return of a number of volumes issued during the week ending 2nd April: Theology and philosophy – 648; history, biography etc – 1,733; law, politics and commerce – 234; arts and sciences – 1,772; poetry and the drama – 630; language – 233; prose action – 716; miscellaneous literature – 2,410. Total – 8,376. Daily average is 1,396, corresponding week last year – 1,144. Total from commencement (5th November 1877) – 1,107,306.' (*Glasgow Herald*)

APRIL 4TH

1765: 'The magistrates hereby intimate that for further preventing carts loaden or unloaden to pass the Bridge of Glasgow, they have caused to put up a folding pole upon the said bridge, at the north end thereof. But in order to accommodate gentlemen and others passing along the said bridge in coaches and chaises, they have engaged a servant who is to lodge in the little house on the east side of, and immediately without the bridge, and on the north end thereof, and to be ready at all times, from five o'clock in the morning till eleven o'clock at night, to open the said folding pole. It is therefore expected that all gentlemen and others, having occasion to pass along the said bridge in coaches or chaises, will endeavour to make their time of passing betwixt the said hours of five o'clock of the morning and eleven at night. If necessity requires them to pass betwixt eleven at night, and five in the morning, they will order their servants to call at the said little house and on the north end thereof, where they will find the said servant who will open the pole to them.' (*Glasgow Journal*)

APRIL 5TH

1820: There was much talk of an insurrection by Scottish radicals, although it never came to serious conflict (albeit three weavers were executed for treason, including James Wilson). With tensions running high, the authorities called out their armed forces on this day as recorded by one of the participants:

As one of the Glasgow Sharpshooters, I leaped at five o'clock from my bed, at the reveille sound of the bugle, and hastened to the rendezvous of the regiment. When I reached the square, it was evident, from the number of green-coated individuals pouring in from every side, that, as the danger increased, the determination to meet it was more decided. Before six o'clock, I found myself among 800 bayonets, ready to act at a moment's notice. For the honour of the corps, the muster-roll showed few absentees, while several individuals answered to their names who were rarely seen on other more showy occasions. The corps never appeared in greater spirits, nor more ready to rush, if need be, against the whole Radical pikes that might muster; although it must in justice be added, that there was as yet no semblance of a single hostile pike to put that courage to the test.

(*Glasgow and its Clubs*)

APRIL 6TH

1932: These notices and adverts were printed in the *Glasgow Herald* on this day:

Enjoy lunch today in Fraser's Restaurant. Undoubtedly the most favoured rendezvous in the city. Distinguished for spacious comfort. Delicious food and unobtrusive service. Luncheons today 1/6, 2/3. Gentlemen may have snack lunch served in the Olde English Smoke Room and enjoy a quiet chat and smoke away from the noise and jostle of the streets. Ladies should not overlook the magnificent display of all that is new in the world of fashion displayed for their delectations in the saloons. Elevators to all floors. 8-12 Buchanan Street C1. 116-120 Argyle Street, C2.

On 26th December a lady who was a passenger on a yellow tramcar proceeding from Netherlee Park Gates to Glasgow sustained an accident by falling down the stairs through the excessive swaying of the tramcar. Will anyone who witnessed the above accident kindly communicate with the subscribers? R Maguire Cook & Co, Solicitors.

Bank of Scotland. Authorised capital – £4,500,000. Paid up capital – £1,500,000. Reserve fund and balance carried forward – £2,315,758. Deposits and credit balances – £30,828,263.
Abstract balance sheet: total liabilities – £38,544,520; total assets – £38,544 420.

APRIL 7TH

1653: A letter dated this day attested to the scale of destruction of the great fire of June 1652. It was signed by, amongst others, Oliver Cromwell and the Earl of Pembroke:

> Whereas we, being credibly informed that, about the 17th day of June last, there happened, in the town of Glasgow, a sudden and very lamentable fire, which, in a very short space, burnt down the best part of the buildings, with a third part of the said town, and almost all the shops and warehouses with the residences of the merchants. In which places so consumed were fourscore bye-lanes and alleys, with all the shops, besides eighty warehouses, which alleys were the habitations of a thousand families; all which losses computed amounts to one hundred thousand pounds Sterling, as by the said certificate and representation, published by the magistrates and ministers, concerning the sad condition of the people there of, by reason of that fire, may more fully appear. We therefore, taking into our compassionate considerations the lamentable and deplorable conditions of the said poor inhabitants, do, upon their earnest requests, recommend them, as an high object of charity, to such pious and well-disposed people as shall be willing to contribute their charity towards the relief of the present and pressing necessities of the said inhabitants.

(*The History of Glasgow*)

April 8th

1626: 'This said day Gabriel Smythie undertook to sharpen all the masons' irons during the time of the building of the Tolbooth and steeple thereof, until the work be ended, for forty pounds money, and in case he be a loser he refers himself in their will, therefore, etc.' (Town Council records)

———◆———

1777: 'On this day, Alexander Stuart, collector of excise, exhibited an information to two justices of the peace for the county of Lanark, setting forth that various persons in Glasgow and its neighbourhood had, betwixt the 8th of January and 2nd of April last, made, brewed, or distilled several great quantities of low wines and strong waters, and have not paid duties for the same, as by the law and statutes of excise they were required and appointed to do. Judgment, therefore, was prayed against various persons after-named for forfeiture of double duty, and expenses, etc.' (*Old Glasgow and its Environs*)

APRIL 9TH

1912: 'The Jungle proved a popular resort for holidaymakers yesterday, large attendances being attracted to the New City Road establishment throughout the day. Several performances were given and each of them drew forth the enthusiastic appreciation of the onlookers. The displays given daily at The Jungle demonstrate in a remarkable manner the extent to which animals of the jungle and the wild can be trained. Lions, tigers, leopards, bears under the direction of their trainers, male and female, give sensational performances, while an elephant entertains and amazes with its intelligence. While the cleverness of the animals call forth nothing but praise, tribute must also be paid to the courage of the trainers. Altogether no one should fail to see the performance which Mr Frank C Bostock is now presenting in Glasgow. The animals do not exhaust the attractiveness of the spacious Bostock establishment. There are numerous free side-shows of an entertaining description and the large patronage extended to these kept the fun going briskly yesterday.' (*Glasgow Herald*)

APRIL 10TH

1639: 'This said day it is concluded by the said provost, baillies and council, that there be sent out one hundred men to the border, to the common defence, and to be maintained upon the common charges of the town, and to intimate with all diligence by sound of drum, to require all able men, who will go on the said service, to enrol themselves.' (*Memorabilia of the City of Glasgow*)

———◆•———

1873: 'Improvement in Photography. The latest and most important discovery which has taken place in connection with photography is that of the autotype process, by which permanency is gained, while the peculiar colouring of the original picture is given to the copy. The Autotype Fine Art Company, to whom the credit of this invention is due, are now showing in the rooms of their representative in the city – Mr Thomas Annan, Hope Street – a large number of prints which have been made by this process from the works of such eminent artists as Turner, Claude, Sir Joshua Reynolds, Sir David Wilkie, Hogarth etc. All of them are very faithfully printed and the tinting is delicately and truthfully rendered.' (*Glasgow Herald*)

April 11th

1791: 'Last Thursday night, about twelve o'clock, a gentleman on his way home was politely attacked in Trongate Street by three men, who first deprived him of his stick, then with a slight stroke across the shoulders demanded his money. At that critical moment he had the presence of mind to grasp his watch in one hand and extending both his arms offered them to take everything but to spare his life. Upon their examining his pocket book at one of the lamps, they found three guinea notes, which they extracted, but returned him the book. The gentleman cannot help thinking he was very handsomely dealt by upon this occasion, especially as he had some silver and other articles in his pockets, which they suffered him to retain.' (*Glasgow Advertiser*)

———— • ◆ • ————

1935: 'The prejudice of boys against the shipbuilding trades, which have suffered so severely from depression, and the distaste of girls for domestic service, are commented upon in the annual report for 1934 of the Glasgow Juvenile Advisory Committee. The boys, it is observed, make a demand for apprenticeships in electrical engineering, motor engineering and printing, while the choice of the girls is more often decided by the opportunities for work which occur locally.' (*Glasgow Herald*)

APRIL 12TH

1757: In the Minute-book of the City on this day: 'Considering that the town-officers have been in use to get buns and ale upon the day on which the Lords of the Council come to town, by which sundry abuses have happened, and for remedying, the Magistrates and Council ordain that the officers be allowed one shilling sterling at each time the Lords come to town at the Circuit.' (*Glasgow and its Clubs*)

———— ◆ ————

1884: 'The Clyde Trustees's new fleet of steamers for passenger service in Glasgow Harbour commenced to run on this day. The first boat left Victoria Bridge at 5 am, while on the upward or return run a start was made from the western terminus at Saw Mill Road, Whiteinch at 5.40 am. The early boats were taken advantage of chiefly by workmen, but during the day they were well patronised by the general public. Bunting was freely displayed at the various landing places on the river, and a considerable amount of interest was taken in the new service, the movements of the tiny vessels being watched by large numbers of spectators.' (*Glasgow Herald*)

These passenger boats, known as 'Cluthas', were withdrawn in 1903 following the advent of the subway and trams. They had been a popular service, with over 2.7 million passengers in 1897.

April 13th

1638: 'This day the provost, baillies, and council, understanding the great abuse done and committed by William Anderson, in taking such great and exorbitant prices for the tails of salmon, far exceeding the prices that was wont to be taking of old, it is ordained, that the said William nor no others, the sellers of salmon of the town's common stock, take no more for salmon tails hereafter, except the prices following: 8 pennies for the tail of one little salmon, and 16 pennies for the tail of a big salmon.' (*Memorabilia of the City of Glasgow*)

———◆———

1803: The Magistrates of Glasgow placed this advertisement, which appeared in the *Glasgow Courier*:

Wanted, for the City of Glasgow, an Executioner. The bad character of the person who last held the office having brought upon it a degree of discredit, which it by no means deserves, the Magistrates are determined to accept of none but a sober well-behaved man. The emoluments are considerable. Applications will be received by the Lord Provost, or either of the Town-Clerks.

APRIL 14TH

1610: 'This said day the provost, baillies, and council, upon complaint made by Mr John Blackburn, Master of the Grammar School and by the deacons and masters of Crafts, and certain other neighbours of this town upon the great and common abuse done by scholars and apprentices towards themselves and their masters in haunting the yards where the alley bowls, French kyles (nine pins) and Glaikis (puzzle game) are used, in withdrawing themselves from the school and their masters service to their great hurt and debauchery, besides the great damage and hurt done by them to the neighbouring yards next to the other yards where the pastimes are played and used in breaking their trees and destroying of their herbs and seeds sewing in the said yards. For remedy it is ordained that all such persons who have the said alleys and yards, that if they receive in the yards to play at the said pastimes, any scholar or apprentice, they be depraved persons, under punishment of ten pounds for each occurrence, and that they permit none to play in the said yards, and that the master of the school ordains his scholars to prepare their bows for the archery to be their pastime.' (*Memorabilia of the City of Glasgow*)

April 15th

1905: 'Seldom if ever have the streets of Kilsyth been the scene of such turmoil as was witnessed on the evening [of this day] and the following morning. The cause of the disturbances, which culminated in a riot, was a visit made to the town by the Anderston Orange Flute Band from Glasgow, who were accompanied by many men and women, evidently of the rowdier class. At Croy, where there is a Catholic population, party tunes were played, with the result that the band followers and the people had a few skirmishes. On reaching Auchinstarry, the band left the main road and paraded up and down the rows [of miners' houses], a man in front waving a huge wand with an imitation Bible at the end of it and covered with Orange colours. Women and men, one after another got a knock on the head from the band followers, many of whom carried short sticks or knuckledusters. Many of the miners were in the town at the time otherwise it would have been an unusual thing for Auchinstarry miners not to have paid back with interest all they got. However some of them got their revenge later on in the evening.' (*Glasgow Herald*)

APRIL 16TH

1853: Harriet Beecher Stowe was a major figure in the anti-slavery movement of the nineteenth century, famous for writing *Uncle Tom's Cabin*. She gave talks in Europe and it was on one of these trips that she first came to Scotland. She described her first sight in a letter to 'Aunt E':

> As we came towards Glasgow, we saw, upon a high hill, what we supposed to be a castle on fire – great volumes of smoke rolling up, and fire looking out of arched windows. 'Dear me, what a conflagration!' we all exclaimed. We had not gone very far before we saw another, and then, on the opposite side of the car, another still. 'Why, it seems to me the country is all on fire.' 'I should think,' said Mr S, 'if it was in old times, that there had been a raid from the Highlands, and set all the houses on fire.' As we drew near to Glasgow these illuminations increased, till the whole air was red with the glare of them. 'Dear me,' said Mr S in a tone of sudden recollection, 'it's the iron works! Don't you know Glasgow is celebrated for its iron works?'

(*Sunny Memories of Foreign Lands* by Harriet Beecher Stowe, 1854)

APRIL 17TH

1909: 'On this day sixty thousands spectators, enraged because the match between the Celtic and the Rangers for the final of the Scottish Cup, culminated for the second time in a draw, broke into rioting. More than 70 persons were injured. The match had been keenly fought, and each side had scored one goal. The crowd thought that extra time should have been allowed for the game, so that it might be fought to a finish. Then the mob, which included much of the Glasgow hooligan element, took the law into their own hands. The few policemen on the ground were swept aside and pelted with stones and bottles. The goal posts were uprooted and the nets destroyed. Foot by foot, however, the crowd were driven back by the truncheons of the police, and it seemed as if they would be forced out of the ground. Suddenly, however, there was another attack. A number of men and lads, tearing up the barricades around the ground, piled them in heaps, with planks and wooden rails, and set them alight. Firemen drove up and did their best to get at the flames but the crowd turned on them. The Scottish Association have decided to withhold the Cup this year.' (*Penny Illustrated Paper and Illustrated Times*)

APRIL 18TH

1939: 'A decision was made last night by the congregation of St Vincent Street Church – popularly known as 'Greek' Thomson's Church – to sell the building to the Glasgow Association of Spiritualists. The sum offered was £4,250. Various organisations in Glasgow made inquiries about the church, among them being a repertory company and the Provincial Grand Lodge of Freemasons. The only definite offer put forward however, was that by the Association of Spiritualists. The Association, it was stated, would take over the building on 30 June. A communion service on 28 May will be the last service in the church and affairs of the congregation will be wound up the following week.' (*Glasgow Herald*)

The church was bought by Glasgow Corporation in 1970. There were plans to open the building as a tourist attraction similar to the Greek Thomson-designed Holmwood House in Cathcart. The church remains a functioning place of worship, currently used by the Free Church of Scotland.

APRIL 19TH

1912: With much interest in the days following the loss of the RMS *Titanic*, this report appeared in the *Glasgow Herald* on this day:

All hope has now been abandoned for the safety of the British steamer *Erna*, wich left the Clyde on February 28 for St John's, Newfoundland, and has not since been heard of, although she was due at her destination some ten days after leaving the Clyde. The generally accepted theory concerning the disappearance of the vessel is that she must have encountered ice floes in the vicinity of the Banks of Newfoundland, and that she has been crushed to pieces and foundered, with the whole of her crew of over 40 men. The *Erna* was a three-masted steamer of 3,476 ton gross, and was built in 1890 by Messrs Caird and Co, Greenock. She signed on her crew at Glasgow on February 12 and a number of the men came over from Newfoundland to take the vessel back to St John's. She was under the command of Captain JM Linklater, Thornwood Avenue, Partick, who had his family with him.

APRIL 20TH

1450: In a gift granted by King James II, the lands including what is now known as Glasgow Green were given to William Turnbull, Lord of Provan and Bishop of Glasgow:

> For the praise of Almighty God, and of the glorious Virgin Mary, and the blessed Kentigern, patron and confessor of the Church of Glasgow, and for the love which we bear to the Reverend Father in Christ, William, present Bishop in said Church, we have given to the said Bishop and his successors for ever, the City of Glasgow, Barony of Glasgow, and lands commonly called the Bishop's Forest, with their pertinents in woods, plains, meadows, marshes, pasturages, etc.

1661: 'This said day, forasmuch as it is sufficiently known to the magistrates and council that William Watson, candle-maker, was apprehended this last night by the guard, with others his companions, drinking in the house of Mr James Hamilton, at two or three hours in the morning and that an honest man that was on the guard had his face broken to the effusion of his blood. It is ordained that William presently be put in the stocks, and to remain during the magistrate's will, and thereafter to remove himself off the town.' (*Memorabilia of the City of Glasgow*)

APRIL 21ST

1589: 'This day Ninian Hutcheson is decreed in the wrong by decision of the court, for the illegal and strong-handed taking away from John Clerk of two salmon fish. Also for the forging of a wrongful complaint against the said John, alleging him to have taken shot of fish which should have belonged to the said Ninian and decreed the said Ninian to pay to the said John immediately 19 shillings for the said fish.' (*Memorabilia of the City of Glasgow*)

———— ◆ ————

1898: This letter was printed in the *Glasgow Herald* on this day:

Sir, I was glad to notice in today's paper reference was made at yesterday's town council meeting to the din made by the city dust carts in their midnight travels. I live in the vicinity of Fitzroy Place and consider the noise and disturbance made by the cart there perfectly intolerable, rendering it impossible to fall asleep till well after midnight. I have slept in many a large town, and have nowhere and never experienced the state of affairs undergone by us in this second city of the empire, and especially in this district of it where high rents are paid, and where the weary ratepayer expects that at least he will be allowed to sleep. I am, Tired Out.

APRIL 22ND

1643: 'This said day, ordains a warrant to be given to the treasurer to pay James Bogle the sum of a hundred pounds for helping of him to pay his ransom from the Turks.' (*Memorabilia of the City of Glasgow*)

———————•◆•———————

1925: '"The National Anthem will be sung at the close of the meeting and if there are any Republicans present I request them to leave the hall now". This was the concluding sentence of the introductory remarks by the Earl of Glasgow who presided at a meeting under the auspices of the British Fascists, held in the Berkeley Hall. There was a large attendance. Brigadier-General Blakeney, the President of the British Fascists, speaking of the ramifications of Communism, said that it was a deliberately organised campaign of subversion and was intended to bring about the world revolution. In the afternoon Brigadier-General Blakeney addressed the members of the Rotary Club in the Ca'doro Restaurant on "For King and Country". Communism stood for the shattering of society. It was a danger in war, and it was a more insidious danger in peace. It was necessary that there should be some form of organisation to deal with the problems which faced them and to counter the Communist movement in every town.' (*Glasgow Herald*)

APRIL 23RD

1762: 'On this day, Dr Joseph Black, professor of Chemistry at the University of Glasgow, explained his theory of latent heat – such was the name he himself gave to it – to the members of a literary society in the town and afterwards laid before his students a detailed view of the extensive and beneficial effects of this habitude in the grand economy of nature. From observing the analogy between the cessation of expansion by the thermometer during the liquefaction of the ice and during the conversion of water into steam, Dr Black, having explained the one, thought that the phenomena of boiling and evaporation would admit of a similar explanation. He was so convinced of the truth of this theory, that he taught it in his lectures in 1761, before he had made a single experiment on the subject. At this period his prelections on the subject of evaporation were of great advantage to Mr James Watt, afterwards so distinguished for his application of steam power. His discovery indeed may be said to have laid the foundation of that great practical use of steam which has conferred so immense a blessing upon the present age.' (*A Biographical Dictionary of Eminent Scotsmen* by Robert Chambers, Thomas Thomson, 1856)

APRIL 24TH

1907: The Prince and Princess of Wales received a warm welcome during their visit to the city, which saw parts lavishly decorated in their honour. This was the focus of this piece in the *Glasgow Herald*:

> Doubtless the time is remote when a city will be daring enough to display herself to Royal eyes as she really is. Even so, Glasgow would bear inspection, but, though a sensible town, she has her moments of vanity, so when august personages grace her streets she must put on her braws.

> She decks her grey buildings with gay flags, and swings garlands of flowers across her matter-of-fact streets. Accepting such trappings are inevitable on such occasions it must be conceded that on this occasion they are well disposed. The host of decorative artists who, for the past week or so, have been engaged transforming the homely face of Glasgow into something pretty, have done their work well, by which we mean that they have not overdone it.

> In any case, we are sure the wealth of decoration was not sufficient to conceal from the eyes of our august visitors the real character of our city, which would, indeed, have been a pity.

April 25th

1682: The following letter direct to the Magistrates and Council of this burgh, by the Marquis of Montrose, was produced and read on this day:

My Lord Provost and Gentlemen, His Majestic having appointed me Baillie of the Regality of Glasgow, in which as in all other capacities, I am or shall be stated, I resolve to embrace every occasion faithfully and zealously to advance His Majesties service and being confident that you will be no less forward, in your respective stations, to promote the Royal interest, and withall, having many reasons to have a singular respect to your city, in which I have my freedom, and intend to have my neighbourhood, I thought none fitter to discharge the duty that office owes His Majesty, both for His Majesties services and my credit, than Baillie Nisbett, your Dean of Guild, whom, for my respect to your city, and the personal kindness I have for himself, I have deputed Baillie of the Regality as by the commission herewith sent appears, and I do resolve to continue it to his successors in that Magistry, without some indispensable cause to the contrary, this being the greatest testimony I can at present give of my respect to your city... I am your really your affectionate friend and servant, Montrose.

(*Memorabilia of the City of Glasgow*)

APRIL 26TH

1892: 'At Glasgow Sheriff Summary Court on this day John Meiklejohn was charged with having sold one pennyworth of sweet milk which contained 4½ per cent of added water. Mrs Meiklejohn stated she bought the milk from a wholesale dealer, the bargain being that she was to be supplied with pure milk. The milk was sold exactly at it was received. The dealer stated that it was guaranteed pure to him and sent out as received. The Sheriff said he quite believed that there was no adulteration on the part of the respondent, but technically that was no protection under the Act. He limited the penalty to 2s 6d.' (*Glasgow Herald*)

1892: 'M & J Lambie, grocers and provision merchants, were charged with having sold 1lb of butter which contined 99 per cent of fatty matter not derived from milk. The respondents had given positive instructions to be careful not to sell margarine as butter. Unfortunately, Mr Lambie's daughter was left temporarily in charge of the shop and when the two lady inspectors called and asked for 1lb of butter at 1s, she naturally thought they wanted margarine and supplied them with it, as there was no genuine butter being sold at that time under 1s 2d per lb. The Sheriff imposed a fine of £2.' (*Glasgow Herald*)

APRIL 27TH

1780: 'By the Sheriff of Lanarkshire. Whereas, notwithstanding the public promonitions that have been given, and the public examples which have been made, the illegal practice of killing salmon fry still prevails in this country, to the great prejudice of the salmon fishing. A reward of half a guinea is hereby offered for each information upon that head left at the Sheriff Clerk's office, mentioning the names and designations of the offenders, and the names and designation of the witnesses by whom the offences can be proved, to be paid upon their conviction. The names of the informers shall be carefully concealed.' (*Glasgow Mercury*)

———◆———

1829: 'On Friday night a disturbance took place in Jamaica and Argyle Streets, occasioned in the first instance by a dispute betwixt two police officers and some carters, who were acting in contravention of the police regulations which, but for the spirited conduct of Messrs McFarlane and Graham, haberdashers, who afforded an asylum to the officers when pursued by an infuriated mob, and the timely arrival of assistance from the office, might have ended in a very serious manner, as it was both of the policemen were very much hurt.' (*Glasgow Herald*)

APRIL 28TH

1869: 'Frightful Murder in Glasgow. On this day Janet Hay, widow, aged 60 years, residing in South Coburg Street, was murdered, by her daughter, Agnes Hay, aged 37 years. The mother and daughter lived together. It seems that Agnes Hay, who is a warehouse worker, had been drinking for some weeks past, and her mind had thus become affected. She left work at 5 o'clock, being commanded to do so, she said, by voices she heard in the clouds. In going home these voices commanded her to murder her mother, which she did by choking her, and striking her on the head with a smoothing iron. She then went to her brother's house and told what she had done. She has been apprehended.' (*Birmingham Daily Post*)

———— ◆ ————

1967: The foundation pile was driven in for the Kingston Bridge on this day. The bridge was part of the planned inner-ring road, to ease city centre congestion and link other sections of the M8 motorway. It had ten lanes and became one of the busiest sections of road in Europe, carrying around 180,000 vehicles a day. In 1999–2000 major strengthening works were carried out that saw the 52,000-tonne structure being jacked up and moved a few inches southwards.

April 29th

1988: The Glasgow Garden Festival was officially opened on this day by Prince Charles and his wife Princess Diana. The festival was part of a series of five National Garden Festivals eventually held in Britain. Two had already been held in Liverpool and Stoke-on-Trent. The festival ran until September and saw over 4.3 million visitors. The location chosen was on part of the old Prince's Dock on the south side of the Clyde. The festival covered 120 acres and visitors were presented with many different attractions. They could enjoy a roller-coaster ride on the Coca Cola Roller (reaching speeds up to 50mph), or go up the 240 feet-high 'Clydesdale Bank Tower'. Railway and tram lines were also included in the site and a new footbridge was built for the occasion situated next to the SECC. The festival was significant as it stood as a welcome sign of the resurgence of the city following years of industrial decline. It was the first major event in the city since the Great Empire Exhibition of 1938. The site remained empty for several years until becoming the location for the Glasgow Science Centre and IMAX cinema. New premises for both the BBC and STV are also located there.

April 30th

1954: Stirling's Library opened on this day on Queen Street. The library remained in situ for almost forty years, before the building was converted to host the city's modern art collection. The Gallery of Modern Art opened in 1996, with many visitors believing the statue of the Duke of Wellington outside, with its almost permanent addition of a red and white traffic cone, to be an art installation. The building had been built by the tobacco lord William Cunninghame of Lainshaw in Ayrshire who had sold it on in 1789 to John Stirling. It was said Cunninghame spent £10,000 on its construction. The wings were then made into the extensive warehouses of William Stirling & Sons, calico printers. It was afterwards purchased by the Royal Bank of Scotland for its Glasgow branch and, after considerable alterations, formed the Royal Exchange of Glasgow. Robert Reid wrote in *Old Glasgow and its Environs*: 'I went through the house in 1778 while it was building. It was built on the site of two small cottages which fronted the Cowloan. The land was rather marshy, in consequence of which Mr Cunninghame was obliged to be at considerable expense in draining it. This property was generally allowed to be the most superb urban place of residence of any in Scotland.'

MAY 1ST

1823: 'This morning, another of those disgusting scenes occurred, which produces horror in the minds of the living, and keeps them in anxious suspense concerning the bodies of the departed dead. As the watchman was on duty near the High Church, he observed a fellow coming over the wall from the burying ground. He instantly sprung his rattle, and with the assistance of some people had him secured. When seized, he had in his possession the body of a man put up in a sack, which, along with the culprit, was taken to the Police Office. The depredator keeps the shop of a medical person in town. The body was claimed this morning by the wife and son of the deceased. The name of the deceased was John Dempster, a labourer, who was hurt some time since at the new building at the foot of Montrose Street. He died in the Royal Infirmary, and was buried on Tuesday afternoon. Such outrages as have lately been committed on the mansions of the dead, calls aloud for some exemplary punishment being inflicted on these worst of pirates, who, afraid of meeting with any person who can offer them resistance, practise their thefts in the lonely church-yard.' (Broadside entitled *Another church yard pirate* published by W. Carse, 1823, National Library of Scotland Rare Books Collection, shelfmark: L.C.Fol.73 (055))

MAY 2ND

1695: 'An act was read from the pulpits in the city, against buying or selling things on the Sabbath; also, against feeding horses in the fields, or hiring horses to ride on the Sabbath, except in cases of necessity, of which the magistrates are to be made acquainted. The ancient and praiseworthy custom of elders visiting the families once a quarter was revived.'
(*Sketch of the History of Glasgow*)

———— ◆ ————

1827: 'This day, the Circuit Court of Justiciary in Glasgow was opened here by Lords Gillies and Alloway: John Leslie, theft, by house breaking, guilty, to be transported 14 years. Margaret Smith, theft in Calton, pled guilty, 7 years transportation. Hugh M'Ilvain, uttering a forged note, pled guilty, 7 years transportation. Robert Smith, for assault and robbery, pled guilty, 14 years transportation. Thomas Howie, theft in Gorbals, pled guilty, 14 years transportation. David Mullin, uttering forged notes, pled guilty, 14 years transportation. James Stewart, uttering forged notes, pled guilty, 7 years transportation. Robert Johnston and W Johnston, sheep-stealing, outlawed for not appearing. Wm M'Pherson, for bigamy, guilty, 18 months in Bridewell. Jn Donaldson, shop-breaking, Argyle Street, guilty, to be transported for life.'
(Broadside concerning the proceedings of the Circuit Court of Justiciary, Glasgow, William Carse, 1827, National Library of Scotland Rare Books Collection, shelfmark: L.C.Fol.73 (095))

MAY 3RD

1938: One hundred thousand people gathered at Ibrox Stadium in Govan to hear King George VI open the 1938 Empire Exhibition. King George, who famously disliked public speaking because of a stutter, struggled through his address:

> The Queen and I are very happy to be in Scotland once more. We shall see today the completion of a great scheme whose inception we saw when we were last in Glasgow 10 months ago. The exhibition is an Empire undertaking but we do well to remember that it owes its origin and to a great extent its execution to the people of Scotland. I have spoken first of Scotland and I am well aware that without the generous help and support of the rest of the empire that this exhibition would not have been possible. Confident as I am that this great exhibition can make a real contribution to the general well being.

The King and Queen then went on a four-hour tour of the exhibition, held at Bellahouston Park. The exhibition was the last to celebrate the achievements of the Empire and showcased Glasgow's heavy industries, which were seeing an improvement in fortunes with the build up to war. In its seven-month run, the Empire Exhibition received over 12½ million visitors.

MAY 4TH

1798: 'Hair Powder Tax. Notice is hereby given that the Hair Powder Certificates will continue to be given out at this office, and the respective offices in the country as formerly advertised, for two weeks longer from this date, from ten o'clock forenoon, for payment of the duty only. Every person wearing Hair Powder since the 5th April current, without having taken out a certificate, forfeits twenty pounds. Alexander Menzies, Head Distributor and Collector, North Britain. NB – Information will be received by the collector against all persons wearing Hair Powder without a licence who will give suitable rewards to the informers. And those still negotiating to take out Certificates after this intimation will have themselves to blame for being prosecuted for the penalty of twenty pounds.' (*Glasgow Advertiser*)

1949: A fire broke out in the ground floor of Grafton's in Argyle Street. The clothes shop was soon engulfed in smoke and flames as the fire spread throughout the building. A crowd gathered to watch, which impeded the arrival of the emergency services. Thirteen of the shop's workers were killed in the blaze. Two of the shop's staff were later awarded the George Medal for bravery in helping five of their colleagues escape along a roof ledge to a neighbouring building.

MAY 5TH

1638: 'This day forasmuch as of before there was an act set down in favour of James Sanders, that no manner of person should be permitted to teach music within this burgh, or keep a school to that effect, except himself, as the act bears. And now, seeing that the music school is altogether decayed within this said burgh, to the great discredit of this city and discontentment of sundry honest men within the same, who have bairns whom they would have instructed in that art. And that Duncan Burnet, who sometime of before taught music within this burgh, is desirous to take up the said school again and teach music there in. Whereupon the said baillies and council convened the said James Sanders before them and after deliberation they, with the consent of the said James Sanders, granted his licence to the said Duncan Burnet to take up a music school with this burgh, he taking from the town bairns such school fees.'
(*Memorabilia of the City of Glasgow*)

———— • ◆ • ————

1970: On this day Bashir Maan became the first Muslim to be elected to public office in Britain, when voted as councillor for Kingston in the municipal elections. He was also the first Muslim Justice of the Peace. He retired from politics in 2003, aged seventy-five.

MAY 6TH

1746: 'This day, John Cochran, Master of Work, represented that, by advice of the Magistrates, he had sent to London to sell the broken necklace of diamonds, which several years ago were found among the rubbish of Daniel Campbell of Shawfield's house, when mobbed by the crowd in the year 1725, and exposed by some of the mob to sale, with a piece of gold coin, and that the same had been offered back to the Lady Shawfield, who refused to take it, and that, accordingly, the said necklace was sold at £30 sterling.'
(*Memorabilia of the City of Glasgow*)

————— ◆ —————

1814: 'Last week, the Magistrates and Town Council of Glasgow forwarded an address to the Prince Regent, congratulating his Royal Highness on the present auspicious era.'
(*Glasgow Herald*)

————— ◆ —————

1989: A new ship was launched on the Clyde on this day. It was the *Paper Boat*, designed by artist and sculptor George Wyllie. The 18 metre-long ship was launched during Glasgow's Mayfest by writer Naomi Mitchison. Wyllie also designed the *Straw Locomotive*, which was suspended from the Finnieston crane in 1987. He was given an MBE in 2005 for services to the arts. He died in 2012, aged ninety.

MAY 7TH

2002: On this day a statue was unveiled by Prime Minister Tony Blair. The statue was of Donald Dewar, who was the very first First Minister of Scotland. Dewar had studied at the University of Glasgow and been an MP for the Glasgow Garscadden constituency. He had been an advocate for devolution in Scotland and in New Labour's first cabinet was given the job of Secretary of State for Scotland. In 1998 he was able to say: 'There will be a Scottish Parliament. I like that.' He was elected First Minister in the new legislature in May 1999 but only served a short time in office as on the 10th of October 2000 he slipped and fell outside his official residence at Bute House in Edinburgh and suffered a brain haemorrhage. He died the next day. The 9 feet-high statue, created by artist Kenny Mackay, was sited in Buchanan Street, outside the Royal Concert Hall and Buchanan Galleries. It was often the target of vandals and had to be repaired in 2005. When it returned after cleaning and restoration, it was placed on a new plinth, 2m high.

MAY 8TH

1740: 'The channel between Port Glasgow and the Broomielaw was still only navigable for the merest shallops, and the magistrates seem almost to have despaired of its ever being useful for anything else, for upon this day, we find the following cautious entry:

> The council agree that a trial be made, of deepening the river, by carrying away the banks below the Broomielaw, and remit to the magistrates to cause do the same, and go the length of £100 sterling of charges thereupon, and to cause build a flat-bottomed boat for carrying off the sand and shingle from the banks.

It was not, however, till 1755, that the magistrates set about the improvement of the river in earnest, by inviting Mr Smeaton, the celebrated engineer, to survey and make a report upon it. He reported that the river at the ford at the Pointhouse, was only one foot three inches deep at low water, and three feet eight inches at high water and he recommended that a weir and lock should be erected at the Marlin ford, four miles below the city, in order to secure a depth of four-and-a-half feet in the harbour. This suggestion was approved of and, in consequence, the first act of parliament for improving the river was obtained in 1758.' (*Sketch of the History of Glasgow*)

MAY 9TH

1918: 'Sedition Charge. Glasgow Socialist Sentenced. John MacLean, the well-known socialist and representative in Scotland of the Bolshevik regime in Russia, was tried and convicted in the High Court of Justiciary in Edinburgh yesterday by the Lord Justice General and a jury of having been guilty of breaches of the Defence of the Realm Acts and sentenced to five years' penal servitude. Considerable interest was taken in the trial and long before the start the public parts of the court room were filled. The Lord Advocate said none of them could see into the dark recesses of the human heart and none of them would ever know what were the motives which tempted a man at home to destroy the liberty and freedom which were being defended abroad. But just because they could not know what the motive was, they must judge the man by what he did and what the prisoner had done his best to do was to spread sedition and disaffection among the civilian population. It became the duty of the state to protect the brave young working men from such insidious teaching, although for himself he did not believe influences of this kind were likely to erode the honesty and integrity of their young men.' (*Glasgow Herald*)

MAY 10TH

1941: On this day Rudolf Hess landed on Scottish soil. Hess was the deputy leader in Hitler's Nazi regime and had flown from Germany on a mission that is still clouded in mystery. He piloted a twin-engined Messerschmitt Bf 110 aircraft on his own from Augsburg. He bailed out, and landed at Eaglesham and was then taken to Maryhill Barracks. Hess was arrested and initially pretended to be a Luftwaffe pilot called 'Albert Horn'. He stated that he wanted to meet the Duke of Hamilton. The Duke, who was in the Royal Air Force at the time, came to meet with Hess at the barracks and then flew to London to give an account of his meeting. It was claimed that Hess intended to act as a peace broker between the British and German governments and that the Duke could help this process. Hess was put on trial at Nuremberg after the war. He eventually became the sole inmate of Berlin's Spandau Prison and died in 1987 aged ninety-three amidst conspiracy theories doubting if the dead man was even in fact Rudolf Hess. Hess, who had been treated for mental illness in 1941 and had attempted suicide before, had killed himself with an electrical cord. He had been imprisoned for almost half a century.

MAY 11TH

1825: On this day John Kean was publicly whipped in front of Glasgow Jail for shooting John Graham, a cotton spinner. This extract describes Kean's punishment and also contemporary attitudes to corporal punishment:

> The culprit ascended the scaffold soon after 12 o'clock, and after having been bound by the hands, and feet to the post, and his back stripped bare, the Executioner proceeded to inflict the punishment when he gave him 80 stripes, and from the appearance of the unhappy man's body, he must have felt great pain. The crowd was the largest since the execution of James Wilson for high treason and with shame do we say it, a great proportion of whom were females ... We trust that the punishment thus inflicted, will have a most salutary effect on those for which the above awful example is intended, and teach them that the arm of the law is strong ... The Lord Advocate of Scotland has given notice of his intention to introduce a bill into Parliament, by which all crimes of the above description, will in future be punished with Death.

(Broadside entitled *Letter from John Kean to the Lord Provost and Magistrates*, 1825, National Library of Scotland Rare Books Collection, shelfmark: L.C.Fol.73 (079))

MAY 12TH

1794: 'A few days ago the following tragi-comic scene took place in a field near Pollokshaws, between two gentlemen farmers; the cause of which we are told originated from one of them addressing the other by letter under the appellation of "Esquire". The person so addressed, perhaps conceiving himself not justly entitled to such a dignified superscription, and that his neighbour treated him in rather too satirical and ludicrous a manner, sent his polite brother farmer a challenge, requiring him to meet him next day. Accordingly the offended party, with his second, attended, with pistols, where he found his antagonist brandishing a broadsword. A dispute now arose which was to be the fighting weapon, when it was at last agreed they should use pistols. The seconds began to load the deadly peas when lo! the offending gentleman, thinking it an improper soil in which they were intended to be sown, and doubtless having a greater regard for the sixth commandment than his opponent, relented. The seconds then proposed that he should ask pardon of the valorous knight, which was done. The evening was terminated in drinking plentifully of that potent and exhilarating liquor "water of life", which was more agreeable than if this affair had ended in death.' (*Glasgow Advertiser*)

MAY 13TH

1568: Mary, Queen of Scots, had been imprisoned in Loch Leven's island castle following an uprising against her. She escaped confinement but on her way to Dumbarton Castle, her forces were intercepted by those of the Regent Moray who heard of her escape while in Glasgow. The Battle at Langside saw the Queen defeated, and she fled south to England. James Pagan in the *Sketch of the History of Glasgow* described the aftermath:

Upon the regent and his army defeating the queen's army at Langside, he returned in great pomp to the city where he was entertained by the magistrates and a great many of the town council very splendidly, suitable to his quality, at which time the regent expressed himself very affectionately towards the city and citizens of Glasgow; and for their kind offices and assistance done to him and his army, he promised to grant to the magistrates, or any incorporation in the city, any favour they should reasonably demand. His grace immediately caused his clerk and secretary extend a charter in favours of Matthew Fauside, present deacon of the baxters (bakers) in Glasgow, and his successors in office, for the use of the incorporation, for erecting and building a mill upon the river Kelvin for grinding wheat, and accordingly they built their mills thereupon.

MAY 14TH

1792: An article bemoaning the misuse of certain words was printed in the *Glasgow Advertiser*:

Elegance. No poor word had been more tortured from its original meaning than this. We have elegant pastry cooks, elegant men-milliners, elegant hair dressers, elegant footmen, elegant fiddlers, elegant tooth-drawers and elegant accoucheurs! I once heard a lady say she had been robbed of her last guinea by an elegant highwayman. Our diurnal prints have weekly advertisements of elegant lap-dogs for old maids, and elegant opportunities for young ones. In one word every thing is now become elegant that administers to either pleasure or convenience.

Delicacy. Few words have been more twisted out of their import than delicacy. I have heard one lady say, she had such a delicate habit that nothing would stay upon her stomach. Another, that her frame was so prodigious delicate she could not walk twice across the room without being in a violent perspiration! Another was so unfortunate in excessive delicacy of digestion that she could not swallow anything except bread pudding without being sick as a dog! I once heard a young lady boast that she had the most delicate, sweet little lap-dog in the world, only the dear little creature was perpetually playing pa pa tricks upon the carpet.

MAY 15TH

1801: 'On this day, the Faculty in Glasgow commenced vaccinating the children of the poor. From commencement to 31st December 1822, being 21½ years, 24,829 children of the poor were vaccinated gratis. It is remarkable, that during the seven years preceding the Institution of Vaccination in Glasgow, no less than 2,104 children died of the small-pox, and during the seven years subsequent to that period, there were only 795 deaths from that loathsome disease. However, during the seven years which preceded the Vaccination, there were only 217 children died of measles and in the seven years which followed it, no less than 1,198 children died of that disease.' (*Analysis of the statistical account of Scotland* by Sir John Sinclair, 1831)

———•◆•———

1890: 'Yesterday, Gardner & Mitchell, umbrella manufacturers, Ingram Street, were re-examined in bankruptcy. William Gardner, re-examined by Mr Downie, stated that the state of affairs showed an apparent deficiency of £3,600. He had thought over the matter carefully, and he had come to the conclusion that a great many of the orders of contracts must have resulted ultimately in loss instead of profit. While a profit was aimed at, orders must have been taken at too low a price, without considering the cost of the business.' (*Glasgow Herald*)

MAY 16TH

1932: 'There is very little likelihood in the near future for at least that Glasgow and London will be connected by a regular service of passenger and cargo air liners. I was officially informed today that there is no foundation for a suggestion that Imperial Airways are to consider a proposal to establish a service between the two cities, and that in fact they have never even had such a scheme placed before them. They would be prepared to run services anywhere provided the necessary financial and business support was forthcoming but at the moment, I was assured, such services are not paying propositions. By financial support is meant the granting by a civic body such as the Corporation of Glasgow of a subsidy sufficient to ensure the commercial stability of the undertaking. In addition to that there would also be required before a scheme for regular services could be even entertained a definite assurance from manufacturers and business men in the area to be served that they would utilise the air liners for the transport of substantial quantities of goods.' (*Glasgow Herald*)

MAY 17TH

1833: This letter to the editor was printed in the *Glasgow Herald* on this day:

Sir, It has been customary of late years for juries, in the circuit criminal courts of this district, to accompany their verdict against the pannel with a recommendation of mercy in his favour and this too in cases where the crime charged was of the deepest enormity. The professional gentleman conducting the defence takes leave of the jury by a pathetic appeal to their humanity, and they, perhaps, are the more readily induced to indulge in its amiable exercise, by the consideration that it is the only service they can render to a fellow creature upon whose guilt they have been constrained to pass judgment. I ask your numerous readers, is not this practice an improper one? I am led to these reflections by the untimely, though well-merited, fate of the two individuals who have this week expiated their crimes on the gibbet in this city, the one for murder, the other for a rape accompanied with revolting brutality. Both were recommended to mercy. I conclude that juries act in the most becoming manner when they strictly confine themselves to the single duty for which they are impannelled. F.

MAY 18TH

1960: On this day, what is regarded as one of the greatest football games ever played took place in Glasgow. It was the final of the European Cup being held at the neutral venue of Hampden Park. The two finalists were the German team Eintracht Frankfurt and Spanish champions Real Madrid. There was local interest in the match as Eintracht Frankfurt had beaten Rangers 12-4 on aggregate on their way to the final. The game was watched by a crowd of 127,621 – the biggest attendance before or since for a European final. Real Madrid started the game slowly and Eintracht went ahead in 18 minutes. The Spanish side reacted and drew equal in the 27th minute. They then went ahead, consolidated their lead and went into the half-time break 3-1 ahead. Although the Germans scored another two goals, the white-shirted Real Madrid finished the game worthy winners with a 7-3 scoreline. It remains the highest-scoring final. The winning team included the legendary Ferenc Puskas who scored four and Alfredo di Stefano who scored a hat-trick. Following the game *The Times* newspaper described Real Madrid as 'the finest football team in the world'. Real Madrid had won each of the five European Cup finals they had contested.

MAY 19TH

1966: On this day Bob Dylan played Glasgow for the first time. The American singer was in the middle of a world tour, that had seen much controversy. Dylan had started his career as a folk singer, playing an acoustic guitar and harmonica. In 1966 he had started performing with electric guitars and was touring with a full band behind him called The Hawks, and later to be known as The Band. Dylan's concert at the Odeon came only a few days after an infamous show at Manchester, where a member of the audience had shouted 'Judas' at him. Dylan's Glasgow set list included She Belongs To Me, Visions Of Johanna, It's All Over Now Baby Blue, Mr Tambourine Man and Like A Rolling Stone. His visit to Glasgow was tainted by an incident when a waiter who brought room service to his hotel room verbally abused him and when he was being thrown out, produced a knife. Despite this, Dylan returned to play in Glasgow a number of times, including a memorable concert at the Barrowlands in 2004.

May 20th

1899: These notices and adverts appeared in the *Glasgow Herald* on this day:

The National Telephone Company Limited. Subscribers to the exchange system in Glasgow can speak to every other subscriber within the city boundary and also to subscribers in: Govan, Ibrox, Partick, Kinning Park, Rutherglen, Pollokshaws, Cambuslang, Clydebank, Kirkintilloch, Bearsden, Milngavie. The company have at present over seven thousand telephone lines and this number is being added to daily. Where the consumer has the alternative of two suppliers, one with the telephone and one without, it may safely be assumed that for handiness he will ring up the man with the telephone. Some people saw the use of the service at the very start, some have only recently been convinced, some have still to be convinced.

Boys Clothing in Washing Materials. For variety in material, beauty of design, exquisite colourings, effect combined with utility, and keen prices, we cannot be equalled. Drill Blouses, frilled collars, special price 1s 11d. Serge Blouses, Art shades, all wool, special price 2s 6d. Odd knickers, drill serge or velvet, 3s 6d.

Bakers are requested to keep away from Cambuslang and Rutherglen.

Ferguson's Safest Sweetmeats, in tins, 6d. Sold by Higher Class Confectioners.

MAY 21ST

1931: Walter Arnott is described by the Scottish Football Association as 'probably the greatest Scottish player of the Victorian era'. His funeral was reported in the *Glasgow Herald*:

Funeral of Famous Scottish Internationalist. The funeral took place today from his residence, Carolside Avenue, Clarkston, to Cathcart Cemetery of Mr Walter Arnott, the famous Queen's Park and International footballer, who died on Monday a few days after celebrating his 70th birthday. Associates of Mr Arnott in the football world and many members of the general public awaited the arrival of the cortege at the main entrance to the cemetery and joined in the procession to the graveside. The mourners included representatives of the Legislative Council of Scottish Football and directors of various clubs, and amongst those who paid a last tribute to an outstanding figure in Scottish football annals were Mr Robert Campbell, president of the Scottish Football Association, Mr Hugh Logan chairman of Queen's Park FC, and Mr RS McColl and Mr John L Hay, former Queen's Park players and Scottish Internationalists.

MAY 22ND

1835: 'In the hiring market there were a great number of male servants, but they were not much in request, a few of the ablest were hired at 8*l* to 9*l* 10*s*, others from 5*l* 10*s* to 7*l*; lads 13 to 17 years old from 1*l* 10*s* to 4*l*. There was a large attendance of women also, but it did not meet the demand and very high prices were asked. Dairy maids asked £5 and in some instances £4 to £5 was given. Women for ordinary work were hired at £2 10*s* to £4, the whole of these for the half year. We observed a few Irish girls for hire, whose attendance at our market, if it were increased, would be a great relief from the scarcity of maid servants.' (*Glasgow Herald*)

1835: 'Two rascals of the names Sutherland and Forsyth made an attempt to break into McCorkindale's extensive hosiery warehouses, corner of St Enoch's Square and Argyle Street. Luckily their intentions were frustrated for the watchman, overhearing the noise of their preliminary operations, sprang his rattle, got assistance, and was just in time to pay the intruders an unwelcome visit when they had got the door forced from its hinges, made their entrance to the premises, and were about to commence their work of spoilation.' (*Glasgow Herald*)

MAY 23RD

1740: 'This day the Magistrates represented that they had made application by petition to the Earl of Glasgow, Lord Ross and Sir John Maxwell of Pollock, overseers, nominated by the Barons of the Exchequer, for overseeing the laying out of the expense for supporting and repairing the Cathedral Church setting forth by the late violent storm and hurricane which happened in the night betwixt the 13th and 14th days of January 1739. Several of the turrets of the Church, and battlement surrounding the same, were thrown down, part whereof fell down upon the roof of the church, and broke through and damnified the roof, and other parts of the said roof which were covered with lead and sclates, was uncovered and tirred by the said hurricane, and the roof thereby much damnified and spoiled and several other parts of the church chattered and disordered, and the top of the spire made to decline and bow down, which will cost a considerable expense for repairing thereof, which will, by the most modest computation, require £50 sterling to repair the stone work and £93 9s 9½d sterling for timber, sclate, nails and scaffolding to repair the roof and £236 2s 8d sterling for cleading the lead roof.' (*Memorabilia of the City of Glasgow*)

MAY 24TH

1927: On this day Scottish inventor John Logie Baird created a new record for sending long-distance television pictures. He sent moving images of his own head 438 miles from London to Glasgow's Central Hotel.

———— • ◆ • ————

1972: On this day Rangers won the European Cup Winners' Cup. They defeated Russian side Moscow Dynamo 3-2 in the final, played in Barcelona. Rangers had shown impressive form in Europe although they had been close to elimination. In the second round they had ended the tie against Sporting Lisbon 6-6 on aggregate. Bizarrely, the referee insisted both teams take part in a penalty shoot-out despite Rangers' three away goals meaning they had already qualified for the next round. Rangers only scored one penalty and thought they were out until the referee's decision was overturned. A semi-final victory over the German side Bayern Munich took Rangers to the final. It was the third they had competed and were determined to not come home again the losing side. The Rangers team included players of the calibre of John Greig, Willie Johnston and Sandy Jardine. They went 3-0 up but had to hold on as the Russians came back to score twice. The final was marred by pitch invasions by fans and confrontations with the Spanish police, and Rangers were banned for a year, denying them the chance to defend their win.

MAY 25TH

1967: On this day Celtic won the European Champions Cup – the first British club to lift the trophy. Over 12,000 Celtic fans travelled to Lisbon to see the Lisbon Lions, as the team became known, defeat Inter Milan. The Italian club had won the prestigious trophy twice. Celtic went an early goal behind when Mazolla scored a penalty in the 8th minute. Celtic went on the attack and in the second half scored when Tommy Gemmell fired in a powerful shot from 18 yards. In the 83rd minute Celtic scored the winning goal after Steve Chalmers flicked in a shot by Bobby Murdoch. Celtic's attacking style of play had overcome the defensive system adopted by the Italians. Congratulations flooded in. Bill Shankly, the Liverpool manager, congratulated Jock Stein by saying to him: 'John, you're immortal now.' The final ended a season where Celtic had won every competition they'd entered. The manager of Rangers, Scot Symon, said after the final: 'Words just cannot express this achievement after such a wonderful season. This win is a fitting climax.' Celtic reached another European Cup final in 1970 but lost to Feyenoord.

MAY 26TH

1939: 'Summer Show in Glasgow. The most pleasing item in the second programme of the summer time show Half Past Eight presented last night at the King's Theatre, was a colourful episode from the life of Napoleon, written by Charles Ross, the producer of the show. It was distinguished by the fact that it had dramatic point, so lacking in most of the other sketches in this entertainment, and also by an acid portrayal of Napoleon by Gordon Rennie. Spectacle was the most attractive aspect of the programme. Despite the work by George West and Jack Raymond the humorous sketches were built up mainly of material that is wearing thin and they dragged in places. George West still shows his unique taste in bizarre outfits. The spectacular items were made more delightful by the dancing of Felicity Andreae, whose grace of movement pleased the audience, especially in Legend of the Waterfall and in a Spanish fiesta number. Pierette's Dream contrasted the modern "hot stepping" with the grace of ballet dancing. Hilda Stewart and Charles Stewart and the Gee Boys, all clever dancers, were not seen often enough.' (*Glasgow Herald*)

MAY 27TH

1861: 'On Saturday afternoon the new steamers *Ruby* and *Rothesay Castle* started from the Bridge Wharf at four o'clock for Rothesay on their first passenger trip. As both steamers had been highly spoken of as very swift boats, considerable interest was manifested on the occasion both at the Broomielaw and along the coast by crowds of persons who were in expectation of witnessing a race. Even if such a contest could, with any degree of fairness and satisfaction, take place in the narrow channel, it would be in contravention of the river regulations, but it so happens that the river is not suitable for any trial of speed. The *Ruby* started first, and after Bowling was passed, and plenty of sea room obtained, they certainly steamed in a most admirable manner. While the *Ruby* proved herself to be a crack steamer, and the swifter of the two, still the *Rothesay Castle* kept her position well, and on reaching Gourock, was not much more than a minute's time behind the *Ruby* – the run being accomplished by the former in an hour and 35 minutes. Seeing that both steamers are so swift, it is to be hoped that no feeling of contention will arise.' (*Glasgow Herald*)

MAY 28TH

1827: An Act 'for forming a carriage road or drive round the park or public Green of Glasgow, and for the better regulation of the fire places and chimneys of steam engines, and other works in the said city and suburbs' was given the Royal Assent on this day. The carriageway around the Green was devised to improve the area and also to relieve unemployment amongst the weavers. The particulars pertaining to chimneys were specific, as can be seen in this excerpt:

…the proprietors or occupiers of all steam engines, or of works of which the machinery is moved by steam, erected, or to be erected, shall be bound to construct the engine chimneys of the said works of, at least, the following heights and dimensions: the engine chimneys of which the open space or inside capacity at the top does not exceed one hundred and ninety six superficial square inches, shall not be less than fifty five feet in height; the engine chimneys of which the open space or inside capacity at the top exceeds one hundred and ninety six superficial square inches and does exceed three hundred and twenty four superficial square inches, shall not be less than sixty five feet in height.

(*Glasgow: Past and Present*)

MAY 29TH

1861: 'Glasgow Bankruptcy Court. Examination of William McGarry. The bankrupt was a furniture dealer and upholsterer. There were present Mr John Miller, accountant, trustee, and Mr John Naismith, writer, agent in the sequestration. The bankrupt deponed: I have been 18 years in business as a furniture dealer. I began without any capital, my only stock being my own house furniture. The business was remunerative for the first seven years. About three years ago I took an additional shop. The rent of both shops was £165 which was more than the business would pay, and this and the dullness of trade brought me into difficulties, as I had increased my stock considerably. I stopped payments in April, there being a decree against me for £12 10s 4d. I latterly offered a composition of 12s, which offer was accepted by a number of my creditors. I was shortly afterwards incarcerated by a creditor, who refused to accept of the composition. Interrogated: Have you any property that you have not handed over to the trustee? Deposed: Nothing, except my wife and ten of a family. (Laughter.) My liabilities are £514 and my assets £345. This concluded the examination.' (*Glasgow Herald*)

MAY 30TH

1791: The *Glasgow Advertiser* dated this day included these articles:

Saturday last, Thomas Walker, belonging to the Society of Porters, was fined by the magistrates in five schillings and twenty four hours imprisonment, for refusing to go on a message from the Cross to the Broomielaw unless he was paid threepence.

Charles Gardner, Thomas Martin and Cecilia Clarke, who were under sentence of transportation, in this jail, were escorted by a guard towards Edinburgh, on their way for New England. The magistrates, whose humanity and benevolence is well-known, were pleased to allow Gardner and Martin two shirts, two pairs of stockings, one pair of shoes and a handkerchief, each and Clarke, two shirts, two pairs of stockings, one pair of shoes, one short gown, one apron, one handkerchief, two mutches, and a duffle cloak, to accommodate them on their passage.

Sunday, his Grace the Duke of Argyle, Lady Campbell, Mrs Campbell Carrick, Lord John Campbell and Doctor Ewart arrived at the Saracen's Head.

MAY 31ST

1864: 'A Sad Case. Miss Watt, the only surviving daughter of the greatest British bibliographer, Dr Watt, has lately died at Glasgow in a workhouse. Last year a petition was presented to Lord Palmerston praying for a grant of £100 a year for the benefit of Miss Watt. The petition was signed by Alfred Tennyson, John Ruskin, Thomas Carlyle, George Grote, Sir Frederick Madden, Holman Hunt, Mrs Gaskell, and many other names of note. An answer was promised in February, but none came till last week, some days after the death of the poor lady had been announced to one of the Premier's secretaries. Then a fellow secretary wrote to ask if Miss Watt could be supported on £50 a year. If so that sum might probably be given to her.' (*Glasgow Herald*)

———•◆•———

'Professor Anderson's Entertainment. The Professor having lately announced his readiness to give any Spiritualist £100 for each rap produced on a table which he could not account for by a natural cause, a numerous audience assembled in the City Hall last night, in the fond hope and expectation of witnessing a "spiritual convention" a sort of miniature séance. No spiritualist appeared and for one night at least Mr Anderson had the satisfaction of still keeping his money in his purse.' (*Glasgow Herald*)

JUNE 1ST

1982: On this day Pope John Paul II held an open-air Mass at Bellahouston Park. It was the first ever visit by a pontiff to Scotland. A quarter of a million attended the Mass, the biggest gathering of people in Scotland to that date. Some had camped on the roadside since the beginning of the week in order to secure a good vantage point. The historic event took place on the hottest day of the year and a number of people were treated for heat-related ailments. The Pope arrived by helicopter and then toured the site by his vehicle nicknamed 'The Popemobile'. In his address, he talked of the success of Scotland's Catholics in being able to flourish after the challenges presented through the centuries. John Paul II was the first non-Italian pope since 1523, and had engaged Catholics around the world more energetically than his predecessors. As he left Bellahouston the crowd sang Will Ye No Come Back Again?. Although Pope John Paul II didn't make a return journey, his successor, Pope Benedict XVI, held a similar Mass in 2010.

JUNE 2ND

1830: On this day Glaswegian Sandy McKay fought the Irishman Simon Byrne in a bare-knuckle bout in England. The *Glasgow Herald* described the later stages of the fight:

Round 31. Sandy came up game as a lion. Simon jobbed him terrifically in the sore places, and, catching Sandy's head under his arm, he jobbed him in the ribs with killing severity. In the struggle both went down. From this round forth Byrne gradually rose in favour, and although still having recourse to the cautious system of going down to avoid the embraces of his still formidable antagonist, the punishment he administered in every round was dreadful. Sandy's face was opened in all directions, and almost tattooed like that of a New Zealander. Still he came up with unshrinking courage, and from the increasing weakness of Byrne, who literally exhausted himelf by hitting, hopes were entertained he might make a turn in his favour. The hope was, however, vain. Byrne maintained his caution and got better in the 47th round, while McKay became more groggy and rolled like a ship in the storm.

McKay died the following day. Rioting occurred in Glasgow when news arrived. The Roman Catholic chapel was attacked and four people were killed.

June 3rd

1930: This article by the Scottish Justices and Magistrates Association appeared in the *Glasgow Herald* on this day:

Flogging. Its use as a deterrent. The recent prevalance of the razor-slashing type of crime in some of our great cities has called forth in some quarters a demand for the use of flogging as a deterrent punishment. Indeed, some of our learned judges have pronounced in favour of the reintroduction of the use of the 'cat' in cases of brutal crime. The law on the subject of flogging differs very much in England and in Scotland. In Scotland flogging was abolished in 1862 and from that time till the passing of the Criminal Law Amendment Act in 1912 the infliction of this punishment was absolutely illegal. Even now it can only be inflicted in the small number of cases which come up under the appropriate section of that Act dealing with men living on the immoral earnings of women. In England on the other hand, there are powers to flog under various Acts and as a recent case reminded the public, flogging is still occasionally carried out. Here we must make it plain that we are speaking only of adult offenders. The birching of juveniles, though perhaps an equally controversial subject, is not one with which we are concerned just now.

JUNE 4TH

1778: 'Yesterday the workmen began to remove the centres from below the additional part of the last arch of the Old Bridge. They proceeded in rather too precipitate a manner, by loosing the wedges on one side, so that the weight of those centres not slackened preponderating, tumbled the whole over. A mason got one of his legs sorely crushed, but happily no other accident happened.' (*Glasgow Mercury*)

***

1890: 'The Scottish Football League. The league was formally constituted at a meeting held in Aitken's Hotel last night, when the following office-bearers were elected: chairman, Mr A Lawrence, Dumbarton; vice-chairman Mr George Henderson, Cowlairs; secretary, Mr JH McLaughlin, Celtic; treasurer, Mr Wilton, Rangers. The fixture list between the following clubs which comprise the league, was completed: Celtic, Third Lanark, Rangers, Cowlairs, Renton, Dumbarton, Vale of Leven, St Mirren, Abercorn, Cambuslang and Heart of Midlothian.' (*Glasgow Herald*)

JUNE 5TH

1952: On this day the Art Gallery and Museum at Kelvingrove put a new acquisition on display. The work was a painting by Spanish Surrealist artist Salvador Dali entitled *Christ of St John of the Cross*. The buying of the painting was not universally welcomed although it soon became the most popular and talked about artwork in the collection. The painting, which measures 2m x 1.2m, depicts Christ on the cross, seen from above so that his face is unseen, seemingly hanging in mid-air looking down on a small landscape featuring some fishermen. The painting cost the corporation £8,200 and included in the purchase agreement was the gallery's rights to the copyright and reproduction. In 1961 the painting was attacked and damaged, and the large tear in the canvas required careful repair by the gallery's conservation staff. For many years the picture was hung at the end of one of the long side galleries, which afforded visitors a dramatic view. 'The Dali' as it was known, was moved to the St Mungo Museum of Religious Life and Art when that museum opened in 1993, although it was returned to Kelvingrove in 2006 following the revamp.

JUNE 6TH

1944: The Allied invasion of France began on this day: D-Day. Operation Overlord saw 160,000 troops take part in the biggest-ever seaborne landings. The majority of the soldiers were from America, but a sizeable proportion were from the Commonwealth, who had been fighting since 1939. Many Scots were part of the invasion force and one in particular made his mark in history through carrying out a very Scottish act. Bill Millin, the son of a Glasgow policeman, was born in the city in 1922. He had joined the army following a spell in the Territorial Army and became part of the 1st Special Service Brigade, the commando force led by Lord Lovat, who asked him to be his personal piper. As they landed on Sword Beach, attracting heavy gunfire, Lord Lovat ordered Private Millin to start playing his bagpipes, which he did, firstly with Hielan Laddie and then The Road to the Isles. Millin was unarmed, except for his skean dhu. He played throughout the day, including when walking over Pegasus Bridge, which Millin described as 'a very long bridge'. When some German soldiers were captured they said they'd refrained from shooting the piper as they thought he was insane. Bill Millin died in 2010, aged eighty-eight.

JUNE 7TH

1963: A four-piece popular music group from Liverpool played Glasgow for the first time. At the Odeon Cinema, they play seven songs: Some Other Guy, Do You Want to Know a Secret?, Love Me Do, From Me To You, Please Please Me, I Saw Her Standing There, and Twist and Shout. The Beatles supported American solo artist Roy Orbison on his tour although their popularity meant they ended the tour as headliners. (*Beatles Bible*)

———◆———

1983: An unusual shape was seen in the skies over Glasgow as the space shuttle made a flying visit. The NASA shuttle *Enterprise* – named after the spaceship in the science fiction TV series *Star Trek* – had flown over the Atlantic to attend the Paris Air Show. It had been a star attraction, mounted on the back of its specially adapted Boeing 747 transporter aircraft. The unique combination of flying machines had visited Germany, Iceland and Italy. On its return voyage it flew over Glasgow, with thousands watching at the airport, although it missed an intended flypast at the Rockwell factory in East Kilbride. The *Enterprise* had been used for test flights, where it carried out glided landing approaches. It never flew in space. It is now a museum exhibit, part of the Smithsonian Institution.

JUNE 8TH

1906: 'The launch at Clydebank yesterday of the new Cunard liner *Lusitania* was favoured with splendid weather, and the many thousands of spectators saw, in the best possible circumstances, the floating of the largest vessel that has yet been built. Everything combined to make the launch a great success. Her 16,000 tonnes of launching weight were released prompt to a second at the time arranged weeks before, and two minutes forty two and a half seconds afterwards, the huge hull was floating peacefully in the waters of the Clyde. The crowd was the largest that has ever witnessed the launch of a vessel on the Clyde, or probably anywhere else. Messrs John Brown & Co had declared a holiday for the occasion but they had granted permission to all their employees to come inside the yard and they had added that each might bring with him a lady friend.' (*Glasgow Herald*)

The *Lusitania* created a number of records for transatlantic crossings after its introduction to service in 1907. In 1915, off the coast of Ireland, it was sunk by a German U-boat. Over 1,000 people died in the incident, which influenced America's participation in the First World War.

JUNE 9TH

1932: 'Street Cleaning. Mr Colin H Macfarlane – Director of Public Cleansing – speaking yesterday at the conference of the Institute of Public Cleansing in Manchester, took as his subject "A Review of Modern Methods of Street Cleansing". Street cleansing, he said, like all other branches of cleansing work, has undergone great changes in the past years. Although the amount of refuse in the streets was now considerably less, the smooth surfaces showed up the slightest dirt and frequent sweepings were necessary. It was, he thought, true to say that "If the streets are dirty it is the Cleansing Department's fault. If they are littered it is the public's fault." Not only did this unnecessary and inexcusable littering look unsightly but it created much needless expense. One despaired of getting the public to correct their habits in this respect merely by education and persuasion. Compulsion in the shape of a by-law, with a penalty for failure to comply, seemed necessary. It was proposed to insert this year in the Glasgow Corporation's Provisional Order a suitable clause to cover this offence. In his opinion it would also be necessary to introduce the system prevailing on the Continent of empowering police officers to impose a fine on the spot.' (*Glasgow Herald*)

JUNE 10TH

1842: On this day a report was printed in the *Glasgow Herald* of an event that drew much attention. It was the arrival of the bicycle in the city. Kirkpatrick Macmillan had ridden from Dumfries on his velocipede, the first pedal-powered cycle in the world. The blacksmith's arrival in Glasgow caused a scene and crowds forced him to ride on the footpath, where he unfortunately caused a child to be knocked over. The newspaper commented on the appearance of this new machine:

> The rider was soon surrounded by a large crowd, attracted by the novelty of the machine. The child who was thrown down had not sustained any injury and, under the circumstances, the offender was fined only 5s. The velocipede employed in this instance was very ingeniously constructed – it moved on wheels turned with the hand by means of a crank, but to make it 'progress' appeared to require more labour than will be compensated for by the increase of speed. This invention will not supersede the railways.

(*Glasgow Herald*)

JUNE IITH

1915: 'Music in the Glasgow Parks. The following bands will play today in the Glasgow Public Parks and open spaces: Glasgow Western and City of Glasgow Pipers in Alexandra Park, at 7.30pm; Springburn Rechabite Band in Ruchill Park at 7.30pm; 1st and 146th GCBB in Tollcross Park at 7.30 pm; His Majesty's Royal Horse Guards (Blues) in Victoria Park at 7.30 pm; Rouken Glen Entertainers in Rouken Glen Park at 3.30 and 7.30 pm; The Crackers Concert Party in Queen's Park at 3.30 and 7.30 pm.' (*Glasgow Herald*)

1915: 'A Renfrew man, William Morton, made his 122nd appearance at the Police Court yesterday when he was charged with creating a breach of the peace in Hairst Street. He pleaded not guilty, but Police Judge Wright, who presided, sent him to prison for 60 days without the option of a fine. Morton declared that he would rather he had been sent to the front to get shot than sentenced to 60 days.' (*Glasgow Herald*)

JUNE 12TH

1782: 'Following the surrender of Lord Cornwallis and his whole British army to the Americans under Washington at Yorktown in March, 1782, the downfall of Britain seemed at hand. Ireland, with forty thousand volunteers in arms, was clamouring for independence, and Britain was without a soldier to oppose an invasion. In the emergency the new British Government called upon the principal towns to arm their inhabitants, and the Lord Provost of Glasgow, Patrick Colquhoun, received a letter from Lord Shelburne, desiring the Town Council to take measures for that purpose on this day. The request cannot be said to have been received with enthusiasm by the main body of the citizens, who seemed to regard any interruption of their business pursuits as a matter not to be thought of. They also regarded the enrolment of manual workers as undesirable, probably for the same reason. The Lord Provost, however, informed Lord Shelburne that a number of the younger inhabitants, who could afford to buy arms and to spend time in learning military exercises, were willing to take up the project.' (*History of Glasgow* volume 3 by George Eyre-Todd, 1934)

JUNE 13TH

1842: 'A week has now passed since a single drop of rain fell in this neighbourhood, during which we have had by day a fierce sun and the wind from the arid north east. Yesterday was amongst the hottest days we have had. In the afternoon the thermometer stood at 103 degrees in the sun and at nightfall it pointed to 70. On the evening of Saturday last, about 8 o'clock, a young man was bathing in the Clyde at the bend of the river near Little Govan when though able to swim, he sunk, in all likelihood from the attack of cramp and was drowned. Mr Geddes, the keeper of the Humane Society's House, recovered the body. On Wednesday night, between nine and ten o'clock a young lad named Duncan McKenzie, about thirteen years of age, belonging to Tradeston, lost his life in the Clyde at the Dominie's Hole. He had gone in to bath at the spring-boards and after swimming nearly across the river he sunk when within two or three yards of the south bank. Upwards of half an hour elapsed before the body was recovered and every effort to restore animation proved unavailing.' (*Glasgow Herald*)

JUNE 14TH

1690: 'Our sovereign lord and lady taking to their consideration, that the city of Glasgow is amongst the most considerable of the royal burrows within their ancient kingdom of Scotland, both for the number of inhabitants, and their singular fitness and application to trade, and the convenient situation of the place upon the river of Clyde: and that the common good of the said city hath been greatly wasted and exhausted, by draining vast sums of money from magistrates, who were not freely elected and chosen, as is usual in other royal burrows and likeways considering the firm adherence, and constant zeal for the Protestant religion of the community of the said city, their majesties did grant a full and ample charter, confirming all former charters granted to them, by any of their royal predecessors, in favour of the community of the said city or gild-brethren, tradesmen, or any society, or deaconry, within the same; and also of new granting and disponing to the said city and common council thereof, a full and ample power, right, and faculty of electing their provost, baillies, and other magistrates, at the ordinary time of election, as freely as any other royal burgh might do within their said ancient kingdom.' (Act of Parliament in favour of the town of Glasgow)

JUNE 15TH

1639: 'This day it is ordained that by sound of drum the inhabitants of this burgh bring their whole silver plate, to be bestowed in defence of the good common cause in hand, and ordains James Stewart, late provost, Walter Stirling, Dean of Guild, John Barnes and Gawain Nisbet, to attend upon the receiving of the silver plate. This day also ordains the treasurer to have a warrant for the sum of 27 pounds money, disbursed by him to John Cuthbertson, drummer, in consideration of the extraordinary pains he has taken in recent times.' (*Memorabilia of the City of Glasgow*)

1693: 'An Act of Parliament was obtained in favour of the city of Glasgow, disponing to the Magistrates and Council, an imposition of two pennies Scots upon the pint of all ale and beer to be either brewed or inbrought and vended, hopped, or sold within the said town, suburbs, and liberties thereof, for any space their majesties shall please, not exceeding thirteen years, for the purpose of paying the town's debt; excepting ale and beer brewed by heritors in the country, and consumed by them and their families in town, also excepting ale and beer brewed and vended in Gorbals.' (*Old Glasgow and its Environs*)

JUNE 16TH

1985: An institution came to an end as the Apollo put on its final show. The legendary Renfield Street venue had started life as Green's Playhouse, opening in 1927. It was the biggest cinema in Europe at the time. A number of rock acts such as Jimi Hendrix and Led Zeppelin played it in the late 1960s and early 1970s. It closed in 1973 before reopening a few months later as the Apollo. The first acts to play were Johnny Cash, the Rolling Stones and Lou Reed. Over the years many singers and bands performed including Paul McCartney, Rod Stewart, AC/DC, David Bowie, Motorhead, Cliff Richard, Billy Connolly, Chuck Berry, Slade, The Jacksons, The Who, Queen and Abba. The Apollo was regarded as being a special place for bands to perform and many live albums were recorded there, including Status Quo's Live, Roxy Music's Viva! Roxy Music, The Stranglers' Live at the Apollo, Gillan's Mutually Assured Destruction: Glasgow 1982 and AC/DC's If You Want Blood You've Got It. The final act to take to the famously high stage was Paul Weller's Style Council. The site is now a multiplex cinema. (www.glasgowapollo.com)

JUNE 17TH

1831: 'W McMillan, the pedestrian, who lately performed the task of walking 100 miles in 24 successive hours, 30 of which were walked backwards, on Tuesday night began the performance of the same feat here, on the Paisley road. He commenced at half past six o'clock, and continued through the night and day, accompanied by crowds of onlookers, some of whom wearied themselves out by following and endeavouring to keep up. The walking backwards, which he performs with amazing facility, he divided into four and five miles at a time. He stopped occasionally at short intervals and partook of wine and other refreshments and on Wednesday morning he appeared to be much fatigued, but trudged on without fagging. He finished exactly at five minutes past four, being nearly two hours and a half within the allotted time.' (*Glasgow Herald*)

1831: 'On Wednesday night a large hogshead, containing about 12 or 14 cwt of soap, was smuggled in one of the steamers from Belfast. It was carried to the back shed of the Market Inn. Here the excise officers got information the contraband soap was deposited, and it was taken possession of but the lock was opened by false keys, and the whole of the property carried off, piecemeal. We understand however, it was again nearly all recovered, secreted in different places in the neighbourhood.' (*Glasgow Herald*)

JUNE 18TH

1794: 'On this day the foundation of a stone bridge across the Clyde, at the foot of the Saltmarket Street, was laid by Gilbert Hamilton, the late Lord Provost. During the subsequent year, the work was carried on, and so far completed, that the arches were thrown across, the spandrils filled up, and the parapets nearly finished when, on 18 November 1795, the lower part of the City was subjected to an alarming inundation of the River, which, at four o'clock pm swept away the northmost arch of the bridge, and, in two hours afterwards, the whole of the arches gave way. This bridge, which was named Hutchison's, consisted of five arches, was 410 feet long, and 26 feet broad, within the parapets.' (*Annals of Glasgow*)

1798: 'Sale tomorrow. Old Scots Cheese. By public sale in A Malcolm's Vendue Rooms, King's Street, on Tuesday, to begin at 11 o'clock forenoon. About eighty old Scots Cheeses, a great part of them made in Dunlop Parish nearly five years ago, which, to persons of taste, are nothing inferior to the famous Parmesan Cheese. They will be sold in single cheeses, without reserve, therefore well worth the attention of private families and tavern keepers.' (*Glasgow Advertiser*)

JUNE 19TH

1912: 'Graduation at Glasgow. The summer graduation ceremony, which took place in the Bute Hall, Glasgow University yesterday, was characterised by somewhat unseemly and discourteous conduct on the part of a number of students. As is usual at the graduation ceremonies, the galleries and a large portion of the area of the building are reserved for the public, and the students, in accordance with old time usage, appropriate the rear of the hall as their own special preserve. Prior to yesterday's proceedings, the undergraduates sang selections of students' songs and topical ditties, varied by humorous displays of ragging, pushing and jostling. When the proceedings opened there was also the customary irreverent interruption of the recital of the Latin prayer. The capping ceremony is always more or less a matter of "dumb show" and the behaviour of the undergraduates during its performance is generally accepted with good-natured grace by the principal participants. At the conclusion of yesterday's capping, however, the students continued their boisterous conduct to such an extent that the Principal felt obliged to abandon the delivery of an address. At the outset he made an appeal for silence, remarking that his voice was not very strong. His appeal fell on unheeding ears.' (*Glasgow Herald*)

JUNE 20TH

1983: A publicity campaign for the city was launched on this day in 1983. It centred around the slogan 'Glasgow's Miles Better' and was devised to help counter Glasgow's 'no mean city' image as a place of crime and deprivation. The slogan – which also played on the punning 'Glasgow Smiles Better' – was used alongside the children's Mr Happy character, from the Mr Men series, drawn by Roger Hargreaves. The campaign garnered much publicity and was seen alongside its inspiration – New York's 'I love New York' – as a successful way of altering popular perceptions of a city with a reputation in need of improvement. The initiative helped pave the way for large-scale, high-profile events being held in the city such as the National Garden Festival (1988), European City of Culture (1990) and the UK City of Architecture and Design (1999). Lord Provost Michael Kelly was heavily involved in its promotion. The slogan was replaced in 1991 by 'Glasgow's Alive' but revived in 1994. The current campaign uses the strapline 'Glasgow: Scotland with Style'. None of the subsequent campaigns have had the impact of the Miles Better one however.

JUNE 21ST

2011: The Riverside Museum opened to the public on this day. *Glasgow Life* issued a press release to highlight some of the features of the new visitor attraction built by the Clyde:

> It is Glasgow's newest visitor attraction, home to the transport, engineering and shipbuilding legacy that made Glasgow great. The Riverside Museum is an architectural masterpiece, designed by Zaha Hadid. The £74 million museum is Hadid's first major public commission to open in the UK. It houses more than 3,000 exhibits, in over 150 interactive displays, telling the stories of the people who made the term 'Clyde Built' one which travelled the world and spoke volumes about unbeatable quality. From massive steam locomotives, to the recreation of a city street during the 1900s, the cathedral-like structure provides a stunning backdrop to showcase the innovation and ambition of what was the 'Second City of the Empire'. The museum reveals the rich and varied stories of Glasgow's great achievements and vibrant spirit; of technological breakthroughs and heartbreaking tragedies; of local heroes and global giants. The museum's major attractions have been designed and built into the structure of the building – with some arriving before the completion of the structure, such is their size.

In just over five months, the museum received 1,068,986 visitors.

JUNE 22ND

1887: A special event was held to celebrate Queen Victoria's Golden Jubilee, as reported in the *Glasgow Herald*:

Yesterday Mr Walter Wilson of the Colosseum Warehouse, treated about 15,000 of the poor children of Glasgow to a trip to Rothesay. The tickets were distributed by clergymen and city missionaries, the superintendents of Sabbath schools, and the officials of kindred organisations, and the class for whom the treat was intended – the deserving and well conducted – were thus reached without difficulty. For so large a number, extensive preparations had to be made. Five river boats were chartered exclusively for the children, and arrangements were made whereby certain numbers of them might travel by the ordinary steamers. For their refreshment during the journey and on their arrival at their destination, 16,000 packages of buns, biscuits, and scones, about 50 cases oranges, 361 cases of sweets, each containing about 640 packages, 8 cart-loads of milk, and 8 cart-loads of aerated waters were provided. As early as half-past six the Broomielaw swarmed with children, ticket in hand, from all parts of the city. Arrived at Rothesay, the various detachments, headed by brass bands which had accompanied them from Glasgow, were formed into procession and marched to the public park.

JUNE 23RD

1763: 'There is established a good stage coach between Glasgow and Greenock, to set out from Glasgow every Monday, Wednesday, and Friday, and from Greenock every Tuesday, Thursday, and Saturday. The stage to commence on Monday the 26th of June, at six o'clock in the morning, and from Greenock on Tuesday the 27th June, at three o'clock afternoon. The time of setting out will be afterwards named, according to the season of the year, and inserted on the tickets at the time. Tickets to be had at Donald Wilson's shop, opposite the Post Office, Glasgow and at Greenock, at Mr George Scot's, at 5s each for inside passengers, and at 2s 6d for passengers behind. That place being commodiously fitted to hold six, secured from all weather, after the best English manner. Every passenger to be allowed ten pounds weight of baggage. No person can be admitted without a ticket. NB The stage goes only twice a week, on Mondays and Fridays, the first fortnight.' (*Glasgow Journal*)

JUNE 24TH

1918. 'Glasgow Picture Houses. The programmes announced for Glasgow picture houses this week present an attractive variety of subjects. At Cranston's Picture House the principal feature during the earlier part of the week will be a drama entitled *The Duplicity of Hargraves* to be followed later by another drama *When Baby Forgot* in which Marie Osborne, the child actress, takes a leading part. An adaptation of Edward E Hale's book *The Man Without a Country* will be shown at the New Savoy. From Thursday a 'problem' drama of New York life *The Price Mark* will be screened. A varied selection of pictures to be shown at La Scala will include *The Flashlight Mystery* in which the principal parts are taken by Dorothy Phillips and William Stowell. Later in the week the outstanding feature will be a war play *On to Berlin*. A screen version of the popular American story *Rebecca of Sunnybrook Farm*, featuring Mary Pickford, will be shown at the City Picture House and during the latter part of the week the chief attraction will be a dramatic film entitled *The Americano*. At the Picture House during the earlier part of the week Bryant Washburn will be seen in a five-act story, *The Golden Idiot*, which will be followed on Thursday by a Lasky drama *Bab's Diary*.' (*Glasgow Herald*)

JUNE 25TH

1725: The imposition of a malt tax was met with much opposition. The target was Duncan Campbell of Shawfield who had supported the unpopular tax. Matters became riotous and troops were called in from Edinburgh to deal with the mob that had ransacked Campbell's mansion:

> The rioters soon made their appearance in augmented numbers before the guard-house, which was then situated at the south-west corner of Candleriggs Street. Stones were thrown at the sentinels, upon which Captain Bushel ordered out his men. This movement was followed by another shower of stones upon the soldiers, upon which Captain Bushel ordered his men to fire. Two men were killed on the spot, and left lying on the street. Other volleys followed, by which two or three additional persons were killed, and several wounded. As is usual in these lamentable cases, the innocent suffered more than the guilty, for the majority of those who were shot were men who had no hand in the riot, or women who had been drawn to the spot from motives of curiosity. A party of gentlemen, who were amusing themselves in a neighbouring bowling green, were alarmed at the firing, and hastily rushing into Candleriggs Street to inquire the cause, had barely time to shelter themselves from the musketry of the soldiers.

(*Sketch of the History of Glasgow*)

JUNE 26TH

1782: The Magistrates and Council were presented with a report into how the city's Grammar School could be improved. On this day they unanimously agreed and ordained the whole Regulations to be carried into effect. Some of the recommendations were:

That the Masters wear gowns in their classes. That each Boy shall pay Sixpence per quarter, for Coals; and that the Master of the oldest class shall be responsible that the Janitor do his duty. That the hours of attendance be, in Winter, from nine till eleven, and from twelve till two o'clock; in Summer, from seven till nine, from ten till twelve, and from one till three. The vacation to be only four weeks, and to commence on the first of July, and the following play-days allowed through the year: at the time of the Spring and Winter Sacraments, from Wednesday afternoon till Tuesday morning; Christmas Day; New Year's Day; last Friday of January; Candlemas-day; first day of May; King's Birth-day; Deacons' choosing, and two or three days after the annual examination, as the Lord Provost may direct; to have only one meeting on the Saturdays during Winter, and none in Summer, and to have no vacation on the Wednesday afternoons, as formerly. (*Annals of Glasgow*)

JUNE 27TH

1832: This proclamation was issued by the Council Chambers on this day:

Proclamation by the Lord Provost And Magistrates. Complaints have been made of the public: profanation of the Lord's Day. In this city and suburbs, for sometime past, in various ways, particularly by disorderly boys assembling on the streets, the Green, and other public places, and playing at games, both during the period of divine service, and after it is finished and also, by older persons assembling in number, in certain parts of the city in the morning, resorting to taverns or tippling houses getting intoxicated and quarrelling, and thereafter crowding, or passing along the streets in a disorderly manner, to the great annoyance of the respectable and well disposed inhabitants. Therefore, the lord provost and magistrates deem it their duty, thus publicly to intimate, their firm determination effectually to enforce the laws for the due observance of the sabbath and that in cooperation with the commissioners of police, they have, accordingly, given directions, that a sufficient number of police officers, shall on Sunday patrol the streets and public places, and apprehend all offenders, in order that they may undergo the punishment prescribed by law.

JUNE 28TH

1749: On this day an account was presented to the corporation by Provost Andrew Cochran and Bailie George Murdoch, who had been sent to London to procure indemnification for the fines and damage which the town sustained by the visitation of Prince Charles Edward, and which they were successful in obtaining to the extent of £10,000:

> To a chaise and maker's servant - £28 2s. 6d. To John Stewart, the servant, at several times, on the road - £6 7s. 2d. To the servant, to carry him, with two horses - £1 10s. To charges on road to London, eleven days - £28 10s. To lodging at London, and house account for coals, candle, tea, sugar, breakfasts, etc - £61 15s. 9d. To William Alloc, the servant, for wages, boarding, and incidentals at London, and for turnpikes and expenses on the road down - £17 13s. 3d. To shaving and dressing - £2 7s. To Mr. Bowden for liquors to quarters (lodgings) - £4 12s. To extraordinary entertainments at London - £30. To writing copies of petition and memorial etc - £7. To expenses and incidentals, ordinary and extraordinary, at London by Andrew Cochran - £125 12s, by George Murdoch - £105 4s. To a writing master, to come down, £5 5s.

(*Memorabilia of the City of Glasgow*)

JUNE 29TH

1832: 'On Saturday afternoon, two individuals arrived in town from Kirkintilloch with the intention of conveying thither a large silk flag, the painting and lettering of which had just been completed, preparatory to the approaching jubilee. Fatigued with their walk, the reforming flag-bearers agreed, previously to leaving the city, to treat themselves to a dram. And with this view entered a house in Wallace Court, Bell Street. While discussing the spirit-stirring contents of the stoup, something on the street attracted their attention, and up went the window, but their surprise may be imagined when on turning round they discovered that the table had not only been suddenly bereft of the nearly full whisky measure as well as the tumblers and glass, but that their richly-adorned flag, in expectation of the arrival of which that night the radicals of Kirkintilloch were all on tiptoe, was nowhere to be found. The alarm was given but the light-footed thief had disappeared, and as yet has managed to keep out of the way. The unlucky erranders departed woefully crest-fallen, not so much it is said for the actual loss of the emblem of liberty itself, but lest they might be (as they were afraid they would) compelled to pay the piper by their reforming brethren.' (*Glasgow Courier*)

JUNE 30TH

2007: 'I seen the guy getting out the car, the car was on flames, and the guy was going to go straight for the police and I'm like that no chance, no chance, that isn't going to happen. That was the only thing I thought: Go for it, go get this guy. All the way across as you turned round to see this guy in flames, lying on the ground, trying to get up and people hosing him down. Just don't expect to see that on your way to work, especially not at Glasgow Airport. We're under attack here. It's your civic duty to just go in and do it. They can try and come to Britain and try and disrupt us any way they want but the British people have been under a lot more things than this and we always stand proud. If you come to Glasgow, Glasgow doesn't accept this. This is Glasgow so, we'll set about you.' (John Smeaton, baggage handler, Glasgow Airport)

———— • ◆ • ————

2009: Glasgow City Council's licensing board voted to allow the film *Life of Brian* to be shown. The film, by the comedy group Monty Python, had been effectively banned from being shown in the city since its release in 1980.

July 1st

1794: 'Notice. Cows will be admitted into the Green at the Fair of Glasgow to graze the remainder of the season on payment of 25s grass mail, and 1s 6d fee for the herd, for each cow, the day before the Fair.' (*Glasgow Advertiser*)

———— • ◆ • ————

1842: 'Yesterday was the last day that the barbarous practice of sweeping chimneys by means of boys was allowed in this kingdom, the late Act, abolishing the disgraceful custom, coming into effect this day. We notice, from the following clause in the Act, that the punishment attached to the infringement of its provisions is most stringent, and that no sum less than £5 can be inflicted for each offence: "And be it enacted that from and after the First Day of July in the year One Thousand Eight Hundred and Forty Two, any person who shall compel, or knowingly allow any child or young person under the age of Twenty One years, to ascend or descend a chimney, or enter a flue, for the purpose of sweeping, cleaning, or coring the same, or for extinguishing fire therein, shall be liable to a penalty not more than £10, or less than £5."' (*Glasgow Herald*)

JULY 2ND

1792: 'A cure for the bite of a Mad Dog, said to be infallible. Take three yolks of hen's eggs and olive oil as much as will fit three half egg shells, put this together into a frying pan, on a gentle fire, by continually stirring it with a knife, mix it well together, and continue doing this till it turns to a conserve, or thick jelly, which will fill a great tea cup. He who is bitten must take (the sooner the better after the bite, the effect of the remedy being uncertain if not applied within nine days) the above mentioned doses two successive days, after he has fasted six hours, abstaining even from drink, which he likewise must do for six hours after he has taken it. The wound must be scratched open twice a day with a piece of fir wood for nine successive days and every day the wound must be dressed with some of the same remedy. He who has only played with and caressed such a dog, or has been licked by the same, takes (for precaution's sake) only the above mentioned dose for some time. To an animal that is bitten must be given two successive days a double portion of the same remedy.' (*Glasgow Advertiser*)

JULY 3RD

1883: On this day the SS *Daphne* was launched from Alexander Stephen & Sons' shipyard. On reaching the water she immediately went over onto her port side and quickly sank. One hundred and twenty four workers were killed, including some apprentices only fourteen years of age. Flaws in the ship's design were blamed for one of the Clyde's worst disasters.

◆

1963: The Clyde Tunnel was officially opened. It was built to speed up the time to cross the river as drivers were finding it quicker to drive into the city to cross the King George V bridge and then drive back out rather than wait for the ferry. Each tunnel tube had a cycle and pedestrian way underneath the vehicle section. The tunnel was half a mile long and during its construction workers suffered from the 'bends' due to working in conditions using compressed air to prevent the tunnel from caving in. Two workers died. The tunnel eventually saw traffic flows of 65,000 vehicles per day, around seven times that originally envisaged. An artwork devised by Roderick Buchanan called 'Gobstopper', consisting of video footage of children being driven through the tunnel holding their breath, won the Beck's Futures prize in 2000.

JULY 4TH

1887: 'Royalty Theatre Glasgow. The Premier Theatre of Glasgow. Tonight (Monday) and tomorrow (Tuesday). Important engagement of the distinguished French artiste Madame Sarah Bernhardt. Who will appear in two of her most famous impersonations: tonight Fedora, tomorrow Adrienne Lecouvreur. Prices: Orchestra Stalls and Dress Circle 19s 6d, Private boxes £4 4s. Boxes and pit stalls 5s, Pit 2s, Gallery 1s.' (*Glasgow Herald*)

1917: 'At Glasgow Sheriff Court yesterday, two men and two women admitted contravening the Defence of the Realm Act by giving false names or addresses to hotelkeepers in Glasgow. One of the men was fined £5 and the other £3. The women were fined £2 and £1.' (*Glasgow Herald*)

1917: 'Damage estimated at about £3,000 was caused by fire last night in the premises at 91 Buchanan Street, recently occupied by Miss Cranston as lunch and tea rooms. The outbreak occurred shortly before nine o'clock. The fire brigade were summoned and a detachment from the Central Fire Station quickly arrived. The building, which possesses several attractive architectural features, was erected about 20 years ago from designs prepared by Mr George Washington Browne, and the internal decorations, which include a good deal of carved woodwork, were carried out by two well-known Glasgow decorators, Mr Charles McIntosh and Mr George Walton.' (*Glasgow Herald*)

JULY 5TH

1791: This advertisement appeared in the *Glasgow Mercury* on this day:

> The 14th of July being the anniversary of the late glorious Revolution in France by which so many millions have been restored to their rights as men and citizens, the Friends of Liberty in Glasgow and neighbourhood are invited to celebrate the second anniversary of that Revolution at the Tontine Tavern, on Thursday next, in order to certify their joy at an event so important in itself, and which is likely so essentially to promote the general liberty and happiness of the world.

1816: 'From the 5th of July 1815 to the 5th of July 1816, there were 1,621 Ale and Porter Licenses issued from the Excise office, for the City and immediate Suburbs; and notwithstanding the vigilance of the Burgh and County Magistrates, upwards of 550 persons have been prosecuted and fined in the above District, in sums amounting to upwards of £8,000 for selling Spirits without a License, and for illicit distillation.' (*Annals of Glasgow*)

JULY 6TH

1871: 'A special general meeting of the Royal Botanic Institution of Glasgow was held yesterday in the Religious Instruction Rooms for the purpose of considering the heads of an arrangement between Mr John Kibble and the directors for the erection of that gentleman's conservatory within the Botanic Gardens, and which, after a period of twenty one years, would become the property of the Institution. Mr J C Wakefield presided and, after having expressed his satisfaction at the proposed terms, moved that it be remitted back to the directors and special council to get the agreement drawn out in proper form and revised by Dr Kirkwood. The motion was seconded by Mr Readman and agreed to. Mr Russell entering his dissent.' (*The Scotsman*)

❖

1938: 'The suggestion that Glasgow's method of disposing of its sewage was unscientific was made by the Lord Provost. The city had tried out various schemes and they were now proceeding with what seemed to him the unscientific method of carrying it down the Clyde in steamers and dumping it at Garroch Head. He wondered if they would ever return to the time when apprentices had to lay it down as a condition of service that they were not to have salmon more than five days a week.' (*Glasgow Herald*)

JULY 7TH

1788: 'The first mail coach from London to Glasgow arrived at the Saracen's Head on this day and such was the interest excited on that occasion that Mr Buchanan of the Saracen's Head, who had an interest in the mail coach, and a crowd of horsemen went out as far as Clyde Iron Works to welcome her approach. Mr Bain, who has been one of the contractors for carrying the London mail since 1790, states that for many years there was such a scarcity of passengers that the contractors lost money by it. It was usual for the mail coach at that time to arrive at the Saracen's Head from London, a distance of 405 miles, in 63 hours, being nearly 6 miles an hour.' (*Enumeration of the inhabitants of the city of Glasgow and county of Lanark, for the government census of 1831* by James Cleland, 1832)

————◆————

1902: 'A lad named William Raeburn (11) was removed to the Royal Infirmary on Saturday suffering from serious injury to his right hand, caused by an explosion of gunpowder. Raeburn and a companion called Higgins are reported to have found the explosive in a tin can behind the Metropole Theatre. Higgins put a lighted match into the receptacle and Raeburn, on seeing a policeman approach, ran off with the can in his hand. The powder exploded and three of the lads' fingers were burst open.' (*Glasgow Herald*)

JULY 8TH

1880: 'The new yacht *Livadia*, the water palace of the Czar, was launched yesterday from the works of Messrs John Elder and Co, Govan. The naming ceremony was gracefully performed by the Duchess of Hamilton and the launch was witnessed by His Imperial Highness the Grand Duke Alexis, Prince Lobanoff-Rostovsky, Russian Ambassador; Prince Shahovskvy and an immense number of spectators. Altogether not fewer than between 30,000 and 40,000 persons collected to witness the memorable event. This wonderful specimen of naval architecture has excited an unusual amount of interest. No Popoff ironclad has been seen in this country and the new yacht, having been designed by the great Russian Admiral and being a novel departure from the beaten track of ordinary shipbuilding, has attracted great attention ever since it began to assume practical shape on the stocks at Fairfield. The vessel has been constructed with a rapidity which is almost marvellous and which demonstrates in a striking manner the extraordinary resources of the builders.' (*Glasgow Herald*)

The yacht had an unusual design, being of a wide, flat-bottomed shape. It was barely used and passengers were unhappy with the effects of the impact of the waves hitting the bottom of the flat boat. The *Livadia* was eventually stripped of her engines and left to rot.

JULY 9TH

1857: The case of Madeleine Smith received a great deal of attention in Victorian Glasgow. The daughter of a well-known architect, Madeleine was in a relationship with a Frenchman Pierre Emile L'Angelier. Supposedly being about to blackmail Madeleine, L'Angelier died, of arsenic poisoning. On this day her trial ended:

The jury retired at five minutes past one o'clock. At 1.35, or half an hour after the jury had retired, the signal was given of their return. Before they entered the Court and when there was great but subdued excitement throughout the dense crowd in every part of the hall, the Lord Justice Clerk warned the audience against an exhibition of any sort when the verdict was returned. The injunction was vain. No sooner were the final words 'Not Proven' uttered than a burst of applause broke forth. This was immediately followed by loud and almost simultaneous cheering, which lasted some time. The officers of Court repeatedly cried 'silence' but they might as well have tried to put back the Falls of Niagara, so intense was the feeling, especially in the galleries.

(*Glasgow Herald*)

Smith eventually left Scotland and after spending time in London, she emigrated to America, where she died in 1928.

JULY 10TH

1990: A singing legend took to the stage in Glasgow. Frank Sinatra made his appearance at Ibrox Stadium in his first concert in the city for thirty-seven years. Despite it being a cool evening, he received a warm reception, so much so he promised to return. Sinatra had been a teen idol in the 1940s but had seen his career slump. It had revived after his Academy Award-winning performance in the film *From Here to Eternity* in 1953. His music career took off again and he recorded some of popular music's classic songs. During this period he played the Glasgow Empire in 1953. With fellow Rat Pack members Dean Martin, Sammy Davis Jr and Peter Lawford, Sinatra epitomised the era of the hedonistic 1960s Las Vegas lifestyle. At his Ibrox concert he played for around an hour and a half. His set opened with Come Fly With Me and included in the rest of his setlist were Strangers in the Night, You Make Me Feel So Young, Mack the Knife, I Get a Kick Out of You, New York New York and the song that he is most identified with: My Way. He didn't return to Glasgow and died in 1998, aged eighty-two.

JULY 11TH

1958: On this day Peter Manuel was hanged in Barlinnie Prison. He had been convicted of seven murders, although he may have killed a further eleven people. After being arrested Manuel had denied any involvement in the crimes, until he was confronted by his mother. She told him to 'Tell the truth.' Manuel sacked his legal counsel during the sixteen-day-long trial and attempted to defend himself. Although the judge praised his performance in court, saying 'the accused has presented his own case with a skill that was remarkable,' Manuel was found unanimously guilty by the jury on seven counts. After donning a black tricorn hat, the judge sentenced him to death, saying, 'This is pronounced for doom.' Manuel was one of the last persons to be hanged in Scotland. Following his execution, he was found by the coroner to have killed a man in Newcastle in 1957. Manuel is regarded as Scotland's first modern 'serial killer' and it is claimed that the term itself stems from his murders.

JULY 12TH

1919: This advertisement appeared in the *Glasgow Herald* on this day:

> The Royal Route. Glasgow and the Highlands. By the Royal Mail Swift passenger steamer *Columba*. Leaving Glasgow (Bridge Wharf) daily (Sunday excepted at 7 am) for Gourock, Dunoon, Innellan, Rothesay, Kyles of Bute, Tarbert and Ardrishaig. Conveying passengers, via Crinan and Caledonian Canals for Oban, Mull, Staffa, Iona, Fort William, Inverness, etc, and the north as per Tourist Programme. The finest day's sail in Britain is by RMS *Columba* to Tarbert and Ardrishaig, and arriving back at Glasgow at about 6.45 pm. Day return fares: Cabin 9s, or with Breakfast, Dinner and Plain Tea 15s. Fore cabin 6s or with Breakfast, Dinner Plain Tea 12s.

The *Columba* paddle steamer was regarded as the finest of the ships used to take passengers 'doon the watter'. It was launched in 1878 and was in service until 1936. The 300 feet-long vessel was the flagship of the David MacBrayne-owned fleet.

JULY 13TH

1845: On this day the first cargo of American ice imported into Scotland was unloaded at the Broomielaw. The *Glasgow Herald* reported:

> From the novelty of the import, it has attracted a considerable degree of curiosity and interest. The cargo was procured at the Rockland Lake, a fine sheet of water situated about 40 miles up the Hudson River. We learn that the loss during the passage has been exceedingly little. The lot amounts to about 220 tons. On Saturday an entertainment in honour of the new importation was given under an awning on the quarter deck of the Acton.

1968: A quantity of weapons were dropped off during an amnesty in Easterhouse. They included axes, hammers, meat cleavers, bayonets and clubs with spikes. The amnesty had been arranged with the help of English singer Frankie Vaughan. Vaughan, who had been appalled at the level of youth gang violence while on a visit to the city, had met with the leaders of four of the gangs: the Pak, the Drummy, the Rebels and the Tot. In return, Vaughan had said he would provide money and other help to set up a youth centre. Although his efforts were appreciated, the problem of gang violence in the area did not go away and there was some opinion that the attendant publicity only made matters worse by glamourising it.

JULY 14TH

1894: 'Orange Demonstration in Glasgow. The annual demonstration associated with the Twelfth of July took place in Glasgow yesterday. The gathering which was under the auspices of the Grand Orange Lodge of Scotland was attended by the members of a large number of lodges in the city and neighbourhood. Meeting at various points previously fixed, the representatives of the different districts proceeded to the Green, where they were marshalled according to their respective numbers. The first contingent arrived about eleven o'clock, and the last at a quarter to twelve. Numerous spectators from pavements and windows watched the processionists, as with bands playing and banners flying they marched through the city. At one or two points in Garscube Road several green flags were displayed, but the opposition was treated with good humour by the processionists. After the public meeting the procession was remarshalled and returned, by way of New City Road to the County Buildings. To prevent disturbance a large force of constables was on duty but so far as is known there was little or no call for the intervention of the police.' (*Glasgow Herald*)

JULY 15TH

1839: 'Our fair has ended in harmony as it commenced in joyousness. On Saturday night, at eleven o'clock, all was bustle and brilliancy, and before twelve the Green was as dark as midnight. The Captain of Police has assured us that he has never known or seen so little of blood and battling as upon their occasion. "Tiling" was unknown and, barring a fight upon the Green, "all went merry as a marriage bell". This time twelvemonth there were twenty-nine cases upon the Police record. Today Bailie Robertson has only to adjudicate upon nine. Prevention is at all times better than cure and the police force was so judiciously placed that outrage could not have taken place, however willing the Donnybrook blades might be.' (*Glasgow Herald*)

1793: 'By the Lord Provost and Magistrates of Glasgow. Within these few days several mad dogs have been seen in this city and neighbourhood, which have bit several other dogs. The inhabitants of the city are hereby strictly prohibited and discharged from allowing their dogs to go loose through the streets for one month; that all persons contravening this order will be fined in five shillings sterling for each offence, one half of the money to be paid to the informer.' (*Glasgow Advertiser*)

JULY 16TH

1888: 'Glasgow International Exhibition. Glasgow Fair Saturday was looked forward to by many as likely to beat the record of attendance at the Exhibition, and had circumstances been favourable the probability is that such would have been the case, but with an almost continuous downpour of rain it is not surprising that the attendance was far below the highest yet attained. In fact, when it is taken into consideration that only about 7,000 season ticket-holders were admitted, it is rather a cause for wonder that so respectable a total was reached under such adverse conditions. The morning was dry though dull, and before the rain came on several thousands passed the turnstiles, but the gloomy prospect after the weather fairly broke down must have deterred large numbers from paying an intended visit to Kelvingrove. In consequence of the rain the buildings were uncomfortably crowded during the afternoon and evening and the sultry atmosphere became very oppressive. A considerable number of excursionists were present from some of the chief towns in Lancashire, from the mining districts in Fife and from some of the outlying towns around Glasgow. Total attendance since opening day: 1,856,573.' (*Glasgow Herald*)

JULY 17TH

1630: The Burgh Records on this day recorded two payments to be made:

> Mr William Wallace, master of the grammar school, got 20 merks to bear his charges for riding to Edinburgh, about the grammar, to be imposed upon the country.

> Ordains the Treasurer to have a warrant for thirty pounds, paid out by him to Valentine Ginking, for gilding the thistle and crown and sceptre above the King's arms, and to gild the town's arms above the entry to the railing of the tolbooth, and to colour the post of the blackfriar's steeple.

1941: 'Vegetables grown in Glasgow parks are now not to be offered for sale to the general public in shops opened for the purpose throughout the city. It has been discovered that legal authority for such an enterprise on the part of the Corporation is lacking. To get over the difficulty the Parks Committee considered the suggestion that huts should be erected in the parks from which the public could be supplied with vegetables. Apparently it has been discovered that produce may only be sold "on the spot". In the meantime, a protest has been received against any direct trading of this nature from traders who use the facilities of the Glasgow Fruit Market.' (*Glasgow Herald*)

JULY 18TH

1748: 'There has been a larger quantity of salmond taken in the Clyde this week than has been known for many years past. It was currently sold in our market for about one penny per pound.' (*Glasgow Journal*)

1791: 'Mr Robert Park, rum and wine merchant in Glasgow, begs leave to intimate to his friends and public that he has now made a junction of this business with Mr James Corbett, junior, of Tollcross, in Gibson's Wynd, where he is now removed and carries on the same business, and where liquors of all kinds, of the best quality, will be sold by Mr Corbett and him on the lowest terms. As it is necessary from said junction that Mr Park winds up his own concern as soon as possible, he requests that those who are indebted to him will pay what they owe with their conveniency, and he begs leave to acknowledge the favours of his former friends and customers, and solicits a continuance thereof in the said new concern of Corbett and Park.' (*Glasgow Advertiser*)

July 19th

1940: On this day the first German air raid targeting Glasgow took place. The *Glasgow Herald* reported the attack but, under wartime restrictions, refrained from naming the location:

> Scottish Tenement Partly Demolished. The South-West Scotland raider flew at a great height above cloud and dropped two clusters of bombs. One cluster of four fell in a working-class area and it was there that the casualties were caused. One of the bombs struck a three-storey tenement near the gable and brought down part of the building. Occupants of the houses were buried among the debris. A second bomb falling in the same district landed in a back-court practically alongside a surface air-raid shelter. This bomb had brought down a portion of the back wall of a terrace of three-storey houses. Two other bombs in this group landed in an allotment, destroying hen-houses and uprooting trees. A woman who was in bed in one of the houses at the gable end of the partly demolished building was buried in the debris along with children in another house. They were extricated by demolition squads. Several children sustained cuts from flying glass.

(*Glasgow Herald*)

This report refers to damage and injuries sustained in Scotstoun. Three people were killed.

JULY 20TH

1820: James Wilson, a sixty-year-old man from Strathaven, was briefly involved in the Radical insurrection of 1820. On this day he was put on trial for High Treason. He was found guilty and his execution was set for ten days later:

Not fewer than 20,000 had assembled. When the old man was made to ascend the scaffold, one universal shout of sympathy was set up for him by the assembled crowds. He gazed upon them with something like bewildered astonishment. He bowed his head once or twice silently then let go the signal and in a little while his dead body was cut down and lay stretched on a black board on the top of a large fir coffin and the ghastly face was then rudely turned over and with one or two shocking terrible blows, the executioner struck the head from the body of James Wilson and snatching it in his bloody hands, with little regard to its innocent grey hairs, he uttered in a sort of horrid yell, the words, 'Behold the head of a Traitor!' At this sight the lingering and petrified audience burst forth with the exclamations 'Shame! Shame! Murder! Murder!' and several of the soldiers on duty absolutely fainted. It was indeed a terrible sight. (*Reminiscences of Glasgow and the West of Scotland*, Volume 1 by Peter Mackenzie, 1865)

July 21st

1870: 'On Tuesday evening two "drouthy cronies" – the one a private in the Ayrshire and Wigtown Rifles, and the other a shoemaker from Glasgow – had been indulging pretty freely together, and as the evening wore on they went in company to a lodging house in Cross Street, Ayr, to stay till morning. Early yesterday morning the shoemaker awoke and found his companion gone, and when he himself arose from bed he was still more astonished to find that his own clothes were also away and instead of them there was lying by his bedside a full suit of regimentals. He had no recourse but to assume the garb of the militiaman and go in search of his companion, in order to make him aware of the mistake he had committed. While on this searching expedition he was met by the police constables of the regiment who were just on the look out for a few absentees from the camp on the previous evening. Much to his surprise, the poor shoemaker was marched off by them to the camp, where, after relating the exploits of the previous evening, he was handed over to the civil authorities. The militiaman is still at large in the civilian's clothing.' (*Glasgow Herald*)

JULY 22ND

1791: This report of strange phenomena appeared on this day in the *Glasgow Advertiser*:

Tuesday last, between two and three o'clock in the afternoon, we had a heavy rain, which lasted about fifteen minutes, and inundated many parts of this city to such a degree that for some time there was no passing along the pavement. Soon after the rain the expanse became amazingly clear and the sun shone uncommonly bright, attended with great heat. About that time an appearance was seen in the Heavens resembling a serpent moving in the direction from west to east. The horizon perfectly clear in that direction it was visible for some minutes and then seemed to part into a great many pieces. Before its separation it was to appearance at least two hundred yards long and its motion resembled that of a ship's pendant displayed at the mast-head in a gale of wind. About the same time of day, in Kilbryde, there was heard in several parts of the parish a noise much the same as that of the going of the great machinery of a cotton mill, but incomparably louder, and terminated in something like a whirlwind which tore the thatch from the houses and carried up into the air, to a great height, every light substance in its way.

JULY 23RD

1907: 'Jabez Wolffe, of the Glasgow Dolphin Swimming Club, yesterday made his first attempt this year to swim the English Channel. Proceeding to the South Foreland from Dover in the steam yacht *Sea Wolf*, he took water at 10.46. The sea was smooth, there was practically no wind and the swimmer started with twenty eight strokes per minute. For nearly an hour he had the flood tide and drifted to the westwards but later he felt the effect of the ebb tide, which brought him towards Dover. A Calais boat brought news that at 3 pm he was seven or eight miles out and going well with his over-arm stroke. A later telegram says that Wolffe had to abandon his attempt owing to his leg giving out. At the time he had covered twenty miles, swim and drift, or about thirteen miles in a direct course. He said he was resigned to his fate, and would not make another attempt.' (*Glasgow Herald*)

Jabez Wolffe did return, in total making twenty-two attempts, and although getting close, he never succeeded. He returned to the Channel in 1926, this time as a coach, and saw his pupil Gertrude Ederle achieve the distinction of being the first woman to swim it.

JULY 24RD

1837: This handbill was issued on this day:

Atrocious Murder. Whereas on the night of Saturday last between the hours of 11 and 12 o'clock, John Smith, cotton spinner, while peaceably passing along Clyde Street, Anderston, with his wife, on his return to his dwelling-house was wickedly and maliciously fired at by an assassin, armed with a pistol, two balls from which entered the body of the said John Smith, and he immediately fell, mortally wounded, and is since dead. And whereas there is reason to believe that this murderous assault has been committed by one or other of the Turn-out Cotton Spinners. And the master of cotton spinners of Glasgow being determined to use every means in their power to bring to condign punishment the perpetrator of this cold-blooded murder, hereby offer A Reward of £500 to any person or persons who will give such information to George Salmond, Procurator Fiscal, as will lead to the apprehension and conviction of the guilty party or his associates.

(Report of the trial of Thomas Hunter, Peter Hacket, Richard M'Neil, James Gibb, and William M'Lean)

The five cotton spinners were sentenced to transportation for the murder and other offences relating to their attempts to intimidate other workers during an industrial dispute.

JULY 25TH

1800: 'By the Sheriff of Dumbartonshire. Whereas certain carters supposed to come from Glasgow and Paisley did, last season, on their way to and from Inverary, commit several depredations in the neighbourhood of Dumbarton, and wantonly drove against and overturned carriages, whereby some of the lieges were much hurt and injured. These are, therefore, intimating to all concerned, that the Act 12th of his present Majesty, entitled 'An Act for the better Regulation of Carters etc', whereby it is enacted that no person shall drive any cart, car or waggon, without the name of the owner, his place of residence, and the number of the carriage being placed on a conspicuous part thereof, under the forfeiture of 20s for every offence, shall, with the whole other clauses contained in that Act, be hereafter strictly put in execution against all such as may be found contravening against the same, within this county, and that constables are appointed in the neighbourhood of Dumbarton and of Luss for the purposes of enforcing that Act.' (*Glasgow Advertiser*)

JULY 26TH

1612: 'Matthew Thomson, hielandman fiddler, is apprendended on suspicion of assaulting a young damsel, called Janet M'Quhirrie. It appears that the charge was denied by him and hard to be verified but the baillies did not give the fiddler the benefit of the insufficiency of evidence for finding him an idle vagabond they ordained him to be laid in the stocks until the evening, and thereafter put out of the town at the West port, and banished the same for ever and should he ever be found within this town hereafter of his own consent, he is to be hanged without any trial.' (*Sketch of the History of Glasgow*)

———— • ◆ • ————

1916: 'At Rutherglen Police Court yesterday forenoon Robert Mackie (18), a miner, and Patrick Morrison (17), miner, were charged with a breach of the peace in the streets of Rutherglen last night. It was stated that the accused, along with a band of youths terming themselves "Redskins" entered the burgh about 8.30 pm and commenced fighting with each other. There were crowds at different parts of Main Street exceeding 2,000 people. Mackie was sent to prison for 30 days and Morrison was fined 20s with the option of 10 days imprisonment.' (*Glasgow Herald*)

JULY 27TH

1789: This advertisement appeared in the *Glasgow Advertiser* dated this day:

For bilious and other complaints of the stomach: Oriental Vegetable Cordial. One of the most valuable medical discoveries which time and even philosophy could ever boast of, sanctioned by Royal Authority and held in such a peculiar degree of general estimation that upwards of 500 persons have continual recourse to its excellent and potent virtues in the prevention and cure of excruciating malodies, which often prove fatal before assistance can be procured. The salubrious powers of this cordial have been long and universally acknowledged by the flattering patronage and testimony of thousands. It is a pleasant, safe and effectual remedy in bilious disorders, violent pain, or spasm of the stomach and bowels, sickness, vomiting, flatulence, crudities and acidities. It greatly increases the appetite, promotes digestion, and fortifies the stomach and bowels, thereby contributing to preserve the just equilibrium of the body. In fainting, lowness of spirits, nervous and hysterical atrophy, it is highly beneficial, by bracing the nerves, cherishing the animal spirits, and giving vigour to the system.

JULY 28TH

1790: Work on constructing the 35-mile-long Forth & Clyde Canal had begun in 1768 and it had experienced problems with funding before its eventual completion. This report from Robert Forsyth's *The Beauties of Scotland* in 1806, relates the official opening:

On this day the navigation was opened from sea to sea. Ceremonial is less regarded in public affairs in Scotland than in most other countries. It appears, however, that all mankind are in some degree fond of solemnity and pomp and, accordingly, the opportunity of opening the canal was seized for a display of this sort. The committee of management, accompanied by the magistrates of Glasgow, were the first voyagers on the completed navigation. On the arrival of the vessel at the termination of the canal, at Bowling Bay, on the river Clyde, and after descending the last lock into the Clyde, the ceremony of uniting the eastern and the western seas was performed by the chairman of the committee, with the assistance of the engineer, Mr Whitworth, by the symbol of pouring into the Clyde a hogshead of the water of the Forth. A vast number of spectators attended, and expressed, by loud acclamations, their joy on account of the completion of the work.

JULY 29TH

1684: In the seventeenth century the Covenanters, who opposed the King in religious matters, were persecuted. One such case was that of a man from Pollockshaws called William Niven Smith:

He lived peaceably, following his trade. Nor was chargeable with anything, but not hearing Mr Fisher the episcopal incumbent. This day, about midnight, a party came and took him out of his bed, and carried him to Glasgow Tolbooth. They alleged he had been at a sermon of Mr. Renwick's, which was false. He lay three weeks there in irons, and then was carried up to the bishop, and examined by him and Colonel Windram. Nothing was found against William save his not hearing Mr Fisher. But nothing could prevail unless he would take the test, which he peremptorily refused, and was sent, with five others, two and two of them fettered together, into Edinburgh under a guard. There he lay in the irons night and day, till May 1685, when he had his share in Dunnottar sufferings, and afterwards was sent to New Jersey.

(*A Complete Collection Of State Trials And Proceedings For High Treason And Other Crimes And Misdemeanors from the Earliest period to the Present Years*, Volume 11, compiled by T.B. Howell (1811))

JULY 30TH

1971: In 1971 the Upper Clyde shipbuilders' yards faced closure due to financial problems. The Conservative government under Ted Heath refused to lend money in order for them to continue in operation and fulfil existing orders. Six thousand jobs were in danger of being lost. The unions organised a work-in, rather than a strike. The campaign gathered strength with support from John Lennon and Billy Connolly, an ex-shipyard worker. On this day one of the shop stewards, Jimmy Reid, gave a speech to the gathered workers:

> We are not going to strike. We are not even having a sit-in strike. Nobody and nothing will come in and nothing will go out without our permission. And there will be no hooliganism. There will be no vandalism. There will be no bevvying because the world is watching us, and it is our responsibility to conduct ourselves with responsibility, and with dignity, and with maturity.

In 1972 the government changed policy and gave money to three yards on the Clyde. Reid was elected Rector of the University of Glasgow the same year and gave another inspirational speech where he exhorted the students to avoid merely joining the rat race and to help forge a more humane society with opportunities available to everyone. He died in 2010.

JULY 31ST

1781: 'By his will, dated this day, Dr Hunter bequeathed to the principal and professors, his splendid collection of books, coins, paintings, and anatomical preparations, in addition to £8,000 for building an erection for the reception of the collection, and for its support and further augmentation. These donations consist of the gatherings and industry of a long and successful life, and of their kind are unrivalled in the kingdom. Originally the collection was valued at £65,000, but by successive additions, it is now computed to be worth upwards of £130,000. The building was erected in 1804, from designs by Mr William Stark of Edinburgh, at an expense of nearly £12,000. The front exhibits six Doric columns rising from a flight of steps and a dome of stone, surmounted by a glass cupola, gives a graceful finish to this beautiful and classic structure.' (*Sketch of the History of Glasgow*)

The Hunterian Museum opened in 1807 at the original site of the university in the East End. The building described was subsequently demolished when the university moved westwards in 1870. The Hunterian is Scotland's oldest public museum and now includes important collections of works by Charles Rennie Mackintosh and James McNeill Whistler.

AUGUST 1ST

1806: The British victory at the Battle of Trafalgar was celebrated all round the country, tinged with great sadness at the loss of Admiral Horatio Nelson, shot during the battle by a French sniper. Glasgow was the quickest in raising a memorial to the hero of the battle, its monument being built three decades before London's:

Nelson's Monument, situated in the High Green of Glasgow, was erected in 1806, by public subscription, at an expense of upwards of £2,000. The foundations of this towering obelisk were laid on this day, being the anniversary of the battle of Aboukir. It is 144 feet in height, including the pedestal, and is fenced in by a handsome iron railing, to protect it from the mischievous depredations of boys and idlers. This elegant structure is, unfortunately, situated too near the numerous smoking brick stalks of our widespread factories, which, from their near resemblance of form to an obelisk, tends greatly to lessen the effect of this graceful cenotaph, erected by our citizens to the greatest naval hero of Britain.

(*Old Glasgow and its Environs*)

AUGUST 2ND

1810: 'On this day the foundation stone of the Glasgow Asylum for Lunatics was laid. When the procession arrived at the site of the building, the Bands played the King's Anthem. Thereafter, the acting Provincial Grand Master laid the foundation stone of the Asylum, with all the honours usual on such occasions. On which, the brethren gave three cheers, and the bands played the Masons' Anthem. The procession was guarded by a detachment of 700 men from the 71st, or Glasgow Regiment, and the Argyleshire Militia. The propitiousness of the day added greatly to the splendour of the occasion. The procession, which consisted of more than 2,000 persons and 240 musicians, was conducted in the most orderly manner and reflected great credit on the judgment, zeal, and activity of Captain John Graham, of the 6th Regiment of Lanarkshire Local Militia, who acted as Grand Marshal. Although the concourse of spectators was incalculably great, from the deep interest which all ranks took in this Institution, no accident occurred. The collection at the Church doors, amounted to £163, 2 shillings.' (*Annals of Glasgow*)

AUGUST 3RD

1305: On this day William Wallace was captured. The freedom fighter had become Guardian of Scotland in the absence of a Scottish monarch and had won notable victories, particularly at Stirling Bridge in 1297. Wallace had also taken part in a successful raid on Glasgow Castle, called the 'Battle of the Bell of the Brae'. By 1305, he had fallen out of favour with the Scottish nobles following the defeat at Falkirk in 1298 and had become an isolated and wanted figure. It is commonly held that Wallace was betrayed by a Scottish nobleman called Sir William Menteith, while staying in Robroyston. Wallace's life was chronicled by Blind Harry, who wrote a long-length poem called *The Wallace*, written two centuries after Wallace's death. Part of the work describes Wallace's last days in Scotland:

> At Robrastoun Wallas was tresonabilly,
> Thus falsly, stollyn fra his gud chevalry,
> In Glaskow lay and wyst nocht of this thing.
> Thus he was lost in byding of his king.
> South thai him led, ay haldand the west land,
> Delyverit him in haist our Sullway Sand.

Wallace was taken to London and after a show trial was executed by being hung, drawn and quartered.

AUGUST 4TH

1763: 'This Is To Acquaint The Curious that there is to be exhibited by the inventor and maker, S Boverick, at the sign of the Mason's Arms, opposite the Main Guard, Trongate, at one shilling each person, the so much admired collection of Miniature Curiosities, consisting of the following pieces: An ivory chaise with four wheels, turning readily on their axis together, with a man sitting on the chaise, all drawn by a flea, without any seeming difficulty, the chaisemau and flea being barely equal to a single grain. A flea chained to a chain of 200 links, with a padlock and key – all weighing less than one-third of a grain. The padlock locks and unlocks. These two pieces are mentioned, with admiration, by Mr Henry Baker, of the Royal Society, in his book called *Microscope made Easy*, which the inventor and maker has by him, to show if required. A pair of steel scissors weighing but the sixteenth part of a grain, which will cut a large horse-hair. Thirty-six dozen of well-fashioned silver spoons in a peppercorn, and still room for several dozens more. To be exhibited here no longer than the 13th.' (*Glasgow Journal*)

AUGUST 5TH

1643: 'The session enacted that adulterers should be imprisoned, and then drawn through the town in a cart, with a paper on their face; thereafter to stand in the jugs three hours, and be whipped. From various entries, it appears that this punishment was frequently inflicted. During this year, two hair gowns were bought for the use of the kirk.' (*Sketch of the History of Glasgow*)

———◆———

1810: 'Near two o'clock there was a violent thunder clap, without any perceptible interval between the flash and the stroke, which seemed to shake the Royal Infirmary. All the flame was suddenly drawn into the wards with a rustling noise, together with a dense column of soot and smoke, which instantly filled the ward. This occurrence, and the injury of Nelson's Monument, suggests the propriety of guarding every building much exposed, by thunder rods, which, when properly constructed, have never failed to prove a safeguard. The lightning also struck a house in Rottenrow Street. In the upper floor a window was shivered to pieces; in the second floor a kettle, which was on the fire, had its spout melted off. In the ground floor several children and their mother were sitting at the fire; the children's hair was much singed, and the mother was thrown a considerable distance.' (*Old Glasgow and its Environs*)

August 6th

1812: Henry Bell brought into service the first commercially successful steamship service in Europe. His ship the *Comet* made its delivery trip on this day. Although slow and cumbersome, it heralded a new era in water transportation:

> The *Comet*'s first voyage was from Greenock to Glasgow when she arrived at the Broomielaw in three hours and a half. It was found, as Robertson (the engineer) had predicted, that the four paddle-wheels were unsuitable. She would not steer. Consequently two were taken off, after which she went to better purpose. The fares were 4s first cabin, and 3s second cabin. After a short time she was lengthened 20 feet. This operation took place on the beach at Helensburgh. The original engine was also displaced by one of six horse-power, made at Cartsdyke, Greenock, by Thomas Hardie. So great became the success of the *Comet* that in 1819 we find her orbit widely extended. On 2nd September in that year she was appointed to sail from Glasgow to Greenock, Gourock, Rothesay, Tarbert, Loch Gilp, Crinan, Easdale, Oban, Port Appin and Fort William. She continued to run until October 1820 when she was wrecked in the Dorus Mhor in an attempt to round the point of Craignish.

(*A Book about Travelling Past and Present*, compiled and edited by Thomas A. Croal, 1877)

August 7th

1641: 'This day it is ordained a proclamation to be sent through the town, concerning the flagons, commanding and charging that no vendor or drawer within this burgh of wine, ale, beer, or any other sort of liquor, to take upon hand to sell any flagon either of their own or of any other person, except such ware sealed with this present year of God, under the punishment of five pounds money, and if any do come to buy with an unsealed flagon, the seller is ordained not to fill the same but to show the same to magistrates, that the owners thereof may be punished accordingly.' (*Memorabilia of the City of Glasgow*)

———•◆•———

1844: The Highland and Agricultural Show was held on Glasgow Green and opened to the public on this day. The *Glasgow Herald* expressed its satisfaction with the event and one particular aspect:

> While this is the largest show ground, we have also no small pride in stating that it is also by far the largest show which has ever been held. The vastness of the Glasgow exhibition may be learned from the fact that enumeration of the various lots, along with the names of the exhibitors, occupies no fewer than 87 closely printed octavo pages.

AUGUST 8TH

1889: These advertisements appeared in the *Glasgow Herald* on this day:

Electric Light, by meter or otherwise. Estimates and advice free. Anderson and Munro, 136 Bothwell St.

15/6 'Desirable' trousers are receiving what it has been my aim they should merit, the complete approbation of thousands of gentlemen who have tried them. G R Husband, 93 St Vincent Street.

The success of the season – Tennent's lager beer. Superior to any imported. Sold everywhere. Wellpark Brewery, Glasgow.

Kelvinside Ladies' College, 21 Athole Gardens. The high-class institution for the board and education of young ladies will be re-opened on Monday 2nd September. Leading features: Carefully graduated curriculum, embracing all the branches of a young ladies' English education; Private lessons and classes for the study of the piano forte on academical principles; Large, airy and well-lit class rooms furnished on the most approved hygienic principles and equipped with the most modern apparatus.German constantly spoken in the house. Terms on application.

Bags! Bags! Bags! Hide Gladstone's from 15s, Saturday to Monday bags from 5s, Leslie Graham's Union Street.

AUGUST 9TH

1844: A festival to commemorate Robert Burns was held on the banks of the River Doon at Alloway. Over 80,000 people attended, including three of Robert Burns' surviving sons and his sister Isabella. People travelled from all over the country to pay tribute to Scotland's Bard, and the departure of those from Glasgow was reported by the *Glasgow Herald* on this day:

The great rush however took place into Ayr on the morning of the great day itself. In Glasgow there was no small commotion from the earliest peep of dawn, for though the morning was dull, lowering and uncomfortable, it did not prevent crowds from rising with the morning light and marching down to the Broomielaw, many of them preceded by bands of music, for the purpose of embarking in the steamers, six of which left between half-past four and half-past five. All were respectably filled and they made the passage to Ayr, calling at intermediate stations, in from five and a half to six hours, thus carrying to the Land of Burns an immense mass of people. The Glasgow and Ayr Railways commenced to carry passengers at six in the morning and continued to forward trains every half hour until far in the forenoon.

AUGUST 10TH

1871: 'On this day the foundation stone of the new Western Infirmary Buildings in connection with the University at Gilmorehill, was laid with masonic honours by PGM Montgomerie Neilson. The weather was fortunately very fine and the procession, as well as the interesting ceremonial at the foundation stone, were witnessed by large numbers of spectators. The new Infirmary, which is intended to provide for the treatment of the sick poor in the Western District of the city, is being erected on a convenient site at Donaldshill, in the immediate neighbourhood of the University and has already been carried up to the basement storey. The site comprises 13 acres of ground and the buildings which are being constructed upon the block or pavilion system, will extend when completed to 500 by 240 feet, including the quadrangles. The hospital is intended to contain 316 beds but it will be constructed with one additional or supplemental ward, giving 352 beds in all and when so completed will cost about £50,000.' (*Glasgow Herald*)

AUGUST 11TH

1638: The burgh records described work requiring to be done, some of it grisly to the modern mind:

> This day ordains the tresaurer to have one warrant for the sum of 50 pounds money disbursed by him to John Boyd, for translating of the stock wall of the High Street and setting the same down in another place, and for taking a wall at the cross, covering the same, and for translating the head that was thereon, and setting it on the said new wall in the Stockwell gate.

'The head which was translated to the Stockwell from the Cross, in 1638, was probably that of some unhappy Papist or Jesuit, whom the Covenanters regarded with the utmost horror as imps of Satan. In revenge for this and for the like barbarities perpetrated by the Covenanters, the Royalists, when they became masters, ordered the head of the godly and reverend James Guthrie to be put on the Nether Bow Port of Edinburgh, in 1661 and the head of Lord Warriston, another Covenanting leader, to be placed on the wall of the same port.' (*Old Glasgow and its Environs*)

AUGUST 12TH

1560: 'Order issued to all Magistrates and people in power, at the Reformation: Trusted friends, after most hearty commendation, we pray you fail not to pass immediately to the Kirk (of Glasgow) and take down all the images thereof, and bring forth to the kirkyard and burn them openly. And also to cast down the altars, and purge the kirk of all kind of monuments of idolatry. And this we fail not to do, as this will do us singular satisfaction, and so commit you to the protection of God. Take good heed that neither the desks, windows, nor doors be in any way hurt or broken, either glass or iron work. From Edinburgh, Signed, Earl of Argyll, James Stewart, (Earl of Moray), Lord Ruthven.' (*Annals of Glasgow*)

The cathedral came under threat in 1579. Andrew Melville, principal of the University of Glasgow, ordered the cathedral to be demolished and the stones to be used to build other churches. Tradesmen of the city surrounded the building to prevent its destruction. The teenage king, James VI, agreed with the tradesmen, saying 'too many churches have been already destroyed'. (*The History of Glasgow*)

AUGUST 13TH

1778: 'In July Barbara Barber had been tried before the Magistrates for keeping a bawdy-house. She was sentenced to remain in prison and then to stand for the space of an hour, bareheaded, on the Tolbooth stairhead, with a label on her breast, having the words: "For keeping a notorious bawdy-house" and afterwards to be banished from the city and its liberties for seven years.' (*Old Glasgow and its Environs*)

On the 13th of August she stood on the Tolbooth stairhead as per her sentence. Two years later, this notice appeared in the *Glasgow Mercury*:

> May 11th, 1780. Yesterday Barbara Barber was whipped through this city by the common hangman. She had formerly been banished by the magistrates for keeping a disorderly house, under the certification of the above disgraceful punishment in case of her returning.

———◆———

1915: 'The directors of the Alliance of Honour have brought into operation a "war time" membership in order that large numbers of men and youths above 15 may be linked together by the pledge: I promise by the help of God to do all in my power to uphold the honour of our Empire and its defenders in this time of war: 1. By personal purity alike in thought, word and deed, and by encouraging at all times a chivalrous respect of womanhood 2. By prayer. 3. By sobriety.' (*Glasgow Herald*)

AUGUST 14TH

1900: 'Grouse Shooting. A Good Opening Day. Big Bags and Healthy Birds. Although Monday is not a good market day in Glasgow the supply of grouse in Glasgow yesterday was about equal to the average. Some birds were on offer in the forenoon, but after noon was well advanced before anything like plentiful consignments reached the city. Up till one o'clock one of the largest dealers had only received 20 brace, which were on sale at 9s. Prices subsequently ranged from that figure up to 15s in some cases, early in the day. The birds for the most part appeared to be well grown. Generally speaking the atmospheric conditions all over the country seem to have been favourable for outdoor sport, as a consequence many parties were afoot and good – in some cases very heavy – bags were got. The birds are reported strong on the wing, wild, and at least an average in number. In the Strathbraan district of Perthshire five guns on the Kinloch grounds had 139 brace, on Glutt, Caithness, 115 brace were bagged, and at Dalwhinnie a hotel party with four guns had 103 brace.' (*Glasgow Herald*)

August 15th

1742: 'Meetings for prayer and praise were for a considerable time held daily, and symptoms of an extraordinary kind began to be manifested. In the New Statistical Account we find the following description of this curious affair, which is known as "The Cambuslang Wark":

> The sacrament on this day was very numerously attended. It has been estimated that not less than 30,000 people attended on this occasion. Four ministers preached on the Fast-day, four on Saturday, fourteen or fifteen on Sunday, and five on Monday. There were 25 tables, about 120 at each, in all 3,000 communicants. Many of these came from Glasgow, about 200 from Edinburgh, as many from Kilmarnock and from Irvine and Stewarton, and also some from England and Ireland. The "Cambuslang Wark" continued for six months, from 8th February to today. The number of persons converted at this period cannot be ascertained.'

(*Rambles Round Glasgow: Descriptive, Historical and Traditional* by Hugh MacDonald, 1860)

AUGUST 16TH

1790: The Glasgow Humane Society was set up on this day to rescue those in the Clyde or recover those who had drowned. *Directions for the Recovery of Drowned Persons* was issued, part of which is reproduced here:

> The body to be laid on a bed and, if taken out from ice, not at first in a warm room; to be gradually rubbed with flannel, heated. The immediate application of heat, when the body has become frigid with cold, would probably destroy life. In summer, lay the body in the sun. Let two or three people undertake the rubbing of the body, first gently, and then more smartly. Never with salt. Warm water to be injected. Two persons must be employed in endeavouring to inflate the lungs. One holds the mouth and one nostril, while the other, having inserted the nozzle of a pair of bellows into the other nostril, blows till the chest is filled. Repeat this operation, and continue the rubbing for some hours, without despairing; by no means blow air from the mouth of the operator into the lungs of the person. Put the person into a warm bed, between two other persons, and after sleep he awakes quite restored.

(*Annals of Glasgow*)

AUGUST 17TH

1929: 'An interesting visitor to Glasgow this week is Hans Weichberger, a 19-year-old Austrian art student who has travelled almost 1,500 miles on foot since he left Vienna on June 10. Emulating the "Beloved Vagaband" so far as his meanderings are concerned, he has rested and slept just where he willed – in farm houses and sheds, but mostly in the shelter of hay ricks and protecting hedges. He tramped on through Southern Germany, Bavaria, along the banks of the Rhine, and thence to Rotterdam and Hamburg. There he met a Glasgow visitor and in appreciation of his services as guide he was offered a trip to this country at the expense of the Scotsman.' (*Glasgow Herald*)

———— ◆ ————

1991: On this day Arthur Thompson Junior was shot dead outside his father's house, his father being one of the senior underworld figures in the country. Ex-Thompson associate Paul Ferris was suspected of the murder. Two of Ferris's associates – Joe 'Bananas' Hanlon and Bobby Glover – were found dead on the day of Thompson Junior's funeral, in a car parked where the funeral cortege would pass. Ferris was found not guilty of the murder after the longest-ever Scottish criminal trial. He was jailed for firearms offences in 1999. Arthur Thompson Senior died of a heart attack in 1993.

AUGUST 18TH

1783: 'On this day the meteor, which had been the cause of general alarm, was seen at Glasgow at nine o'clock in the evening. Its appearance was that of a fiery ball, with a conical tail and it moved in a direction from north-east to south-west with inconceivable velocity. Its light was so strong and brilliant, that a pin might have been picked up on the street and, what is remarkable, it was seen over all Britain nearly at the same instant – a proof that its height must have been very great.' (*The Picture of Glasgow*)

———— ◆ ————

1807: 'The city, between three and four o'clock pm, was the scene of a violent storm of rain, hail, lightning, and thunder. The streets were inundated with torrents and, amid the cataracts of hail and rain, fell several large pieces of ice. Many panes of glass were broken, and sky-lights and cupolas dashed in pieces.' (*The Picture of Glasgow*)

AUGUST 19TH

1872: 'On this day the system of tramway travelling was inaugurated in Glasgow. The Lord Provost, Magistrates, and Town Council and a large number of gentlemen assembled at St George's Cross in order to formally open the line. Seven cars were brought from the depot in Cambridge Street and ranged along the Great Western Road – two or three being drawn by three horses abreast. The crowd assembled to witness the ceremony was very large.' (*Glasgow Herald*)

———— •◆• ————

2010: On this day the poet Edwin Morgan died, aged ninety. Born in Glasgow's West End he went to school in the then-separate burgh of Rutherglen. He had served in the Second World War as a conscientious objector in the Army Medical Corps. He became a lecturer, then professor, of English at the University of Glasgow where he worked until retiring in 1980. His poetry ranged from space exploration to Marilyn Monroe, from sectarianism to the Loch Ness Monster. Morgan was made Poet Laureate of Glasgow in 1999 and of Scotland as 'Makar' in 2004. In his will he left over £900,000 to the Scottish National Party. He also bequeathed £1 million to set up an award for young poets.

AUGUST 20TH

1819: Sir John Moore, who was born and educated in Glasgow, was killed during the Battle of Corunna while leading his forces against the French. On this day the *Glasgow Herald* reported on a statue in his honour:

> On Monday, the workmen finished the erection in George Square of the monument of Lieutenant-General Sir John Moore, on which is the following inscription :
>
> TO COMMEMORATE
> THE MILITARY SERVICES OF
> LIEUTENANT GENERAL SIR JOHN MOORE, K.B.,
> NATIVE OF GLASGOW,
> HIS FELLOW-CITIZENS
> HAVE ERECTED
> THIS MONUMENT.
> 1819.
>
> It consists of a full-length bronze statue of the hero, about 8½ feet high, dressed in military costume, having a cloak thrown round, the left hand leaning on the sword, and the right placed in easy position across the breast. It is supported by a pedestal of Aberdeen granite, about 10 feet high. The statue is chiefly made from brass cannons. The whole cost is between three and four thousand pounds. The weight of the statue is upwards of three tons, and that of the pedestal ten. The whole confers the utmost credit on the taste and execution of Mr Flaxman, the artist. The monument has a grand appearance, and is placed on the south side of the square, a few feet from the railing, fronting Miller Street.

AUGUST 21ST

1907: 'Glasgow Steeplejack's Terrible Death. A steeplejack named John Goldie met with a terrible death yesterday morning by falling from the top of the well-known chimney-stalk at the works of Messrs Joseph Townsend and Company, chemical manufacturers, situated in Crawford Street, Port Dundas. Goldie was engaged in repairing the top of the great chimney by pointing the parts which showed signs of decay. Goldie ascended the chimney about seven o'clock by the usual method which is adopted nowadays, namely, a series of ladders, which has superseded the former method of kite flying. About eight o'clock Mr Hall, who was working at the base of the chimney, happening to look up, was horrified to see his workman in mid-air immediately above him and descending rapidly to the ground. He sprang out of the way and shortly afterwards saw Goldie strike the wooden roof of the works, through which he fell onto the floor 30 feet below. Townsends' chimney is the tallest in the world, being 468 feet high and the terrible nature of Goldie's fall may thus be realised. When picked up life was extinct but the body, it is stated, was not much mangled although nearly every bone was broken.' (*Glasgow Herald*)

AUGUST 22ND

1803: The poets William Wordsworth and Samuel Taylor Coleridge spent six weeks on a tour of Scotland. With them was William's sister, Dorothy, who wrote about their experiences. When they arrived in Glasgow they found lodgings at 'a new building' – the Saracen's Head:

> Having dined, William and I walked a considerable time in the streets, which are perhaps as handsome as streets can be. The Trongate, an old street, is very picturesque – high houses, with an intermixture of gable fronts towards the street. The New Town is built of fine stone, in the best style of the very best London streets at the west end of the town, but, not being of brick, they are greatly superior. One thing must strike every stranger in his first walk through Glasgow – an appearance of business and bustle, but no coaches or gentlemen's carriages. I also could not but observe a want of cleanliness in the appearance of the lower orders of the people, and a dullness in the dress and outside of the whole mass, as they moved along. We returned to the inn before it was dark.

(*Recollections of a Tour Made in Scotland AD 1803* by Dorothy Wordsworth, 1874)

AUGUST 23RD

1656: 'The council ordains Bailie Walkinshaw and the deacon convener to meet with James Colquhoun and agree with him about the making of the engine for casting of water on land that is in fire, as they have in Edinburgh. The treasurer is to pay James Colquhoun for his charges the last time he went to Edinburgh to see the said engine. The engine was accordingly constructed, and the master of works is ordered to make a timber-shed for its reception.' (This was no doubt the first fire-engine provided for the town.) (*Sketch of the History of Glasgow*)

———◆———

1851: 'A heavily-laden scow, proceeding from Glasgow down the Forth and Clyde canal, came in collision with a schooner, and was capsized. The men on board got to land, but in the cabin were a woman and child. The boat had been turned completely over, and the water did not enter the cabin; for half an hour the woman's screams were heard. The men hastened to cut a hole in the bottom of the boat but their well-meant zeal was fatal: no sooner was a hole made, than the air escaped from the cabin, and the water rushing in from below to supply its place, both mother and child perished.' (*The Household Narrative of Current Events* edited by Charles Dickens, 1851)

AUGUST 24TH

1920: 'Rent Strike. The Campaign Opens. The twenty-four hours strike to mark the opening of the movement against the increases of house rents sanctioned by the recent Act took place yesterday. Many departments of industrial activity were suspended through the workers participating in the demonstration, and considerable inconvenience was caused to the public in Glasgow by the enforced withdrawal of the tramway service. Though the procession of "rent strikers" through the city was not so numerically strong as was anticipated, a crowd estimated at about sixty thousand gathered on Glasgow Green, where resolutions were adopted protesting against the increases of rent and pledging resistance to the payment thereof. A number of notices of increases in rent were publicly burned. The day's proceedings passed off without disorderly incident, with the exception of some interference with tramway employees who had remained at duty, in connection with which two men were arrested. Generally speaking it is computed that about two thirds of the workers in the Glasgow area were idle yesterday, those remaining at work in the shipyards and engine shops varying from about 5 per cent to 30 per cent, while in some instances establishments were closed entirely.' (*Glasgow Herald*)

AUGUST 25TH

1819: James Watt died on this day. Watt had worked as an instrument maker at the University of Glasgow and was walking on Glasgow Green in 1765 when he came up with the idea of a separate condenser for the steam engine. His improvement was to have a huge effect on the Industrial Revolution. An obituary paid suitable tribute:

> By the death of this truly great man, our country is deprived of one of its most illustrious ornaments. Mr Watt may justly be placed at the very head of those philosophers who have improved the condition of mankind by the application of science to the practical purposes of life. His steam-engine is probably the most perfect production of physical and mechanical skill which the world has yet seen while in the variety, extent, and importance of its applications, it certainly far transcends every similar invention. So great was the activity and power of his mind, that he not only embraced the whole compass of Science, but was deeply learned in many departments of Literature: and such was the felicity of his memory, that it retained, without effort, all that was confided to it.

(*The Gentleman's Magazine and Historical Chronicle*, Volume 89, 1819)

AUGUST 26TH

1989: On this day Rangers player Maurice Johnston made his first appearance at Parkhead since signing for the Ibrox club. Johnston had been a Celtic fans' favourite until he signed for Rangers. He had scored fifty-two league goals in three seasons before being sold to French club Nantes in 1987. In the summer of 1989 it was revealed that Johnston was returning to Glasgow. In a press conference in May he said: 'I had six or seven offers…but there was only one place I wanted to go. I always wanted to play for Celtic and I still do.' However, no contract had been signed. Doubts emerged about the deal and Celtic eventually withdrew their offer. Rangers pulled off a sensational coup in getting the player, only the second to have played for both Rangers and Celtic since the Second World War. Johnston's Catholicism also presented problems for fans of both teams. Rangers supporters stated they wished to return their season tickets; Celtic fans called him Judas. Johnston played two seasons for Rangers before leaving to play for Everton in England. He later emigrated and after a time playing, became a coach in North America.

AUGUST 27TH

1928: 'The trades holiday was observed in shipyards, factories and other public works in on Saturday. The weather was favourable and large crowds took advantage of the facilities afforded for travelling to the coast and country. The new weekend fare concessions, which came into operation on the railway on Friday, made a strong appeal to the public and the principal stations were thronged with day-trippers as well as those taking advantage of the longer weekend allowed at cheap rates. There was also increased traffic in the stations on Friday evening, and large numbers availed themselves of the extended facilities to travel to popular English resorts for the few days. The greater part of the crowds that travelled from the city, however, made their way to Clyde resorts for the day, and the demand for accommodation on coast trains and river steamers was very great, particularly on the pleasure steamers sailing to Dunoon, where the Cowal Games proved a great attraction. The special tours organised by the bus companies drew large numbers of holiday-makers and long queues waited for the buses which were running to the well-known resorts around the city. On the Glasgow tramway system the cars were well patronised, and large numbers were carried to municipal parks and elsewhere.' (*Glasgow Herald*)

AUGUST 28TH

1792: In a letter dated this day, English clergyman John Lettice described arriving in the city:

> Leaving Hamilton we proceeded toward Glasgow, through a well cultivated and pleasant country. At the distance of only two miles from the town, our view of it was interrupted by large plantations of fir. Having, at length, passed them and a multitude of stinking brick-kilns in black succession, for half a mile farther, we traversed a dirty street, consisting of brick-makers cottages, and crowded by these useful manufacturers. Before we had advanced far beyond this unpromising scene, we were suddenly surprised by a coup d'oeil of fine lofty houses, wide and beautifully paved streets, many of them running to a great length till their sides meet in perspective, and others at right angles to these. The whole crowned with turrets and spires of churches, and of public buildings, rising lightly and gracefully into the air. At length we found ourselves under the lofty tower of the Tolbooth and alighting at the piazza which joins it, supported by handsome columns, we entered the Tontine hotel behind them, a house of public accomodation, worthy of this magnificent city.

(*Letters on a tour through various parts of Scotland, in the year 1792* by John Lettice, 1794)

AUGUST 29TH

1812: 'By an alarming fire on the evening of 29th August 1812, the work-shops and upholstery-warehouses of the late Mr John Reid, in Virginia Street, were totally destroyed and goods to the value of £20,000 consumed. The property was insured but seven persons were killed by the falling of the roof, and many others severely hurt. Two days elapsed before all their bodies were recovered from the ruins.' (*The Picture of Glasgow*)

———— •◆• ————

1866: 'Victoria Gardens, Govanhill. It will be seen from our advertising columns that these beautiful gardens are to be thrown open, at almost a nominal charge, to the public on Saturday first, on the occasion of their Autumn Flower Show and Promenade. These are possibly the most finely situated allotment gardens in the neighbourhood of Glasgow, both for site and command of scenery, and as they are at present in excellent condition and profuse bloom (in addition to the attraction of the show) they will well repay a visit to all lovers of the beautiful, as well as those who are disposed to countenance the extension of horticultural pursuits among the inhabitants of this city.' (*Glasgow Herald*)

August 30th

1792: In another of his letters, John Lettice describes part of his walk around the city:

> The respectable companion of our walk, with some hesitation, led us to the door of a large reeking edifice. From the threshold we beheld some hundreds of females, all in the busy acts of rubbing, scrubbing, scouring, dipping, and wringing all sorts of linen clothes, accompanied by a loudness, volubility, and confusion of tongues, and such as naturally recalled the polyglot of Babel. We thought ourselves well off to have made our retreat, without having been the objects of any of that delicate wit and raillery, which distinguish the place and from which, we were told, few strangers so fortunately escape.

(*Letters on a tour through various parts of Scotland, in the year 1792* by John Lettice, 1794)

———— • ◆ • ————

1983: On this day three Concorde airliners were at Glasgow Airport. They were taking part in the launch of British Airways' 'Super Shuttle' service to London Heathrow. Despite being able to fly at twice the speed of sound, the Concordes only flew at subsonic speeds for the journey. Standard fares were used, costing £58 single, and there were some empty seats.

AUGUST 31ST

1644: 'Ordained a proclamation to be sent through the town, commanding all manner of persons between 60 and 16 to be in readiness with their best arms and to this effect to come out presently with their several captains, with match, powder and lead and also to provide themselves with 20 days' provisions, to march according as they shall get orders, under the pain of death, and suchlike that no manner of person presume, or taken upon hand, to go within any hours to drink or stay there in time of the night watch, under the punishment of their persons being imprisoned in the Tolbooth.' (*Memorabilia of the City of Glasgow*)

1939: 'Fifty thousand volunteers enrolled in Glasgow. With hundreds still coming forward to offer their services in the various branches of civil defence, it was estimated yesterday that more than 50,000 volunteers – including Territorials but excluding those who have joined ARP (Air Raid Precautions) schemes in works and offices – had been enrolled in National Service from the Glasgow area. The gap which existed last week in the city's civil defence organisation is rapidly being closed. In respect of ARP services alone, 2,500 new recruits have been enrolled at the City Chambers and district headquarters during the past four days.' (*Glasgow Herald*)

SEPTEMBER 1ST

1800: This article on fashion was printed in the *Glasgow Advertiser* on this day:

Female Fashions for September. Full length walking dresses. Round dress of white muslin, black lace cloak made to hang full on the shoulders and trimmed on the outside edge and on the ends with broad lace. Bonnet of yellow silk ornamented with a wreath of roses, and tied under the chin with a yellow ribbon. Dress of white muslin made to wrap over with one lappet, which is tied in with the girdle and which hangs down before in a long end, finished with a tassel, square silk shawl, small round chipped bonnet wreathed with oak leaves.

General Observations. In bonnets the Swinley Slouch and the Weymouth Shade and Slouch are the newest and most favourite shapes in chip, straw and Leghorn. Flowers continue to be universally worn and the Weymouth trimming, which consists of a very small flower wreath, is generally adopted. The prevailing colours are the geranium, the marone, pea-green and crimson.

SEPTEMBER 2ND

1962: The last scheduled tram finished its route on this day. Trams had been introduced to the city in 1872 and had covered 100 route miles. With the increasing popularity of private motor cars and the Corporation's own bus service, it was decided to retire them. The service had been gradually wound down since the mid-1950s. The last scheduled journey was from Yoker to Dalmarnock, carried out by tram number 1313. An official procession was held a few days later that saw an estimated 200,000 people turn out to witness the passing of an era. Twenty tram 'caurs' were driven through the streets, including a horse-drawn example from the previous century. Some people created their own commemorative coins by placing them on the lines to be flattened. Glasgow was the last major city in Britain to operate a tramway system before modern trams were brought in, beginning with Manchester in 1992.

SEPTEMBER 3RD

1787: 'During this year, the operative weavers having made an unsuccessful application to the manufacturers for an advance of their prices, a great number of them struck work, and assembling together in multitudes, paraded the streets, and began to annoy the families of those manufacturers. They then went deliberately to the work-shops of those who had not struck work and, having cut out their webs from the looms, burned them on the streets of the Suburbs. On this day, the mob having destroyed a number of webs in the Calton, repaired to the foot of the Drygate, and were burning webs, when the Magistrates arrived with a detachment of the 39th Regiment of Foot. The Riot Act having been read, the people were admonished to disperse, but without effect. At length, it was found necessary to order the military to fire, when three persons were killed on the spot, and a number of others severely wounded. This severe, though necessary, example had the effect of dispersing the mob. The last great assemblage on this memorable occasion was at the burial of the three persons who were shot: they were interred in the Calton Burying-Ground, accompanied by at least 6,000 persons, consisting of men, women, and children.' (*Annals of Glasgow*)

SEPTEMBER 4TH

1760: These vacancies were advertised in the *Glasgow Courant*:

• Wanted. To go to Virginia, under indentures for a few years: A young man, who understands Latin, Greek and Mathematics, to serve as a Tutor in a gentleman's family.

• A lad who has served an apprenticeship as a surgeon, to live with one of his profession.

• Two gardeners, who understand their business well, particularly the work in a garden.

• These, properly recommended, will meet with suitable encouragement, on applying to Buchanan and Simson, merchants in Glasgow.

———— • ◆ • ————

1860: A century later the *Glasgow Herald* Situations Vacant section included these vacancies:

• Wanted, a stout, active Message Boy. Apply at Paton's, Buchanan Street.

• A first class soda water bottler wanted, for Greenock.

• Wanted, for a factory in town, an active, intelligent man, to draw over cloth and keep weaving books. Wage 20s a week. Must be of exceptionable character. One who has been similarly employed and accustomed to coloured work preferred.

• Wanted for a house in London, a stout, active woman, about 40, who can wash and dress linen and who would make herself useful. Wages good.

• Wanted, a married woman as wet nurse, to take the child to her own house. Milk young. Apply to Mrs Denmark, Carrick Street.

SEPTEMBER 5TH

1853: The *Glasgow Herald* printed advertisements on this day for sailings from Glasgow to different destinations around the world:

Emigration to Australia. Loading at Lancefield Quay. At Glasgow for Melbourne, Port-Philip, direct. Landing passengers at the City Wharf, and carrying only a very limited number. The magnificent new frigate-built clipper ship *Sapphire*, 1,140 tons register, 1,700 burthen, A1 at Lloyds for 7 years, will sail on a day shortly to be named. This truly noble vessel requires only to be seen to secure approval, the excellence of her mould and the convenience and comfort of her passenger accommodation, being such as have seldom been equalled. All the cabins and berths will be fitted up in the best style, and so as to afford the essential advantages of abundant light and ventilation. An ordained minister, and duly qualified surgeon, will accompany the ship. Intending passengers are requested to inspect the ship at Lancefield Quay. For dietary scale, terms of freight or passage, apply to MacCallum, Graham & Black, 41 St Vincent Place.

SEPTEMBER 6TH

1983: A pilot of a new detective show first aired on this day. The programme started at 9 o'clock on STV and was called *Killer*. It was a three-parter featuring a Maryhill police detective called Jim Taggart. He was played by Mark McManus and Neil Duncan played his sidekick Detective Sergeant Peter Livingstone. The show took off and was shown on the national ITV network. As *Taggart* it became Britain's longest-running police series. McManus played the dour detective for eleven years. He died in 1994 and was replaced as Detective Chief Inspector by Michael Jardine, played by James MacPherson, although the title of the show remained the same. Some of the famous faces who have appeared in the show include Robert Carlyle, Ken Stott, Clare Grogan, John Hannah, Billy Boyd, Amanda Redman and Dougray Scott. Over a hundred episodes were made, but in 2011 ITV declined to commission any more episodes. *Taggart* was famous for the phrase 'There's been a murder' but there is some debate over whether the line was ever said, even amongst the cast themselves.

September 7th

1863: 'On this day the defender sent two carriages drawn by two horses each, from Glasgow to Port Glasgow, and passed through the pursuer's toll-bar. The carriages were to attend a funeral at Greenock on the following day. The defender's driver, when asked for toll, claimed exemption on the ground that he was going to a funeral. The pursuer, believing that the defender was not entitled to exemption, raised this action for 2 schillings of toll to try the question. Its solution depended on the meaning of the section which is in these terms: "No funeral procession, or carriages in such procession, and no foot passenger shall, while going to or returning from the place of interment on the occasion of any internment, be liable in any toll or pontage." The pursuer maintained that the two carriages formed at the time they passed through the toll-bar no part of a funeral procession, no corpse having been present. The Sheriff held that were was no exemption in this case and gave decree.' (*Scottish Law Magazine and Sheriff Court Reporter*, Volume 2, 1863)

SEPTEMBER 8TH

1831: This day saw the coronation of King William IV. William was the oldest person to become a British monarch, being sixty-four when he succeeded his brother George IV the previous year. Celebrations were held around the country and Glasgow saw a procession and fireworks show. The *Glasgow Herald* reported one particular event:

> In every tavern in the town there were parties of happy people, drinking to the health of his Majesty, but we cannot help mentioning, in a particular manner, that a most respectable company of upwards of eighty gentlemen, sat down to a most excellent dinner in the Royal Exchange Coffee House (Mrs Allison's) to celebrate the all-engrossing event – Thomas Atkinson Esq in the chair, David Hamilton Esq, the architect of the Exchange, croupier. By the well-known tact and capability of Mr Atkinson for the situation he occupied, the hilarity and good humour of the company were kept at the very highest pitch during the evening. (*Glasgow Herald*)

William was King for only seven years, until he died in June 1837 of heart failure. His niece Victoria acceded to the throne. She reigned for considerably longer – nine times longer – at sixty-three and a half years.

SEPTEMBER 9TH

1935: 'Glasgow Boxer's Success. Benny Lynch, the Scottish Fly-weight Champion, won the World's, European and British Fly-weight Boxing Championships after 4 minutes 42 seconds actual fighting at Manchester, before a crowd of 7,000 onlookers. Tumultuous scenes were witnessed at Belle Vue when Lynch made ring history by scoring a technical knock-out in two rounds over Jacky Brown (Manchester). The Scot fought like a human tornado from the first bell, and completely outpunched Brown who was down ten times in all during the short time the bout lasted. The end came in dramatic fashion after exactly 1 minute 42 seconds of fighting in the second round. Brown had been so badly punished that he was reeling helplessly round the ring. Suddenly he threw up his right hand in token of surrender, and referee Moss Deyong thereupon intervened, and raised Lynch's hand as winner and new World's Champion. Lynch's performance must rank as one of the most spectacular ever recorded in a World's Champion fight. Seen after the fight Lynch said: "I knew I had him going when I put him down the first time, after that it was merely a matter of time."' (*Glasgow Herald*)

September 10th

1933: On this day the Boys' Brigade held a special parade as part of a whole weekend celebrating the organisation's fifty years of existence. The *Glasgow Herald* reported on the events the following Monday:

The celebration of the Boys' Brigade jubilee in Glasgow at the week-end produced imposing demonstrations of the strength of the organisation and the public esteem of the movement. His Royal Highness Prince George acted as reviewing officer at a parade of the boys, numbering with their officers 30,000, which took place in Queen's Park Recreation Ground on Saturday afternoon. A host of spectators witnessed the proceedings and the spectacle presented was of a memorable description. Prince George communicated a message from the King expressing His Majesty's pleasure at being a patron of the institution, congratulating the organisation 'on reaching the 50th milestone in its life of valuable service to the youth of our country'. The conventicle held on Sunday afternoon was remarkable in its evidence of the popular interest. Hampden Park was used for the purpose, and the large enclosure was filled with the congregation. It was estimated that 100,000 were accommodated, while thousands were denied admission. The gates were closed about an hour before the appointed time of the service.

(*Glasgow Herald*)

SEPTEMBER 11TH

1885: 'By an explosion of gas at 25 Lyon Street, several persons were injured, at least one of them seriously. For some time Mrs Jane Lafferty or O'Donnell, who occupies the house, felt a strong smell of gas about the place, and she called in the assistance of two constables, Charles Stewart and William Rust. As the gas pervaded other parts of the tenement besides O'Donnell's house the constables divided their efforts, Stewart taking the house in which the accident took place, and Rust going to the flat above. The former officer procured a table and placing it in the lobby of the house, he got up on it and with his lamp endeavoured to ascertain where the gas was coming from. Directly an explosion occurred, the force of it throwing the unfortunate man violently to the floor. The explosion was attended by a loud report, which attracted many of the neighbours, and subsequently it was discovered that some of the furnishings of the house had been set on fire. Attention was in the first place directed to the injured constable and the people who happened to be in or about the house at the time. Stewart had sustained serious injuries. He was removed without loss of time to the Royal Infirmary.' (*Glasgow Herald*)

September 12th

1832: On this day Joseph Levy became the first person to be interred in the Necropolis. Levy, who died of cholera, was the first of 50,000 to be buried there. James Pagan in his *Sketch of the History of Glasgow* described it:

One of the most pleasing institutions connected with Glasgow, however, is the Necropolis – a burying ground of recent institution, and laid out according to the plan of the celebrated Pere la Chaise in Paris. Previous to the opening of this cemetery it was known as the Fir Park – a property belonging to the Merchants' House – and though almost valueless for any other purpose, it is scarcely possible to conceive a locality better fitted for the solemn and sacred purpose to which it is now devoted. It rises to a height of 300 feet above the adjacent level, and is only separated from the cathedral and its olden cemetery by the Molendinar burn. The view from the summit is picturesque, interesting and beautiful. To the south-west the city extends in all its mighty proportions, with its many spires rising far above the roofs of the dwellings; while to the east the eye is refreshed by a long vista of hill and dale, with agricultural and woodland scenery.

SEPTEMBER 13TH

2006: On this day Kelvingrove Art Gallery and Museum reopened. The famous red sandstone building had been closed for renovation in 2003, and the £28 million refurbishment saw a complete redisplay. The building had first opened in 1901, built to house the city's art and museum collections, as part of the Glasgow International Exhibition. The Art Gallery and Museum became the city's most-visited attraction, with around a million visitors per year. It was a story of the city that the museum's architect, on first seeing the completed project, ran up to the top and jumped off to his death, so disappointed was he that it had been built back to front. This urban myth is still told by taxi drivers to tourists. One story that has some foundation is that the building is haunted by a ghost. A member of staff was in the staff canteen, which at the time was situated in one of the front turrets. He became so frightened upon seeing an apparition of a woman in a long dress appearing in front of him that he resolved never to work in the building again.

SEPTEMBER 14TH

1939: These notices appeared in the *Glasgow Herald* on this day:

During the War. Your Dogs. Owing to the numerous appeals from clients, Miss Trotter has decided to continue to run the Deancourt kennels as a boarding kennel during the war. Would all those who contemplate sending their dogs into the country please communicate with Miss Trotter immmediately as space is limited, and bookings are already being received. Owners' dogs will receive every care and attention whilst in Miss Trotter's charge and her own personal kennel staff will be remaining with her.

The Time for Women. Nurses! ARP Workers! Members of the ATS! Make certain you have the right time by wearing an Angus wrist watch. Sold only by Hendersons, 84 and 145-7 Argyle St.

'Black Out'. Light reading for 'black out' nights. Jackson's Bookshop, 73 West George Street.

Troon Golf Club. All competitions are cancelled until further notice.

Escape the Alarms! Come to the peace, safe comfort and beautiful surroundings of Perthshire. Accommodation available at the Bailie Nicol Jarvie Hotel, Aberfoyle.

Sunset today is at 7.37. All lights must be obscured by that time.

September 15th

1737: Hutchison's Hospital was founded by two brothers: George and Thomas Hutchison 'for the entertainment of as many aged and decrepit Men to be placed therein'. The foundation stone was laid by Thomas Hutchison in 1641 but the building was not finished until 1660. Its location was to the west of the town's West Port. Despite its original aims, the remit was widened and on this day it was decided that it was not just men who were to be admitted:

> Original Regulations respecting the Qualification of Pensioners. The Patrons enacted, that such part of the surplus funds as they may judge convenient, after paying the repairs, etc, of the Hospital, and the stated maintenance of twelve old Men and twelve Boys, should be applied to the maintenance of poor old decayed Women of fifty years of age and upwards, Widows and Relicts of persons who had been in credit and reputation in this City during their widowhood.

(*Annals of Glasgow*)

September 16th

1769: On this day Lieutenant George Spearing was only half-way through an unusual ordeal. He had accidentally fallen into an old coal-pit in North Woodside while out collecting hazel nuts. He remained undiscovered for seven days and seven nights. On this day, he failed to attract the attention of some potential rescuers:

> There fell but little rain, and I had the satisfaction to hear the voices of some boys in the wood. Immediately I called out with all my might, but it was in vain, though I afterwards learned that they actually heard me but being prepossessed with an idle story of a wild man being in the wood, they ran away affrighted.

Lieutenant Spearing described his conditions in the 17 yard-deep hole:

> The pit I had fallen into was about five feet in diameter but the subterranean passages were choked up, so that I was exposed to the rain, which continued with very small intermission, till the day of my release and, indeed, in a very short time, I was completely wet through.

He was rescued on the 20th, after a party of men came out to find his body. They were surprised he was still alive. He lost his left leg, due to injuries sustained in his ordeal. (*Rambles Round Glasgow: Descriptive, Historical and Traditional* by Hugh Macdonald, 1860)

SEPTEMBER 17TH

1819: The *Glasgow Herald* reported on rioting that took place in the city over a number of days:

Monday evening we had one of the most alarming riots in this city that has occurred for many years past. In the afternoon a considerable body of men assembled in the Green, armed with weapons of various descriptions, with the avowed intention of joining their brethren in Paisley who, it was known, had been rioting for the two previous days. The whole party then proceeded on their way to Paisley, but had not gone far on the road when it was agreed to return and raise a disturbance in Glasgow, which would serve the double purpose of harassing the constituted authorities there and dividing the military force. They accordingly put about and a scene of riot and confusion, unparalleled in this part of the country, immediately took place. A great proportion of the city lamps in Trongate, Candleriggs, Stockwell, Glassford Street and almost the whole in the Gallowgate, Kent Street and Great Hamilton Street were broken and the windows of the shops of a number of respectable individuals were also demolished. From two to three hundred city lamps have been broken.

September 18th

1658: A proclamation was made by the town's authorities, regarding traffic using the bridge:

> On this day the tacksman of the bridge is ordained not to suffer any carts with wheels to go along the bridge, until that the wheels be taken off, and the body of the cart alone is drawn by the horse.

'In the ease of a heavily loaded cart this would surely be a prohibition with a vengeance. The magistrates of these times must either have been jealous of the introduction of wheeled carriages, or suspicious as to the stability of the bridge, which is still in existence, and up till January 1847 was in ordinary use for every kind of traffic between the north and south banks of the Clyde. Carts, minus the wheels, are still used in Argyleshire and other parts of the Highlands.' (*Sketch of the History of Glasgow*)

———— • ◆ • ————

2006: On this day the Clyde Arc Bridge was officially opened. Known as the 'Squinty Bridge' the road bridge connects Finnieston on the north of the Clyde with Govan on the south. It was the first city centre traffic-bearing crossing built since the Kingston Bridge almost forty years before. The £20 million bridge was closed two years later for repairs when one of the support cables snapped.

SEPTEMBER 19TH

1775: 'On this day the town council gave John Golborne £1,500, as a remuneration for deepening the river ten inches more than he was bound to do by his contract. They farther honoured him by the gift of a silver cup, and made his son a present of £100. In 1768 Mr Golborne had been called in. The principle upon which Golborne proposed to act was to narrow the channel for several miles below Glasgow, and, by thus confining the water, to enable it to act with greater effect upon the bottom, and thus to scour out for itself a channel deeper in proportion as it was narrower. This plan he proposed to carry out by constructing jetties from the banks, at different distances apart. In January 1775, Golborne had erected 117 jetties, including both sides of the river, and improved it so effectually, that vessels drawing more than six feet of water came up to the Broomielaw at flood tide. This improvement – vast at that time – was appreciated as it ought to be.' (*Sketch of the History of Glasgow*)

SEPTEMBER 20TH

1793: 'This day the following gentlemen were elected Deacons of the Incorporated Trades of this city for the year ensuing: Hammermen – Patrick Maine, Taylors – Archibald Brodley, Cordiners – James Bryce, Weavers – William Hunter, Bakers – William Gentle, Skinners – John Howie, Wrights – James Young, Coopers – John Hoods, Fleshers – William Lang, Masons – Daniel Wardrop, Gardeners – Robert Wilson, Barbers – Walter McIndoe, Dyers – Adam Grant.' (*Glasgow Advertiser*)

❖

1793: 'A Horse Race. There is to be run for over the course at the west end of Partick on the first Friday of October, at two o'clock, a subscription purse of five guineas, viz four guineas to be won by the best of three heats and one guinea by the second best, and three times round the course each heat. There will be no race unless three horses start, and no horse will be booked that has run for fifty pounds. Any horse, mare, or gelding that is intended to run must be booked within three hours of the time above specified, at the house of Allan Craig. There is to be a foot race immediately preceding the horse race and an after-shot race in the evening in case the subscription is filled up.' (*Glasgow Advertiser*)

September 21st

1860: Cooking depots were established by merchant Thomas Corbett on this day in 1860 for the poor to eat properly. A journalist recorded his experiences of dining:

The favour extended towards these cheap dining rooms in Glasgow is unmistakeable, and they now occupy the place of a local institution. I have recently had dinner in both the Jamaica and Argyle street depots, and on both occasions fared sumptuously for four pence half-penny. The basin of broth or pease-soup, which costs one penny, is, if anything, superior in quality, and quite equal in quantity, to the same dish charged for in restaurants, 4*d*, 5*d* and 6*d*. Among the objectionable features are the knives and forks which have a decided charity school look. The spoon is never scoured clean, and improved in shape by various geniuses, intent upon making the article utterly useless for the conveyance of meat to the mouth. The knives and forks appear to have been raked out of some thieves' den, no two of them being alike. Another disagreeable feature is the number of visitors who are apparently suffering from incipient diphtheria, and who betray their sufferings by clearing their throats and spitting abundantly over the floor.

(*Southland Times*, National Library of New Zealand)

September 22nd

1820: This letter appeared in the *Glasgow Herald* on this day:

Sir, I observe that there is the intention of renewing the Police Act. I take the liberty of suggesting that the unequal and therefore unjust, tax on Foot Pavements should undergo revision. It is only twenty years since the inhabitants of this City were first compelled to make foot pavements in front of their properties, under the authority of the first Police Act, which contains the following compulsit: 'That when the floors or stories of front houses or buildings belong to more proprietors than one, the several proprietors of the said house, or building, shall cause the ground before their respective houses of building to be paved, and the pavements to be kept in repair, the expense being defrayed in proportion to the rents of the respective parts of the house or building belonging to each of them'. From this act it is evident that the tax is unjust, the whole of the expense of making and maintaining the pavements being defrayed by a small proportion of the inhabitants, to the total exemption of those proprietors who have houses in the closes. I suggest that the Foot Pavements should be made by the Board of Police from their common fund. I am, A Citizen.

SEPTEMBER 23RD

1820: There was much popular support for King George IV's estranged wife Queen Caroline. The public protests about her treatment resulted in bonfires being lit on Glasgow Green, and the city's fire engines being shoved into the river. *The Scotsman* reported on citizens' attempts to sign an Address in support of the Queen:

> The Magistracy of Glasgow drove a body of individuals out of the Tron Church session house, where they were subscribing an address to her Majesty the Queen. No riot nor disturbance could be alleged to afford a pretext for this interference, which it is impossible to view in any other light than as an insult to the citizens. One scarcely knows whether to feel more contempt for the paltry spirit that dictated such an act or indignation at the flagrant partiality it displayed. Had the object been to address the King, these same men would no doubt have thrown open every public building in the city. Their petty efforts, however, will only expose their own littleness, and will have no effect in preventing the inhabitants from expressing their opinions on a great public question. The number of names is said to be immense and the pressure of individuals to get their names put down altogether unprecedented.

The Address received over 35,000 signatures.

September 24th

1740: 'This day it is statuted and ordained that the wheat being at 19s sterling the boll, including the manufacturing, that the wheat bread, whether white, wheaten, or household, be prepared, marked and sold by the baxters conform to and according to the assize fixt and determined by the Act of Parliament, etc. The Magistrates and Council do now further statute and ordain that the baxters for the future affix upon their bread the initial letters of the bakers name, and upon the several sorts, whether white, wheaten or household, the letters following, viz, the letter F on white bread, the letter W on the wheaten bread, and the letter H on the houshold bread. As also affix distinct figures, such as I for a penny loaf, II for a two penny loaf, and so forth for larger loafs. And likeway agree and ordain that there be scales and weights provided and fixt in the Clerks Chamber and that any of the inhabitants who have any suspicion of the weight of the bread furnisht to them may bring the same to the Clerks Chamber to be weighted, and if found light, do impower the Magistrates to pay for the loaf, and give half a crown of reward to the person who brings the loaf.' (*Memorabilia of the City of Glasgow*)

September 25th

1970: On 30th December 1969 three armed men held up a Clydesdale Bank in Linwood. They were spotted afterwards and the resulting events were described in this citation, dated this day, for two George Medals that were awarded to Inspector Andrew Hyslop and Constable John Campbell:

Inspector Hyslop, travelling in a police van, saw three men carrying two heavy suitcases and a metal box into a common entry of a house in Allison Street. Inspector Hyslop entered the hall of the house where he was confronted by one of the men. The Inspector heard the sound of the pistol misfiring and immediately made to close with the gunman who took deliberate aim and fired a shot which struck the Inspector on the face, and caused him to lose the power of his limbs. The sound of the shot was heard by the other police officers, two of whom ran into the hall and, in attempting to disarm the man, were both shot in the head at close range. The gunman was about to fire another shot at Inspector Hyslop when his attention was distracted and this gave Constable Campbell an opportunity to enter the hall where he grappled with the gunman and after a struggle disarmed him. The two shot constables died as a result of bullet wounds.

(Supplement to the *London Gazette*)

September 26th

1973: On the evening of this day a crucial football match took place at Hampden Park. It was between Scotland and Czechoslovakia, a qualifier for the World Cup to be held in Germany the following year. In front of a crowd of 95,000 the Czechs scored first, in 32 minutes. Scotland increased their pressure and came back into the game with a goal by Jim Holton in the 40th minute. In the second half, Kenny Dalglish was substituted and his replacement Joe Jordan was able to score with a header with just 15 minutes to go. Scotland had qualified for the World Cup for the first time in sixteen years. Denis Law, who was thirty-three years old, said it was the greatest moment of his sporting life. The Scotland team was: Ally Hunter, Celtic; Sandy Jardine, Rangers; Danny McGrain, Celtic; Billy Bremner (Captain), Leeds Utd; Jim Holton, Manchester Utd; George Connelly, Celtic; David Hay, Celtic; Denis Law, Manchester City; Willie Morgan, Manchester Utd; Kenny Dalglish, Celtic; Joe Jordan, Leeds (63); Tommy Hutchison, Coventry City. Despite not qualifying for the later rounds of the World Cup, Scotland were the only team to remain undefeated in the championships, as winners West Germany were beaten in the early group round.

SEPTEMBER 27TH

1929: The BBC was formed in 1922, and the station in Glasgow opened a year later. This is the schedule of 'Today's Wireless Programmes' from Glasgow for this day:

4.0	The Station Orchestra.
5.15	The Children's Hour.
5.57	Weather Forecast for Farmers.
6.0	London Programme relayed from Daventry.
6.15	Time Signal from Greenwich; Weather Forecast and News.
6.30	Scottish Market Prices for Farmers.
6.40	Musical interlude.
6.45	Pianoforte Duets by Weber, Mendelssohn and Schumann.
7.0	Mr Ernest Newman – The BBC Music Critic.
7.15	Musical interlude.
7.25	'The Village and the Village Craftsman – Village Life and Village Industries' by Lieutenant Colonel WR Little.
7.45	'Wind Up', a broadcast sketch by J Jefferson Farjeon. Followed by 'The Split in the Cabinet' a play in two acts.
8.25	Mabel Constanduros and Michael Hogan – The Bugginses at the Seaside, Alfredo Rode (violin); English and Viennese Songs, by Greta Kellar; Buying a Gun by Harry Gratton; Piano Duets by Edgar Fairchild and Robert Lindholm; Jack Payne and the BBC Dance Orchestra.
9.40	Weather Forecast and Second General News Bulletin.
9.55	Scottish News Bulletin.
10.0	Time Signal from Greenwich. Topical Talk.
10.15-11.15	
	A Recital by the English Singers and Henri Casadesus.

SEPTEMBER 28TH

1687: 'This said day the Provost, Baillies, etc, being certainly informed that several of the inhabitants marry and baptise their children at the meeting houses, they hereby ordain all the inhabitants within the said burgh, to book their marriages and what children they shall baptise, in the public and authentic Register as formerly, that risk may be avoided, and minors may not be prejudged, when extracts of their age may be called for at the public Register, and that they pay the ordinary dues thereof to the Clerk, Beadles, and others concerned, under the punishment of three pounds Scots to be exacted off the contraveners, "toties quoties" (on each occasion).' (*Memorabilia of the City of Glasgow*)

1781: 'The Council appointed a Committee to consider what steps are proper to be taken for bringing the posts from London (via Carlisle, Moffat, etc) to arrive at Glasgow as early as they arrive at Edinburgh and to have six posts from London weekly, as Carlisle and Dumfries now have.' (*Glasgow and its Clubs*)

SEPTEMBER 29TH

1822: 'Another prophet has lately sprung up, David Ross, who has been lecturing and preaching in a house in Great Dovehill, called the "Church of Smyrna". For some time past, he has been uttering violent tirades against other sects, particularly the Ministers of the Established Church. He states that the wickedness of Glasgow is such that before now it would have shared the fate of Sodom and Gomorrah, were it not for the existence of one righteous man, ie, himself. The Prophet, attended by the Prophetess and another person, entered the hall, when the audience began to laugh, upon which the Prophet said: "Don't laugh, for I am endowed with the spirit of the Holy Prophets of old." After this the Prophet drew back, and Miriam advanced. When the audience laughed she angrily said she was neither daft or stupid. She here seemed to falter and the confusion and laughter increasing she sat down. About 8 o'clock the prophet left the hall along with his female convert, and during their progress they were hissed and pushed and so roughly used that they were obliged to be taken under the protection of the police, who conducted them in safety to their earthly habitation in the Calton.' (Broadside *The Awful Prophecies of David Ross*, National Library of Scotland Rare Books Collection, shelfmark: L.C.Fol.73 (040))

September 30th

1560: 'Statute by magistrates and council that there be sold no dearer ale than 4 pennies a pint, under the penalty of 8 schillings. And ordained, by the provost, baillies and whole council that the 4 penny loaf weighs 32 ounces, and the 2 penny loaf 16 ounces and that the same be good and sufficient stuff. And ordained, that a stone of tallow be sold no dearer than 8 schilling. And ordained that a pound of candles be sold no dearer than 6 pennies the pound. And ordained, that the peck of horse-corn be sold no dearer, for this present year, than 8 pennies the peck.' (*The History of Glasgow*)

———•◆•———

1850: 'Turtle! Turtle! McLerie, Davidson & Ferguson, Buchanan Street, have now the pleasure of offering to the public upwards of 30cwt of live turtles in excellent condition, varying in weight from 40lbs to 300lbs each. Early application is necessary as the whole will be prepared next week and preserved in cannisters, which may be obtained at 15s each.

Turtle soup, ready as usual, every day, at 12 o'clock noon.' (*Glasgow Herald*)

OCTOBER 1ST

1662: 'The Restoration of Charles II as King and so-called Defender of the Faith sounded the death knell of Presbyterianism in Scotland. The royal mandate had gone forth from the former Covenanted King, that all persons were to acknowledge the bishops. Heavy fines were levied on those who were believed to have had complicity with Cromwell. No fewer than 439 persons in the Glasgow diocese were fined, the total sum taken from them being £350,490 Scots (£29,207 10s sterling). So far as Glasgow and the West of Scotland were concerned, these measures failed to procure honour to Archbishop Fairfoul and his suffragans, and this nonconformity resulted in a meeting of the Privy Council in Glasgow. It was termed the drunken meeting, as it was affirmed that all present were flustered with drink, save Sir James Lockhart of Lee, who was the only dissentient. This drunken meeting passed on this day an Act of Conformity, and such as did not obey were to remove themselves and their families from their parishes within a month. As a result of the Act, nearly four hundred ministers were cast from their charges, fourteen of them being of the Presbytery of Glasgow.' (*The Anecdotage of Glasgow* by Robert Alison, 1892)

OCTOBER 2ND

1936: 'Visit of Nazi Team. Members of the Independent Labour Party unsuccessfully endeavoured to extract from the Lord Provost and the Senior Magistrate, assurances that they had no intention to entertain the German football team which is to meet a Scottish eleven at Ibrox Park. The Lord Provost indicated that he had had no application to entertain the team, but if he did receive such a request he would exercise his own discretion. In reply to a question by Mr Thomas Taylor (Dalmarnock – LLP) asking for assurance that he would "in no way entertain the representatives of Fascist Germany in connection with the visit of the Nazi football team," the Lord Provost said that he had received no application to entertain the team but as Lord Provost he was allowed a considerable discretion in such matters. He intended to maintain his position as the representative of the city. Mr William Shaw (Springburn – Soc) who, as secretary of the Glasgow Trades Council, forwarded a resolution on the previous day to the Scottish Football Association protesting against the German team being permitted to play in Glasgow, asked the Senior Magistrate that if the magistrates received protests from a representative organisation in Glasgow would these by duly considered? Baillie McClounie answered "Most certainly".' (*Glasgow Herald*)

OCTOBER 3RD

1878: The *Glasgow Herald* described the aftermath when the City of Glasgow Bank closed its doors:

Though the news of the stoppage of the City of Glasgow Bank created great excitement throughout the country, nothing in the shape of a severe panic took place anywhere. The decision of the managers of the other Scotch banks to accept the City of Glasgow notes undoubtedly assisted in a great measure to reassure the public, and to prevent any such run on the banks as that which formed so marked a feature of the 'scare' of 1857. On the Glasgow Exchange no such commotion has been experienced since the panic of 1870. It would be idle to disguise the fact that the stoppage of the Bank is not an event which will stand by itself. No commercial concern of such magnitude can go to ruin without dragging others in its train. The public should be warned against the natural tendency to make the worst of such an event. This is not the first time we have heard of a bank which has been compelled to shut its doors through reckless trading rather than through a prevailing state of commerical unsoundness.

OCTOBER 4TH

1793: 'R Hamilton, begs leave to inform his friends and the public that he proposes to open an Academy for the instruction of young gentlemen in the English and Latin languages in the school room in Virginia Street, for some time past occupied by the Reverend Mr Dickson. The great object in his plan of Education will be to combine the study of English grammar with that of the Latin, and to teach his scholars not only to understand their own language grammatically but to read it with propriety, taste, and expression. The pupils will be divided into classes according to their degrees of improvement and taught on the usual terms. Advanced pupils, intended for any of the learned professions, will be assisted by example as well as precept in forming an address proper for the Bar, Pulpit or Senate. Pupils who desire it may likewise be instructed in the elements of Geography and History. It is proposed likewise to open, at the same time, a class from twelve till one, for young ladies in which they will be taught English grammatically and to spell and read with accuracy and propriety. NB Elocution taught in families, or to classes and individuals. For terms please apply to Mr Hamilton.' (*Glasgow Advertiser*)

OCTOBER 5TH

1918: This appeal was printed in the *Glasgow Herald* on this day:

What the Coal Shortage means to YOU! The Coal Shortage is so grave that none but the very poorest houses will have as much as they want and even for these that is not certain. Unless immediate steps be taken to reduce the amount of coal used at home, serious hardship will come – that is what it means to YOU. *But hardship may be avoided* if you take steps now, without a day's delay to meet your difficulties.

Make a tour of your house.

Look in the coal cellar. Calculate how long your coal will last. How often you can have a fire. What you must reserve for illness.

Look in the coal scuttle. Are you mixing coke with your coal? If not – see to it at once.

Put a notice up in the bathroom: 'Fewer hot baths'.

Go round the house at night. Turn out any unnecessary light and *see that it is never lit again.*

Remember that the coal you go without is taking the Americans to the Front. It is warming the wounded in hospitals and the men who are fighting. It is bringing Victory nearer. Do your share in winning the War.

Do With Less Coal

OCTOBER 6TH

1883: On this day the foundation stone was laid for the new municipal buildings:

A grand Banquet, given by the Corporation, took place in the City Hall in the evening. The hall was tastefully decorated, the walls being hung with red cloth, and the windows draped with white muslin. About five hundred gentlemen sat down to dinner, and unusual interest was given to the proceedings by the presence of a large number of ladies, who, on the invitation of the Lord Provost and Mrs Ure, occupied seats in the side galleries, and heard the speeches and the music. The musical arrangements were of the most perfect description. The band of Messrs Adams was stationed in the western gallery, while in the orchestra was the Balmoral Choir, under the leadership of Mr H A Lambeth, the city organist. The members of this choir sang suitable airs between the toasts. From half-past five till six o'clock Mr Lambeth played a selection of appropriate pieces on the organ. The Banquet was purveyed by Messrs Ferguson & Forrester, Buchanan Street, under the direction of Mr William Guilford.

(Description Of Ceremonial On The Occasion Of Laying The Foundation Stone Of The Municipal Buildings In George Square, 1885)

OCTOBER 7TH

1812: 'Glasgow Circuit Court of Justiciary. James Stewart and William McArthur were accused of breaking into the vestry of the English Chapel and feloniously carrying off one minister's gown, silk, one minister's cassock, ditto, two minister's gowns, bombazeen, three linen surplices, one black silk scarf, one table cloth, five towels, and one great coat. Lord Gillies delivered an admirable charge to the jury, who returned a verdict unanimously finding Stewart and McArthur guilty, and they were both sentenced to be hanged, on the 18th of November. The sentence was commuted to transportation for life.' (*Old Glasgow and its Environs*)

———◆———

1818: 'On this day at the Circuit Court, Margaret Kennedy was convicted of issuing forged notes of the Stirling Banking Company, and sentenced to be executed. The poor woman, who is young, was totally unable to read or write, and was earnestly recommended to mercy by the Jury. This is the only instance of any person being tried in Glasgow for forgery since 1805, when two young men were convicted of engraving the plates for forged notes, and issuing the notes. She is the only individual now in custody in Scotland on a similar charge, and only one has been executed the last fifteen years for forged notes.' (*Morning Chronicle*)

OCTOBER 8TH

1844: 'A bronze equestrian statue, in honour of the Duke of Wellington, was erected and inaugurated on the open space in front of the portico of the Exchange. The monument was erected by subscription, which was originated at a public meeting of the inhabitants held on 18th February 1840.' (*Sketch of the History of Glasgow*)

———— ◆ ————

1895: 'On this day at a meeting of the Synod of Glasgow and Ayr, the Reverend WF Stevenson submitted the report of the Committee on Sabbath Observance. While acknowledging some little improvement in the observance of the Christian Sabbath, there were other points which they had to deplore. Chief among these was the great increase during the past summer of the Sunday bus traffic with places in the neighbourhood of Glasgow. The traffic in some cases was almost incessant from early forenoon till late in the evening. They felt bound to call attention to the disturbance of the quiet of these places on the Lord's Day and to the intemperance and disorder which prevailed. It was very notable that Sunday bus traffic seldom or ever converged on places where there were no opportunities of getting spiritous liquours. It generally converged on places where there were licensed premises.' (*The Scotsman*)

OCTOBER 9TH

1993: On this day Nelson Mandela addressed a crowd of 10,000 people in George Square. He thanked the people of Glasgow for their support during the campaign against apartheid in South Africa. Earlier that day Mandela had received his Freedom of the City award. He had been awarded it in 1981 but the South African authorities had refused permission for him to receive it then. Glasgow was the first city in the world to grant him this honour. He had been in jail for almost twenty years at this point, after being sentenced to life imprisonment for plotting to overthrow the South African government. In 1986 Glasgow's City Council changed the name of St George's Place to Nelson Mandela Place in his honour. It was the location of the South African consulate. One Conservative politician said at that time it was a 'terrifying, irresponsible decision' and the move would 'make Glasgow a laughing stock'. Some businesses refused to acknowledge the name change. During his three days in the city Mandela impressed all those he came into contact with by his gentle manner and charismatic presence. A year after his visit he was made President of South Africa following the country's transition to a democratic state.

OCTOBER 10TH

1859: These notices and adverts appeared in the *Glasgow Herald* on this day:

I, James Houston, will not be responsible for any debts contracted by my wife, Margaret Kirk or Houston, after this date.

Mr George Moffat, not being in our employment any longer, is not entitled to uplift any debts due to us. Bertram & Co.

A Safe and Effectual Remedy. Ladies suffering from headaches, lowness of spirits, nervous tremors, indigestion, neuralgia and weakness of the nervous system, are respectfully invited to make trial of Galvanism, which is applied without shock or pain by Mr W Harthill, Medical Galvinister, 53 West Regent Street. Certificates from the Highest Mobility, Gentry and Medical Men attest the success of this simple and safe treatment. At home from eleven till four and in the evenings from seven to nine. No charge for consultation merely.

Coals! Coals! Coals! Good household coals 9s. Most excellent coals at 10s 6d and 11s. Finest Wishaw 11s 6d. Best Soft Coals in the market at 12s 6d per waggon, delivered in the city. Coal Office, 28 St Enoch Square.

OCTOBER IITH

1623: 'It is stated and ordained that no manner of person stamp or wash any clothes, plaiding, yarn or any other thing in the foregate, or backside, where they may be seen, but only in houses and private places, each person under the punishment of 11 schillings for every occasion.' (*Old Glasgow and its Environs*)

———— •◆• ————

1890: A letter, signed 'Annoyed', appeared in the *Glasgow Herald* on this day:

> Sir. Can nothing be done to put a stop to the everlasting and horrid cries of Coal! Coal! Coal! which rend the ears of residenters in private houses – not flats – in Hillhead? In former years such a thing was unheard of in front of private houses, like, for example Ashton Terrace, and we were never pestered in this way. But now it is quite common for lorries to ply up and down with bags of coal. If these coal dealers found they were never patronised they would very soon cease to ply their wares in quarters where they are not wanted, and where their presence is distasteful. Trusting residenters generally in this neighbourhood, who own private residences, will on no account encourage this street selling of coal.

OCTOBER 12TH

1821: The following letter, dated this day, was sent from Thomas McCulloch, stocking-weaver, addressed to his wife in Glasgow. McCulloch had been transported to Botany Bay following a demand for greater political rights:

> I send you these few lines, hoping they will find you and the children in good health. We arrived here on the 18th of May, all in good health (after being at sea five months). I was taken off the stores by a Mr Panton, a native of Scotland, and employed by him as a labourer but not agreeing with me, he was so kind as to transfer me to a Captain Irvine, and I am to be with him as a house-servant, and I am going to remove about 40 miles up the country. If you think of coming here, there shall be nothing wanting on my part to bring you, as I have every encouragement from several gentlemen that can enable me to do so, as your presence here will free me from bondage as any man's wife that comes here as a free settler, can take her husband from Government employment, or being a servant to any of them.

(Broadside *Copy of a Very Interesting Letter from Botany Bay*, National Library of Scotland Rare Books Collection, shelfmark: L.C.Fol.73 (022))

OCTOBER 13TH

1846: The Faculty of the University of Glasgow met on this day and admitted a twenty-two-year-old man as professor of the Natural Philosophy department. His name was William Thomson and he remained in post for fifty-three years. Later known as Lord Kelvin, he made many advances in physics, including the devising of an absolute temperature scale, that was named after him. He formulated the Second Law of Thermodynamics – that heat will not flow from a colder body to a hotter one. He assisted the laying of the first transatlantic cable and also developed an improved ship's compass. A keen yachtsman, he also invented a depth sounder and a tide predictor. It was claimed that his house in the university quadrangle was the first to be lit by electricity in the city. The University of Glasgow said of Lord Kelvin that he was 'universally recognized as the leading figure in the world of science for thirty years'. He was knighted in 1866 and made a lord in 1892. He died in 1907 and, showing the regard in which he was held for achievements in science, was buried beside Isaac Newton in Westminster Abbey.

OCTOBER 14TH

1777: 'On this day the Magistrates and Council, considering that there are only two men employed in cleaning the streets of the City, and which have not been properly cleaned, therefore agree that a third person should be employed, in cleaning the streets in time coming. And in the winter season, the said three men, if they clean the streets properly, shall be paid one pound sterling weekly, and ten shillings weekly in the summer.' (*Glasgow and its Clubs*)

1859: Glasgow's fresh water supply was inaugurated on this day by Queen Victoria at Loch Katrine. One of the Water Commissioners outlined the scope of the project:

> Empowered by Act (of Parliament) the Commissioners came to these wild and romantic regions for that copious supply of pure water of which the large and rapidly increasing population of Glasgow stood in need. The rugged district of thirty four miles in extent, which intervenes between the Loch and the City has been penetrated by tunnels, crossed by aqueducts, or traversed by iron pipes, in the execution of the necessary works for ultimately conveying to the city no less than fifty million gallons of water per day.

(*Glasgow Herald*)

OCTOBER 15TH

1743: 'There was a proposal produced, signed by John Walker, merchant in Edinburgh, for erecting a stage-coach betwixt Edinburgh and Glasgow and to set out twice a week from Edinburgh to Glasgow and twice a week from Glasgow to Edinburgh; and the coach or lando to contain six passengers, with six sufficient horses, for twenty weeks in the summer; and the rest of the year once a week; and each passenger to pay ten schilling sterling, and to be entitled to fourteen pounds' weight of baggage; and that as long as he continues the stage-coach, that the town should insure to him that two hundred of his tickets shall be sold here each year.' (*Minute of the Council of Glasgow*)

The proposal wasn't accepted.

———◆·———

1912: This advertisement appeared in the *Glasgow Herald* on this day:

> What the doctor smokes. The doctor's choice in tobacco is Craven Mixture, and he is supported in that choice by the verdict of the greatest medical journal in the world: the *Lancet*, which published on August 24th, 1912, an analytical report showing that of all well-known tobaccos Craven is unmistakably the purest and best – the smoke Craven yielding only one sixteenth of the nicotine found in any other well-known tobacco. Therefore the doctor smokes and should recommend Craven mixture as the best for health.

OCTOBER 16TH

1589: 'It is ordained that there be no playing at golf, carri, or shinty, in the High Kirk or Kirkyard, or Blackfriar Kirkyard, either Sunday or workday.' (*Burgh Records of the City of Glasgow*)

This was the first recorded mention of golf in the city.

———•◆•———

1971: A march took place through the streets of the city on this day. It was organised by the Irish Solidarity Movement and around 250 people took part. Disturbances broke out when the marchers were met by a counter-march of Protestants, led by the Reverend Jack Glass. Around fifty policemen were in attendance, and were able to prevent an escalation of the trouble witnessed by Saturday afternoon shoppers. Thirty men were arrested, most for breach of the peace offences. A sixteen-year-old was charged with attacking four men with a razor, three of them policemen. One of these was Detective Inspector George Johnston of the Special Branch and a series of photographs of him being slashed by a razor in the middle of the street and then responding by pulling out his own baton were seen around the world. The attacker was sentenced to prison. DI Johnston later retired from the police to live on Arran.

OCTOBER 17TH

1850: On this day James Young obtained a patent for 'treating bituminous coal to obtain paraffine and oil containing paraffine therefrom'. His discovery earned him the nickname 'Paraffin' Young and would lead to the beginnings of the modern oil industry. From his distillation methods, Young was able to produce viable products such as paraffin, lubricating oil, and material for candles from coal and then oil shale. The world's first commercial oil works were set up at Bathgate in 1851 and within a short number of years 120 shale refining plants were in operation in the Central Belt. With his patent in place Young was able to make a large fortune, earning profits estimated to be around £70,000 a year. Young, who was born in Glasgow, studied at Anderson's College where he met David Livingstone, who was studying medicine. Young remained friends with the missionary and explorer and used some of his money to help finance Livingstone's expeditions in Africa. Livingstone laid the foundation stone of Young's factory at Addiewell. Livingstone said: 'Young's friendship never faltered.' (*New Scientist*)

OCTOBER 18TH

1850: 'On Monday afternoon an incident, which might have been attended with serious consequences, occurred in connection with the omnibus which plies between Whitevale and Cowcaddens. While standing at the former locality, the driver and guard, chancing to be both absent from the horses, they, from some cause or other not explained, broke into a trot and proceeded along their accustomed route at the usual pace. A number of scavengers at work on the road, observing the state of matters, endeavoured to stay their progress by elevating their brooms. But this display only alarmed the animals the more, the trot became a gallop and the frightened creatures set off at the most furious pace along Gallowgate Street, spreading dismay on every side, almost frightening to death four unfortunate passengers, who had taken their seats before the horses set off. One of them, an elderly lady, afraid, apparently, to encounter the chance of running against a lamp post, succeeded in getting out of the vehicle while at full career by allowing herself to roll off the lower step of the omnibus on to the street, by which means she reached terra firma in comparative security. The horses, of their own accord, stopped after a run of fully a mile.' (*Glasgow Herald*)

OCTOBER 19TH

1832: William Cobbett was an English reformer, one of several noatable figures, who made tours of Scotland. On this day he wrote of his arrival in Glasgow:

And now what am I to say of this Glasgow, which is at once a city of the greatest beauty, a commercial town, and a place of manufactures also very great. It is Manchester and Liverpool in one (on a smaller scale) with regard to commerce and manufactures but, besides this, here is the City of Glasgow, built in a style, and beautiful in all ways, very little short of the New Town of Edinburgh. The new Exchange is a most magnificent place and, indeed, the whole of the city, compared to which the plastered-up Regent Street is beggarly, is as fine as anything that I ever saw, the New Town of Edinburgh excepted. The whole is built of beautiful white stone and doors, windows, and everything bespeak solid worth, without any taste for ostentation or show. The manufacturing part, with the tall chimneys and the smoke, is at the east end of the city, and somewhat separated from it, so that there is very little smoke in Glasgow.

(Cobbett's tour in Scotland: and in the four northern counties of England: in the autumn of the year, 1832)

OCTOBER 20TH

1918: As the First World War was drawing to a close, another threat to life emerged with the spread of what became known as Spanish Flu. The influenza pandemic killed an estimated 40 million people around the world, far more than in the war itself. A quarter of a million died in Britain alone. In Scotland the death toll was calculated to be 17,515, although this is now thought to be only a quarter of the true figure. The epidemic was deemed to be over by April 1919, having started in May the previous year. Glasgow was one of the first places in Britain to report infected cases. In October, the infection was rampant with around 300 people dying each week in Glasgow alone. On this day this product advert appeared in the *Glasgow Herald*. Its effectiveness is not known:

Kill the Influenza Germ! Chloramine-T tablets. One tablet dissolved in water forms an antiseptic solution, as recommended by the highest medical authorities for douching the nasal passages. To be followed by the insertion of a little Chloramine-T Cream. This simple treatment prevents infection by effectively destroying the Influenza germ. Chloramine-T Tablets - Bottle of 25 tablets 1/8. Chloramine-T Cream 9d, 1/4 and 2/6. Boots Pure Drug Company Ltd. Local branch: 101-105 Sauchiehall St.

OCTOBER 21ST

1971: A gas leak caused a massive explosion at a shopping precinct at Clarkston Toll. Twenty-two people were killed and a hundred injured after the explosion brought down a rooftop car parking area. A passing bus was caught in the blast, the force of which was compared to that of a 1,000-pound bomb.

———— • ◆ • ————

1983: The Burrell Collection was opened. Sir William Burrell had amassed a vast inventory, numbering over 8,000 objects. It included paintings, sculptures, furniture, tapestries, ceramics, medieval stained glass and much more. Burrell bequeathed his collection to the city of Glasgow in 1944, but with certain conditions. He was concerned about the effects of pollution on his artefacts and so had stipulated that any site must be 16 miles from the city centre. A location was found in Pollok Country Park and the terms of the bequest relating to its distance from the city were waived by the trustees, the park being just 3 miles from the city centre. The building was tailor-made for both displaying and storing all the different varieties of artworks. It cost £17 million. The official opening was performed by the Queen. The building was an instant success and received 500,000 visitors in its first six months.

OCTOBER 22ND

1937: 'Drunkenness in Glasgow. "Glasgow is one of the most drunken cities in Scotland," declared Mr William Fletcher, vice-chairman of the board of management of the Scottish Temperance Alliance, in presiding today at the National Temperance Bazaar in St Andrews' Hall. Mr Fletcher said there was twice as much crime in the highest licensed towns in Scotland as in the lowest, while in the no-licence towns the amount of crime was very much reduced. In Glasgow, "red biddy" addicts, who were a definite produce of the public house, were very numerous. These people drank "red biddy" when they had wasted their substance and when they had no more money to spend on legitimate liquor. Lord Rowallan, who opened the bazaar, said it was to the young generation they must look for any real improvement in the temperance cause. They had much prejudice to overcome, but he believed that the general attitude towards the cause of temperance was now more favourable than it had ever been. From 1931 to 1935 the sum of £509,000,000 he said had been spent on housing in Great Britain while during the same period £1,018,000,000 had been spent on drink.' (*Glasgow Herald*)

OCTOBER 23RD

1971: On this day Partick Thistle won the 1971 Scottish League Cup. The Jags claimed their first major piece of silverware for fifty years in front of 62,740 fans at Hampden Park. The final score was 4-1 with the Maryhill team going 4-0 up after only 37 minutes. What made their victory more remarkable is they had beaten Celtic, who were in the middle of one of the most successful periods experienced by a club in Scottish football. Celtic were managed by Jock Stein and had at that point won six league titles in a row and had appeared in two European Cup finals, winning one in 1967. Partick Thistle had only been promoted to the First Division a few months previously and half of the team had part-time jobs. Their manager, Davie McParland, said: 'We had nothing to lose and everything to gain.' The match had been previewed by BBC's *Football Focus*. The presenter had said: 'In Scotland, it's League Cup final day at Hampden Park, where Celtic meet Partick Thistle – who have no chance.' The following Saturday, the enigmatic Thistle were beaten 7-2 by Aberdeen.

OCTOBER 24TH

1650: 'Arriving in Glasgow on the afternoon of this day Oliver Cromwell found that the magistrates, ministers, and leading inhabitants had fled but this was unnecessary, as that morning Cromwell, "at a rendezvous, gave a special charge to all the regiments of the army to carry themselves civilly and do no wrong to any". He also stated that the town of Glasgow seems a much sweeter and more delightful place than Edinburgh. On the Sunday following his entry into the city, Cromwell and his officers made a procession to the Cathedral to hear sermon. Zachary Boyd, minister of the Barony parish, was the preacher for the day, and as he was a man of great boldness, he did not hesitate to rail on them all to their very faces. So enraged was Thurlow, the secretary to Cromwell, that he asked leave "To pistol the old scoundrel". "Tuts," replied the Protector, "you are a greater fool than himself. We'll pay him back in his own coin." He accordingly invited his reverend foe to dinner, held pious converse with him during the evening, and wound up with a three hour prayer, which lasted till 8 o'clock in the morning.' (*The Anecdotage of Glasgow* by Robert Alison, 1892)

OCTOBER 25TH

1808: 'A fatal accident happened at ten o'clock to the Glasgow mail-coach which runs to Carlisle, at Avon-bridge, about seven miles from Moffat. An excessive quantity of rain had fallen during the day, and swollen the river to a very unusual height, by which means the bridge was carried away, but whether before the coach was on it, or not, is unknown. The coach, horses, passengers, guard, and driver, were all precipitated into the river, where they remained till assistance could be afforded, when it was found that the two outside passengers were killed, and three of the inside severely wounded. The other, a lady, escaped unhurt, and was found clinging to a piece of the bridge. The driver had one of his arms broken in two places, and the guard was much injured on the head. Three of the horses were found alive next morning, but one of them, when taking out, was accidentally killed by the falling of part of the bridge. The mail-coach passing to Glasgow would have shared the same fate, had not timely intimation prevented its too near approach to the bridge.' (*A Picture of Glasgow*)

OCTOBER 26TH

1838: An enquiry was held into the behaviour of certain members of the 15th Hussars who were barracked in the city. One of the soldiers had been fined for dog-fighting and another had been involved in an incident at the city's Argyll Arcade. A report in the *Glasgow Herald* described it:

> Lieutenant Knox of the 15th Hussars appeared before Bailie Johnston, at the bar of the Police Court, to answer a charge against him of wantonly and recklessly riding through the Arcade, to the alarm and danger of the lieges, and thereby causing a crowd to assemble. The Lieutenant acknowledged that he had gone through the Arcade and that he was so far wrong, knowing that it was not a thoroughfare for cattle, but he denied that he had endangered any one, or caused a crowd to assemble. The thing was done for a bet. Bailie Johnston said the conduct of the prisoner had been most reckless and wanton – he had treated the citizens with gross contempt, and it could not be tolerated. He regretted exceedingly that his powers in this case were so limited, but he would award the highest fine allowed by law, namely five pounds, which was instantly paid.

For bringing such public disgrace, the regiment were reportedly sent to India.

OCTOBER 27TH

1851: 'Our city was afflicted with one of those sickening spectacles which take place form time to time – a public execution. The crime for which the unhappy man, Archibald Hare, suffered death, was the murder, by stabbing, in the main street of Blantyre, of Ronald McGregor, apparently from drunken frenzy or bravado. The wretched culprit ascended the scaffold with an unfaltering step and on taking his place on the drop faced the multitude with great firmness. Having signified to the chaplain that he was going to address the people, Hare spoke as nearly as follows: "Fellow men I am going to die for a crime of which I am innocent, but I pray God to forgive all those who have persecuted me. All of you beware of dram-drinking and beware of Matthew Miller and take warning by me this day to keep out of bad company." The rope was then adjusted by the executioner and the cap having been drawn over his head, a white handkerchief was put into his hand. After a lapse of a few seconds the handkerchief dropped out of his hand, and the executioner instantaneously withdrawing the bolt, the drop fell with a crash, and the wretched man, after a severe and protracted struggle, ceased to be of this world.' (*The Glasgow Citizen*)

OCTOBER 28TH

1588: 'On this day it is stated and ordained by the baillies and the council, in consideration of the apparent danger of the pest (plague) now in Paisley that no person inhabiting the town, because of the market of Paisley and Kilmacolm approaching, shall pass forth of the town thereto, under the punishment of five pounds, to be taken off every person repairing thereto and banished forth of the said town for a year and a day. It was subsequently resolved that the bridge port be kept by two honest men of the Briggait.' (*Sketch of the History of Glasgow*)

———————•◆•———————

1966: On this day the Red Road flats were officially opened by Willie Ross, the Secretary of State for Scotland. The high-rise flats were built to house those displaced by slum clearances. They could accommodate 4,700 people. The site was situated across the boundaries of both Balornock and Barmulloch and contained nine blocks of flats, with some of them the highest residential towers in Europe at the time. The flats were designed to sway as much as 4 inches in strong winds. The decision to demolish them was taken in 2005.

OCTOBER 29TH

1773: 'Professors Reid and Anderson, and the two Messrs Foulis, dined and drank tea with us at our inn, after which the professors went away and I left my fellow-traveller with Messrs Foulis. Though good and ingenious men, they had that unsettled speculative mode of conversation which is offensive to a man regularly taught at an English school and university. I found that, instead of listening to the dictates of the Sage, they had teased him with questions and doubtful disputations. He came in a flutter to me, and desired I might come back again, for he could not bear these men. "O ho! Sir, (said I,) you are flying to me for refuge!" He never, in any situation, was at a loss for a ready repartee. He answered, with a quick vivacity: "It is of two evils choosing the least."' (*Journal of a Tour to the Hebrides with Samuel Johnson* by James Boswell, 1785)

━━━━━◆━━━━━

1929: 'No solution has yet been found of the mysterious rappings which have been heard in a tenement house in Cowcaddens, although they have been the subject of investigations by the police and others, including spirtualists. The "haunted house" attracted a good deal of interest over the weekend, and on Saturday evening a large crowd gathered outside the entrance, which was guarded by two policemen.' (*Glasgow Herald*)

OCTOBER 30TH

1816: 'Abstract of Regulations for Steam-Boats and other Vessels, Plying on the Clyde, enacted by the Magistrates and Council, on this day: That for the accommodation of passengers, a particular part or parts of the Quay of the Broomielaw of Glasgow, shall, in future, be allowed for the use of the Steam-Boats. That when the said boats sailing in opposite directions, meet, each shall keep to the larboard side. That none of the said Steam-Boats shall ply in the twilight, or in the dark, without having lights ahead, and without having one of crew stationed at the bow of the boat, as a look-out, to give notice in due time, of any obstruction or danger. That in all cases where either passengers or goods are to be taken in by, or landed from, such Steam-Vessels, by means of small boats of any description, the paddles of the Steam-Boats shall be stopped in proper time, and remain so till the boat gets out of the surge of the Steam-Vessel. That no ballast, ashes, or rubbish of any kind, shall be put overboard of any vessel into the River, between the Broomielaw and Dumbarton Castle.' (*Annals of Glasgow*)

OCTOBER 31ST

1969: On this day the body of twenty-nine-year-old Helen Puttock was found in Scotstoun. She had been at the Barrowland Ballroom the previous evening and had left with her sister Jean and a man she had met. Jean got out of the taxi near her home and Helen and the man went off together. It was the last time Jean saw her sister alive. She was able to give police a description of the man. He was of medium build, between twenty-five and thirty years of age, and 5 feet 10 inches in height. He was thought to be called John and had talked of being from a strict religious background, making references to the Bible. A local newspaper initially referred to him as 'The Bible Man' although he became known as 'Bible John'. Helen Puttock was believed to be the third victim of the same killer. Jemima McDonald had been killed in August 1969 and Patricia Docker in February 1968. All three women had attended dances at the Barrowland. Although there were several suspects, no one was ever brought to trial for any of the murders.

NOVEMBER 1ST

1779: 'It may be mentioned that on this day a fox was found at Tollcross, at nine o'clock, and was followed till half-past four in the afternoon. He crossed the Clyde three times, ran over a great tract of country, and at last got to ground in Hamilton Wood. The chase could not be less than fifty miles. This great run recalls an unfortunate occurrence which took place some time afterwards, when Mr Struthers, in following hard after the pack, came to the Clyde near Bothwell, which was at that moment swelled with rain, fearlessly leaped into the stream, and urged the huntsman to follow, which he did with hesitation. The consequence was that Mr Struthers and the huntsman's horse with difficulty reached the opposite bank, but the huntsman and Mr Struthers' horse were drowned.' (*Glasgow and its Clubs*)

1889: Twenty-nine workers were killed when part of an extension being built at James Templeton's carpet factory on Glasgow Green collapsed in high winds. The dead, all women, were working in nearby weaving sheds. The extension's façade was based on the Doge's Palace in Venice. The factory later became a business centre.

NOVEMBER 2ND

1772: 'The inferior Civil Court, commonly called the Conscience Court, from the matters at issue being often left to the oath of parties, was instituted on this day for the determination of small civil claims, which are now fixed to be not under five, nor exceeding forty shillings. An Assessor attends, to give legal advice, if it be found necessary, and to minute the verbal debate. Procurators are not admitted; nor is this a Court of Record.' (*Annals of Glasgow*)

1775: 'The inhabitants of Finnieston request of those gentlemen who send their horses to the fields for exercise, that they will desire their servants not to ride through the village in such crowds, and at such speed, as has been done for some time past. The bleach-fields, from the quantities of dust dispersed by the horses, are almost ruined, and the lives of the inhabitants, from the number and fury of the riders, have been often in danger. They request also that no person after this will carry away sand from the High Street, as they propose at their own expense to form that street in such a manner as to be convenient for those who have occasion necessarily to pass along it.' (*Glasgow Journal*)

NOVEMBER 3RD

2002: On this day Lonnie Donegan died, aged seventy-one. Donegan was from Bridgeton but his family had moved to London in the early thirties. He was the main figure in British Skiffle, skiffle being a style of music played on simple instruments such as guitars, washboards and tea-chest basses. It was thus able to be adopted by young and inexperienced musicians. Those influenced by skiffle included the members of The Beatles, the Rolling Stones and Led Zeppelin. John Lennon and Paul McCartney's first group The Quarrymen played several Donegan tunes. Lonnie Donegan racked up hits with Rock Island Line, Puttin' on the Style, Cumberland Gap, Battle of New Orleans and Does Your Chewing Gum Lose Its Flavour (On the Bedpost Overnight). He had been a member of the Chris Barber Jazz Band before setting out on his own.

NOVEMBER 4TH

1935: 'Reference to the recently published novel *No Mean City* was made in Glasgow today by the Reverend Dr John A Hutton, when he spoke at a social meeting of Belhaven Church. "Glasgow has been having a pretty bad time at the hands of writers," he declared, "and this last book is an extremely severe reflection on the position of this great city." Dr Hutton explained that he had read the book with great care and said that although one's general reaction was perhaps hostile to it, on a more balanced judgment one had to recognise a real background of truth and also a very remarkable absence of any charges. There was not a single word to suggest that the Christian Church had neglected these sad places that were such a menace to social life. During the past 60 years no city had received more attention from the Church than Glasgow. There was hardly a street that was not within call of some Christian organisation; there were missions everywhere. It may have been however that the Church during these 60 years, parallel with its evangelical appeal, ought to have been equally insistent that conditions should have been provided for people in which human life was more possible.' (*Glasgow Herald*)

NOVEMBER 5TH

Late eighteenth century: 'At this time too it was customary for the schoolboys, on the anniversary of the Gunpowder Plot, to "burn Wilkes", instead of as formerly, Guy Fawkes. (John Wilkes – an English radical reformer who had supported the American revolution.) An effigy of Wilkes was kept suspended all day near a large fire, while certain of the band of boys which surrounded it collected money from passengers and at the houses. Towards dusk the stock was divided among the juvenile fraternity, after which the effigy was paraded, and having placidly suffered all manner of indignities, it underwent the ordeal of being consumed in the fire, amid the shouts and huzzahs of the spectators.' (*Glasgow and its Clubs*)

1833: On this day the first elections took place for the city's council, as a result of the 1833 Burgh Reform Act. The era of the 'Old Lady of Self-Selection', as Glasgow's corporation had been described, was over. There were five wards across the city, electing six councillors each. With a representative from the Trades and Merchants houses, the council was composed of thirty-two councillors. The electorate were those whose yearly rent was of the amount of £10 or higher. There were just over 7,000 electors in Glasgow. (*Glasgow* by David Daiches, 1977)

NOVEMBER 6TH

1901: 'As the closing day draws nearer the interest in the Exhibition is increasing. Although the weather yesterday was again disagreeable owing to fog, there was a fairly good attendance of visitors, and in the evening the display of fireworks given by Messrs James Pain and Sons accounted to a great extent for the large crowd within the enclosure. The display, however, was bereft of much of its effectiveness by the thick state of the atmosphere. If the weather is of a favourable character there should be a very large attendance at the Exhibition today. The crowd will consist to a considerable extent of excursionists, parties being promised by the various railway companies from Stranraer, Girvan, Maybole, Ayr, Irvine, Troon, Largs, Fairlie, Saltcoats, Ardrossan, Mauchline and other Ayrshire towns, also from Morecambe, Carlisle, Moffat, Aberdeen, Forfar, Perth, Dundee, Lanark, Crieff, Denny, Larbert, West Calder and Kilbirnie. The attendance yesterday was 116,947, and the drawings amounted to £1,562 4s. The total attendance is now 10,937,879 and the drawings amount to £161,034 19s.' (*Glasgow Herald*)

The Glasgow International Exhibition ran for just over six months. The total attendance figure was 11 million.

NOVEMBER 7TH

1707: The Acts of Union had been passed and Scotland's Parliament was to merge with England's in London. The move was not universally accepted as being a positive by all Scots. A sermon by the Reverend James Clark of the Tron Church inflamed the situation:

> In the conclusion of his discourse he reminded his audience of the humiliating condition they were about to be reduced to, and of their former efforts in the good cause; he told them that addresses would not do, and prayers would not do—there must be other methods. It was true that prayer was a duty, but they must not rest there and finished with the climax of "Wherefore, up and be valiant for the city of our God". This was regarded as a direct encouragement and injunction to insurrection. The people, inflamed enough before, broke out into open violence; the mob drum was beat through the back streets, and an immense and excited populace gathered together. The provost endeavoured to calm the emeute but, instead of his efforts being successful, the rabble broke his windows, stormed his house, and took away all the arms which it contained, amounting to about twenty-five muskets. The provost, finally alarmed for his personal safety, fled from the town and took refuge in Edinburgh.

(Sketch of the History of Glasgow)

NOVEMBER 8TH

1973: A by-election for the Westminister parliament was held on this day in the constituency of Glasgow Govan. The seat had been held predominantly by Labour since 1918 but was taken in a shock result by the Scottish National Party (SNP) who won only their fourth Westminster seat. The elected MP was Margo MacDonald, a former teacher who received just over 41 per cent of the vote. The SNP had seen a rise in popularity following the discovery of North Sea oil. A year later, in the General Election, the Govan seat was won back by Labour, although the SNP won a total of seven seats and doubled their share of the vote. Margo MacDonald won election to the Scottish Parliament in 1999 and again in 2003, 2007 and 2011 as an independent. Her freedom from party political strictures enabled her to campaign on specific issues, such as proposing the legalisation of assisted suicide for the terminally ill.

NOVEMBER 9TH

1815: 'Applications for aid from the Session funds are made to the Elder of the proportion or district of the parish in which the applicant lives. If the Elder, after he has investigated the case, is satisfied that the petitioner is poor, and has established a domicile of three years, he gives a temporary supply, and desires him or her to attend the next monthly meeting, when the case is laid before the whole members of Session. If no sufficient objection is made, the applicant is enrolled, and usually receives from 2 to 5 shillings per month. The General Session appointed a Committee to investigate the books of the several Sessions, in order to ascertain the number of paupers on the funds. The Committee on this day reported these figures:

> Middle, or St Andrew's parish – 212;
> South-West, or Tron – 209;
> North, or Inner High – 204;
> South, or College – 191;
> East, or Outer High – 144;
> West, or St George's – 129;
> St Enoch's – 111;
> North-West – 70.

Total Paupers on the funds of the Sessions – 1,270.' (*Annals of Glasgow*)

November 10th

1745: George Brown was some years in the Town Council, and was several times Dean of Guild. This diary extract gives an insight into how a Sunday could be spent in Glasgow:

> Rose about seven—called on the Lord by prayer—read the 9th chapter of Job—then attended on family worship, and again prayed to the Lord for his gracious presence to be with me through the whole of the day, and went to church at ten of the clock— joined in the public prayers and praises in the assembly of his saints—heard the 17th chapter of Revelations lectured upon, and sermon from the 81st Psalm, 13th and 14th verses. In the interval of public service I thought on what I had heard, and wrote down some of the heads of it; went again to the house of the Lord, and heard sermon from the same text—came home and retired and thought on the sermon. About five at night joined in family worship, and afterwards supped—then retired again and wrote down some things I had been hearing—then read the 9th chapter of Romans, and prayed. After this I joined in social worship a second time, and went to keep the public guard of the City at ten o'clock at night.

(*Diary of George Brown*)

NOVEMBER 11TH

1779: On this day the following notice from the Magistrates was published in the *Glasgow Mercury*:

All cattle for slaughter brought into this city must be driven agreeable to the following direction: Cattle coming by both bridges to be driven the shortest road to the Slaughter House. No cattle of any kind, upon any account whatever, to be driven through any part of the Town's royalty on Sunday and if any cattle are hunted through the streets at any time, the owners as well as the drivers will be punished with the utmost rigour of law. No cattle of any kind, upon any account whatever, to be hung in any of the entries to the markets. No dogs are to be allowed in this market. Any butcher who attempts to bring bad or unwholesome meat, or to blow, or put webs on his meat, will have it confiscated, and be turned out of the market. The Candleriggs market is to be kept entirely for a potato market, after which day all potatoes are required to be carried there, as none will be allowed in the Fish market in King Street.

NOVEMBER 12TH

1901: This letter appeared in the *Glasgow Herald* on this day:

Sir, I read that in the inquiry on the death of a van driver, due to an electric car collision, the jury declared that the car was being driven at an undue rate of speed, but held that no blame was attachable to the driver, who was compelled to run up to time. I believe this is calculated to have a most pernicious effect on the minds of electric-car drivers, for it will certainly give many of them the idea that the orders of their superiors are sufficient to exonerate them in driving at any speed, however reckless. The Corporation time-tables can scarcely be pled in defence of a crime. Assume that a driver by grossly reckless driving kills someone, can they avoid all criminal responsibility by showing that he had to drive with gross recklessness in order to keep to time? Surely not! It is to be hoped that the drivers will be made to understand that no orders of any tramway official can justify them in reckless driving. Every man must answer for his own crimes, and not even a Corporation official can grant a dispensation to commit such acts. I am, etc. Lex.

NOVEMBER 13TH

1866: The *Glasgow Herald* reported a recent meeting of the Police Board:

Mr William Wilson said that as a member of the City Parochial Board he had sat last week on some relief cases. A wretched woman was brought before him, who had been stabbed by her husband. The man committed the crime while under the influence of a liquor called 'finish' bought on Sunday in some druggist's shop. He had the curiosity to go and examine this business and he found that in three of four wards of the city, this 'finish' could be bought in large quantities by the poor wretches whose thirst for strong drink was such that they could not wait till Monday morning. He had heard that the board of Inland Revenue had had their attention called to this matter, and intended to put down the sale of the liquor as soon as possible. The samples of the drink which he got were as like whisky as anything ever he saw and the taste was awful. (A laugh.) Mr Whyte said the liquor was spirit of wine. It was used by polishers for polishing furniture and was saturated with naptha. The Dean of Guild said it was what the excise termed 'methylated spirit'.

NOVEMBER 14TH

1583: 'The Session enacts that there should be no superfluous gatherings at banquets or marriages; that the price of the dinner or supper should be 18*d* and person married should find caution to that effect.' (*Kirk-Session records*)

———◆———

1715: 'The first newspaper published in Glasgow appeared on this day. It was entitled the *Glasgow Courant* "containing the occurrences both at home and abroad." It was to be sold at the Printing House in the College, and at the Post-Office. The price was three-halfpence. Regular customers to be charged only one Penny. It is not known how long this paper was continued. A file of it is preserved in the university library, extending to the 1st of May, 1716, being in all, sixty-seven numbers. It was printed three times a-week, with twelve small pages, and was made up of extracts from the London journals, original letters, poetry, and very little local news.' (*Sketch of the History of Glasgow*)

NOVEMBER 15TH

1733: 'The Town's Hospital was opened on this day. Prior to this, the accommodation for the poor was very indifferent, and by no means adequate to the extent of the Town. The Faculty of Physicians and Surgeons made offer of their services to attend the sick in the Hospital, and find medicines, for free. By February 1735, there were one hundred and fifty-two persons in the House, of which there were sixty-one old and ninety-one young persons. The following scheme of diet is from 1734. The Diet for all Persons in the Hospital, above Fifteen Years of age: Breakfast – every day throughout the week, Oat-Meal Pottage and Ale. Dinner – *Sunday,* Bread and Ale; *Monday,* Broth made without Flesh, with the addition of Bread and Butter, or Cheese; *Tuesday,* Broth made without Flesh, with the addition of Bread and Herrings; *Wednesday,* Broth made with Flesh, with the addition of Bread; *Thursday,* Broth made without Flesh, with the addition of Bread and Cheese; *Friday,* Broth made with Flesh, with the addition of Bread; *Saturday,* Broth made without Flesh, with the addition of Bread and Herrings or Butter. Supper – *Sunday,* Broth with Flesh and Bread; *Monday,* and every other day, Oat-Meal Pottage and Ale.' (*Annals of Glasgow*)

NOVEMBER 16TH

1891: This advertisement appeared in the *Glasgow Herald* on this day:

Ready – Scotland's Unique Amusement Event. Preparations are now complete for the positive inaugural of the first appearance of the original and only: Buffalo Bill's Wild West. Tonight at eight o'clock. Representation of Indian and Frontier Life in America. More complete in every detail than when presented to London – Queen's Jubilee year, New York – Washington's Centennial Year, Paris – Universal Exposition Year, Rome – Pope Leo XIII's Jubilee year and other chief continental cities.

250 Indians, cowboys, scouts, hunters, marksmen and women, frontier girls, Mexicans etc. 175 animals – horses, Indian ponies, wild bucking broncos, mustangs, a herd of buffaloes, wild deer etc. A three years tour, illustrated in 20 animated tableaux of living characters and historical events in conjunction with The Grandest And Largest Scenic Effects Ever Produced. The location is in Duke Street, Dennistoun in the entirely reconstructured East End Exhibition Buildings.

Hours of performance 8 pm daily. Doors open 6.45 pm. Morning performances Wednesdays and Saturdays. The whole of the premises occupied by last year's exhibition are devoted to the uses of this mighty spectacle, and have been transformed into the Grandest Amphitheatre in Europe. Seating capacity 7,000.

NOVEMBER 17TH

1866: The *Glasgow Herald* published the following letter on this day:

Knowing the sympathy which the press and public have for the Great Unwashed, I make bold to bespeak in behalf of a section of that dirty community of which I form a unit. I work with many more on the canal bank, close to Townsend's stalk. All day long we breathe smoke, from six to six we smell smells, but when six comes we rush home and have a wash. A wash! Ah you clean people who live 'doon the toon' don't know what a wash is. It is new life – it is bliss unimagined – it is a luxury enjoyed only by the grimy. But to reach home and to enjoy our wash is a work of much peril. We have to descend from the canal bank by the long flight of stairs at the head of the Port Dundas Road. The stairs are very long, very dilapidated, and there are no lamps on them. At 6pm it is now pitchy dark and with fear and trembling we have to grope our way. Common stairs have all now to be lighted, why is such a public stair an exception? We have wives and bairns to whom, though dirty, we are dear and the prospect of a broken neck is not pleasant. I am, etc, Dirty Dick

NOVEMBER 18TH

1707: 'The kingdoms of Scotland and England were united under Queen Anne in the year 1707 upon which occasion, the citizens of Glasgow showed great discontent and propensity to riot. On this day the Magistrates and Council made an Act for keeping the peace, whereby more than three persons were prohibited from being together on the streets after sunset. At this period, the City was bounded by the original ports: on the east, by the Gallowgate Port, which stood near to St Mungo's Lane; on the west, by the West Port, near to where the Black Bull Inn is erected; on the south, by the Water Port, near the Old Bridge; on the north, by the Stable Green Port, at the Bishop's Palace; and on the north-west, by the Rottenrow Port: the adjoining ground without the ports, and that upon which Bell Street, Candlerigg Street, King Street, Prince's Street, etc are now formed, being then corn fields; and even where a number of the streets were formed within the ports, there were but few houses built, and these chiefly covered with thatch. The population, at this period, was reckoned to be about 14,000 souls.' (*Annals of Glasgow*)

NOVEMBER 19TH

1918: 'Food Control. The Food Controller has decided to allow turkeys, geese, ducks, fowls, chickens and game to be sold free of the coupon either by retailers or in the form of meat, meals in establishment during the Christmas season, from Monday December 16th to Saturday January 4th. In view of this concession the announcement previously made as to the increased value of the coupon for the purchase of poultry during the period from Sunday December 1st until Saturday January 11th is cancelled. The public are reminded that every person selling poultry or game by retail are required to keep posted in a conspicuous position a notice showing in plain words and figures the maximum prices for such poultry and game for the time being fixed by the Food Controller.' (*Glasgow Herald*)

'Scotch Currant Bun. The Food Commissioner for the West of Scotland announces that the manufacture and sale of Scotch currant bun is to be permitted during the period from December 1st 1918 until February 1st 1919. This concession has been granted on the understanding that genuine Scotch currant buns are made; the manufacture or sale of any other similar article will be subject to the provisions of the Cake and Pastry Order 1917.' (*Glasgow Herald*)

NOVEMBER 20TH

1925: This report in *The Scotsman* recounted just one of Johnny Ramensky's arrests for 'cat burglary'. In 1943, 'Gentle Johnny' joined the army and took part in commando missions that utilised his safe-blowing skills. He died while imprisoned, in 1972. Despite escaping from the notorious Peterhead Prison five times, he had spent over forty of his sixty-seven years in jail:

Glasgow Housebreaker. Young Man Sent to Prison. Described as a dangerous criminal, John Ramensky, a sturdily built young man of 20, remitted from Glasgow, was sentenced to 18 months imprisonment by the Lord Justice Clerk at the High Court of Justiciary at Edinburgh yesterday on eleven charges of theft by housebreaking, three of housebreaking with intent to steal, two of attempted housebreaking, and one charge of assault. The offences were committed in the Hillhead, Hyndland, Partick, West End and Crosshill districts of Glasgow, between 30th September and 24th October last. The property stolen included War Savings Certificates, jewellery, watches, and money. The total value being £1,500 of which £172 worth had been recovered. On one night Ramensky entered no fewer than six houses and seven nights later, when he was caught, he broke into three houses.

November 21st

1638: The General Assembly that met on this day was the first to sit in twenty years, during a turbulent time for Scottish religion and society:

The assembly accordingly met, in the Cathedral church, and formed one of the most numerous and imposing gatherings that had ever taken place in the kingdom. The majority of the aristocracy of the country were present, in the capacity of either elders or assessors from burghs; three commissioners were present from each of the sixty-three presbyteries, and a like number from each of the four universities. The great mass, however, though not members of the assembly, consisted of the trains or following which accompanied the barons; and to effect this 'demonstration', a little trickery or ruse is said to have been used. At least, contemporary writers affirm that the friends of the Presbyterian form of worship, the better to ensure a full attendance, not only of the members, but of the nobility and gentry, who were friendly to their cause, gave it out that, as the Highlands were infested with robbers, it would be necessary for all those who were zealous in the cause, not only to escort the commissioners to Glasgow, but to guard them there during their sittings.

(Sketch of the History of Glasgow)

NOVEMBER 22ND

1588: The Magistrates investigated a 'trublance' in regard to which James Scott, painter, burgess of Glasgow, complained against Adam Elphinstoun, glassin-wright (glazier), and others and the result is as follows:

> The said Adam is found in the wrong for the striking of the said James Scott on the breast with a pistol, through the force whereof he hit the said James to the ground, and effusion of his blood in great quantity. And suchlike the said Adam is found in the wrong, for coming to the said James Scott's house on Lammas last or thereby, and pursuing of George Scott, son to the said James, with a drawn sword, and saying, if he had him, he should lay his bowels about his feet and bidding of the said George Scott come forth or else he should have a cold armful of him. An act is passed ordaining the assailants to find security.

(*Sketch of the History of Glasgow*)

November 23rd

1785: The Italian gentleman Vincent Lunardi came to Scotland in 1785. He made a long-distance flight from Glasgow on this day. A crowd of 100,000 watched as the intrepid aviator took to the skies from St Andrews Square. A contemporary account described his flight:

The celebrated aeronaut Mr Lunardi ascended from Glasgow. He took possession of the car about two o'clock in the afternoon, the wind south-west, and advanced north-east for about 25 miles. Having then changed his direction, he proceeded to the south-east, and attempted to anchor but the wind blowing with great violence, the cable gave way, by which accident the anchor, weighing about 10lb, was left on the ground, and the balloon re-ascended with wonderful velocity, to a considerable altitude. After floating for sometime in the air, Mr Lunardi at last descended in Selkirkshire, having performed an expedition of 125 miles in the space of two hours. It is worthy of observation that during Mr Lunardi's expedition a very remarkable circumstance occurred. When at a considerable distance from the Earth, he felt himself much need to sleep, and at last he yielded to this strong propensity, and slept for about 20 minutes on the bottom of the car.

(*The Gentleman's Magazine and Historical Chronicle*, volume 55, 1785)

NOVEMBER 24TH

1869: 'Dense Fog in Glasgow. Throughout the whole of yesterday, the city was enveloped in a thick fog. Gas was brought into general use during the greater part of the day and traffic along the streets was only conducted in safety by the exercise of great caution. Foot passengers were exposed to considerable danger at crossings, but so far as we have heard, no serious street accident occurred, the darkness laying an arrest on anything like swift locomotion. Between 4 and 5 o'clock in the evening when the fog was densest passage along the streets was alike difficult and dangerous. Omnibuses and vehicles moved slowly and cautiously – the driver sometimes mistaking their route, while cabmen were observed in some of the busiest thoroughfares groping their way at the horses' head and with the carriage lamps in their hands. Traffic in the river was entirely suspended and passengers along the harbour and docks were exposed to great risk of falling into the water. Several accidents occurred and one of them terminated fatally. A seaman named James McCormick, employed on board of the schooner *Alfred*, when returning to his vessel, slipped into the water. The only intimation of the occurrence received by his shipmaster was a splash in the water.' (*Glasgow Herald*)

NOVEMBER 25TH

1916: 'The Special Committee of Glasgow Corporation on the Shops Acts recently received a deputation representative of grocers, fleshers, bakers, fishmongers, drapers, hosiers, hatiers, and watchmakers carrying on business in the city who advocated the earlier closing of their premises. The deputation asked the local authority to make a new Closing Order fixing the hours of closing in these trades at 9pm on Saturdays and 7pm on other days of the week when there is no half-holiday, instead of the present hours, which are, under the Shops Act, 10pm and 8pm respectively. The Closing Order issued lately under the Defence of the Realm Act, which fixed the hours at 9pm and 8pm respectively, is only current for six months and expires on April 30, 1917. The Shops Acts Committee subsequently considered the representations of the deputation, and being satisfied that a prima facie case had been made out in favour of a new Closing Order for all the trades mentioned, instructed the Town Clerk to take the necessary procedure under the Shops Act of 1912 to ascertain the opinion of all the shopkeepers interested as to whether they approve or otherwise of the proposed new Order. This will involve a plebiscite.' (*Glasgow Herald*)

NOVEMBER 26TH

1316: On this day Robert Wishart died. As Bishop of Glasgow he played an important part in Scotland's War of Independence against England. Wishart – or Wiseheart – crowned Robert the Bruce as King following Bruce's killing of rival John Comyn in Dumfries' church – a sacrilegious act that should have seen Wishart excommunicate him. Wishart's support of Bruce led to him being captured by Edward I. He was released following the Scots' victory at Bannockburn after eight years' incarceration, during which he had gone blind.

———◆———

2004: On this day a fire broke out in one of the city centre's landmark buildings. The Greek-style temple construction at the corner of Pitt Street and Bath Street had opened in 1856 as the Elgin Place Congregational Church. Over a century later it had become a nightclub, opening in 1982 as Cardinal Follies. The former place of worship escaped the late twentieth-century fashion of stone-cleaning and its blackened exterior finish stood as a testimony to the years of pollution the city had endured. It was designed by John Burnet, whose other buildings included the Glasgow Stock Exchange in Buchanan Street and the Clydesdale Bank building in St Vincent Place. Unlike those buildings the Congregational Church did not survive, being demolished on Christmas Eve, 2004.

November 27th

1647: These pronouncements from the burgh records were reproduced in *Memorabilia of the City of Glasgow* for this day:

The said Baillies and Council granted to the widow of George Anderson, printer and his bairns, as long as they continue in printing in the town, the pension that is required to be paid by the town to the said George Anderson, for their better encouragement there until.

In answer to the Doctors of the Grammar School, their supplication for their straits at the time of the pestilence being in the town, it is agreed that the treasurer shall give equally between them fifty five pounds for which their receipt and their presence shall be his warrant.

Concerning the two hundred and forty marks due by John Auldcorn for the bridge in the year 1645, there is remitted to him nine score marks thereof, for the recompense of his loss by public enemies, and warrants the treasurer to take forty pounds, in satisfaction of the said sum of two hundred and forty marks Scots money.

NOVEMBER 28TH

1864: 'On Saturday two boys, named Daniel Martin and Michael Cooney, each about twelve years of age, were brought before Sheriff Strathearn, charged with having stolen upwards of 60 brass and iron locks from the dwelling house in Maxwell Street occupied by Jane Shearer or Templeton, or otherwise with having resetted the locks. Martin pleaded guilty to the theft, and Cooney to the reset, and they were sentenced to receive in prison each twelve stripes with a birch rod and if the prison surgeon certified that they were unable to bear the whipping, they were each to be imprisoned, for fourteen days.' (*Glasgow Herald*)

———— ◆ ————

1864: 'On Saturday evening a melancholy accident occurred at the Bridge Street Railway Station, which resulted in the death of a woman. It appears that after a train for Greenock had been shunted from a centre line to the one alongside the platform, the train was being backed into its proper place when a crowd of passengers rushed towards the carriages. The unfortunate woman was amongst the first to make the rush forward and in her endeavour she missed her footing and fell between the moving train and the platform. The wheels of a carriage passed over the poor woman's body, causing instantaneous death.' (*Glasgow Herald*)

November 29th

1897: 'At a meeting of the Glasgow Egg Merchants' Association held in Whyte's Hotel, Candleriggs, the following resolutions and recommendations were agreed to: That we, the members of the Glasgow Wholesale Egg Trade, disclaim all responsibility for the return of empty egg boxes, but will use our best endeavours to return as large a percentage of same as possible. We beg to call the attention of Irish egg shippers to the serious injury done to the trade every summer and autumn by the practice of storing eggs for the advancing market, and we hereby resolve that in future we refuse to pay for stale and rotten eggs. We also call the attention of shippers to the practice now so widely prevalent of packing eggs in dirty and foul-smelling straw. The time has come when, if Irish egg shippers wish to preserve the trade, they must send their eggs out fresh, and packed in good clean straw. That we call the attention of Irish railway companies and the shipping companies to the practice of carrying eggs in open waggons, and carting them to the ships' side in wet weather uncovered, also of careless and rough handling in loading and discharging, and express the hope that they will remedy this in future.' (*Glasgow Herald*)

NOVEMBER 30TH

1872: The world's first official international football match was played on this day. The Scottish team was made up completely of players from Queen's Park Football Club:

> This match came off on the West of Scotland Cricket Club, in the presence of the largest assemblage seen at any football match in Scotland, there being close on 4,000 spectators, including a good number of ladies. Ottaway, the English captain, standing conspicuous, and astonishing the spectators by some very pretty 'dribbling'. The English uniform consisted of white jerseys, with the arms of England as a badge, dark blue caps, and white trousers and knickerbockers. Dark blue jerseys, with the Scottish lion for a badge, white knickerbockers, blue and white striped stockings, and red cowls completed the Scottish uniform. The match, after an hour and half's play, ended in a draw. A goal is scored when it is kicked *under* the tape, the ball not being allowed to be carried, thrown, or knocked in. Hacking, tripping, holding, or charging an adversary from behind are among things forbidden. Such are some of the differences of the two styles of play, and it will readily be admitted that the Association game is one which will commend itself to players who dread the harder work of the Rugby mode.

(*The Scotsman*)

DECEMBER 1ST

1800: 'At a meeting of the Lord Provost, Magistrates, Ministers and other Gentlemen of this city, called together by the Lord Provost to take into consideration the state of the poor, the meeting was unanimously of opinion that some extraordinary measures were necessary to be taken for the assistance of the indigent of the city. For this purpose they resolved that it would be expedient to take a General Survey of the State of the Poor, to mark in a schedule prepared for the purpose, the name of the head of every poor family, his or her occupation, the number of the family and their ability for labour, with the allowance which they may receive from any charitable institution, and that the ministers and elders of the different parishes be required to use, without delay, such measures as they may think proper for carrying this into effect. That a general subscription through the city should be immediately begun, for the relief of the poor of every description. That from the produce of this subscription a number of soup kitchens shall be established in different quarters of the city from which soup shall be distributed gratis to the poor.' (*Glasgow Advertiser*)

DECEMBER 2ND

1864: A ferry capsized while crossing the Clyde and the *Glasgow Herald* published its reaction to the disaster on this day:

We have had another terrible warning in the awful catastrophe which occurred at the Broomielaw on Wednesday evening, and we earnestly trust that it may be turned to a profitable account. The story may be told in a very few words. There was an over-crowded boat – a flooded river – a dark night – an unskilful rower – an upsetting of the craft – and the rest is known. At least nineteen men, the majority in the prime of life, have lost their lives by the catastrophe. It is an awful list of mortality – it is a sad and agonising commentary on the manner in which these ferries have been conducted. Looking to the sad result, we may now express surprise that calamities of this kind have not been of more frequent occurrence, when we regard the enormous and ever-increasing passenger traffic at the river ferries which has been carried from side to side in such clumsy boats. The calamity was the natural and almost inevitable consequence of negligence on the part of the authorities, or carelessness or indifference on the part of the boatman and of ignorance on the part of the unfortunate passengers.

(*Glasgow Herald*)

DECEMBER 3RD

1832: 'There is at present a good number of base sixpences in circulation which the public should be on their guard against receiving. They may be easily known by their shining appearance, and a sort of greasy feel they have. On Saturday evening John Christie and John Leckie, criminal officers, apprehended a woman of the name of Elizabeth Dickson, in a house in Gallowgate, in the very act of casting these base sixpences. She had 105 beside her, some of them warm.' (*Glasgow Herald*)

———————•◆•———————

1863: 'Mr Salmon, in his Report on Graveyards to the magistrates and council of Glasgow, dated this day writes: St Andrew's Episcopal Burying Ground entirely surrounds the church with which it is connected. The space applicable to interments extends to about 694 square yards. The outward appearance of this graveyard has all the disagreeable characteristics inseparable from such places, while its locality in the immediate vicinity of a dense and sunken population renders these characteristics all the more objectionable. The effect is repugnant to every just conception of taste and propriety. When we observe what a trifling extent the space is now used, it is most unfortunate that the above church, long ere now, has not been redeemed from its present obnoxious influence.' (*Old Glasgow and its Environs*)

DECEMBER 4TH

1922: 'The annual Scottish concert of the Glasgow Orpheus Choir began its course on this evening in the St Andrews Hall and will be continued on four subsequent evenings, for the Choir have again succeeded in completely selling out the available accommodation five times over. It was remarkable to have done this once or twice but to be able to do it habitually is surely without precedent. By adopting a broad and quite legitimate interpretation of the word Scottish, Mr Roberton and his Choir are able to present year by year a considerable variety of items and last evening the programme, as on former occasions, included not only Scotch folk-songs but compositions by Scotch composers and arrangements and original work on Scottish subjects by "foreigners". The choir sang throughout the evening at a high level of finish. The soloists were very successful in their various items and were, like the choir, warmly received by the large audience.' (*Glasgow Herald*)

DECEMBER 5TH

1783: 'William Scott was executed here for housebreaking. He acknowledged the justice of his sentence, but inveighed heavily against one Thomas Wotherspoon for advising and assisting him in his various depredations. About half an hour previous to the execution, a decent-dressed woman was detected stealing handkerchiefs from a merchant's window immediately opposite the gallows, but being pursued she dropped them and got clear off amongst the crowd.' (*Glasgow Advertiser*)

'A few days ago the wife of a journeyman weaver in Paisley was delivered of three boys, who are all likely to do well. What is remarkable the woman has been eight years married, and never had a child before.' (*Glasgow Advertiser*)

———•◆•———

1800: 'For a short time only. The Panorama of the Burning of His Majesty's Ship *The Boyne* is now open for public inspection in that building formerly occupied by the Panorama of London, in Ingram Street. This grand but awful subject, painted in oil, upon two thousand four hundred and sixty four square feet of canvas by R Dodd, Marine Painter, to His Majesty. Esteemed one of the finest ships in the British Navy she took fire by accident in May 1795, whilst lying at Spithead. Good fires are constantly kept in stoves to warm the place. Admittance one shilling.' (*Glasgow Advertiser*)

DECEMBER 6TH

1892: The *Glasgow Herald* reported on the city's Police Commission meeting held the previous day:

The Inspector of Fires reported that the brigade had received and answered 58 calls during the month. Of these 50 were fires, 3 were false alarms given with good intent and 5 were malicious alarms. With the exception of the fire in the Leather Currying Works, Boden Street, all the city fires were of a comparatively trifling nature so far as property was concerned, but he regretted to report that an old lady was burned fatally at a small fire in Hillhead through her clothing becoming ignited. Sixteen fires were due to defective building construction, 7 to dropped lights, 6 to goods in contact with lights, 3 to sparks from fires, 2 to heat from stoves, 1 to candle, 1 to vapour in contact with light, 1 to a plumber at work, 1 to hot ashes, 1 to escape of gas, 1 to friction of machinery, 1 to heat from kiln, 1 to spark down chimney, 1 to fat boiling over, 1 to children playing with fire, while in 6 instances the causes were not apparent, and they are recorded as 'unknown.' The report was approved.

DECEMBER 7TH

1905: 'Beauty and brightness are combined in an eminent degree in *Aladdin* at the Theatre Royal. If first impressions are to be trusted, the management need have no anxiety as to their latest venture. Seldom has a similar show received such a flattering send-off and those responsible, one may be sure, will make it their business not only to retain but to deepen the impressions produced by the initial performance. The house was crowded in every part and as the scenes were unfolded – each seemingly more dazzling and enchanting than the one which had gone before – there was great enthusiasm, which Mr Wyndham had frequently to acknowledge. From a spectacular point of view nothing more attractive has been seen on the stage. It may be doubted whether any similar production in Glasgow, or even in London, was ever staged on a more lavish scale. The principal comedians are Mr Harry Lauder and Mr Dan Crawley, to whom much of the success is due. The pantomime will be produced until further notice. (*Glasgow Herald*)

During this run, Harry Lauder introduced a new song to audiences entitled 'I Love a Lassie', which became one of his trademark songs.

DECEMBER 8TH

1641: 'Regarding transporting men for Ireland. This day, my Lord Marquis of Argyll exhibits, in presence of the council, a commission from the secret council, regarding the transporting of 5,000 men to Ireland, and to provide boat and small ships for their transport. After reasoning, it is thought fitting that the cost of ferrying of each soldier be 30 schillings, and that each person, both of soldiers and boatmen, have six schillings in the day for victualls during the time they are at sea, to be paid by the public, and some proportion to be advanced before they go aboard. To agree with such boats for transport that it may be lawful for them to return back when they have discharged their companies at Ireland, and that each boat be in readiness at a port, within 48 hours, as they shall be required, and that each boat get half the fare before their going away, and the rest when they come to Ireland.' (*Memorabilia of the City of Glasgow*)

DECEMBER 9TH

1836: 'A Flesh Shop to Let. At the populous and daily increasing village of Maryhill, near Glasgow. A flesh shop, with slaughter-house under it and other conveniences attached, with the goodwill of the business which has been established for more than nine years. Such an opening for a person of experience and capital is rarely to be met with. Apply to David Thomson, Maryhill.' (*Glasgow Herald*)

———•◆•———

1911: 'Glasgow Bills. Extension Order Approved. The Provisional Order for the extension of the city boundaries was discussed and approved yesterday at a private meeting of Glasgow Corporation. Lord Provost D M Stevenson presided over the meeting, which was largely attended. The bill provides for the inclusion within the city of the burghs of Govan, Partick, Pollokshaws and Rutherglen and of a certain area of territory at present within the counties of Lanark, Renfrew and Dumbarton. With some slight modification in the boundaries of the area proposed to be acquired, the proposals of the Parliamentary Bills Committee are practically identical with the scheme in the Order as originally drafted. After discussion the motion to approve the Order was carried by 57 votes to 5. One member declined to vote.' (*Glasgow Herald*)

DECEMBER 10TH

1928: On this day the architect, designer and artist Charles Rennie Mackintosh died aged sixty. 'Toshie' was part of the 'The Four' group along with his wife, the artist Margaret Macdonald Mackintosh, her sister Frances Macdonald, and designer Herbert McNair. Mackintosh designed the Glasgow Herald's 'Lighthouse' building extension, the Martyr's School, the Glasgow School of Art (commonly regarded as his finest work), Kate Cranston's Tea Rooms, and the Hill House in Helensburgh for the publisher Walter Blackie. He also designed the Queen's Cross Church, the only church design of his to be built, which was completed in 1899. Mackintosh was not able to sustain his career north of the border and moved south, to Suffolk. While there in 1914 he was arrested for suspected spying during the First World War, the police confusing his Glasgow accent with German. The couple moved to London, then spent four years in the south of France for financial reasons where Mackintosh painted watercolours. They returned to Britain to stay in London, where Mackintosh died of cancer. His work experienced a revival of interest in the latter part of the twentieth century and featured in calendars, art reproductions, mousemats and other products. Some of the derivative works were termed 'Mockintosh'.

December 11th

1766: 'The magistrates having received information that some of the inhabitants keep in their shops and cellars within the burgh, considerable quantities of gunpowder, from which the most fatal consequences may ensue, hereby order all persons who have gunpowder in their shops, cellars, or other repositories within the city, immediately to carry and lodge the same in the common magazine for powder, at the Castle of Glasgow. If any gunpowder, exceeding six pounds weight, shall be found in the shops, cellars, or other repositories, of any of the inhabitants within this burgh, the proprietors of such powder shall be fined and punished in terms of law. Any persons who inform shall receive a reward of ten shillings from the magistrates, upon conviction of the offender.' (*Glasgow Journal*)

1866: The *Glasgow Herald* paid tribute to 'a well-known and much respected' figure:

> Death of Mr Robert Wylie. Mr Wylie was born in the East End, sixty eight years ago, and spent all his life in his native place. Along with Mr Lochhead, he started in business as an upholsterer and funeral undertaker in Trongate in 1830, and by dint of hard labour, great perseverance, and shrewd business tact, he formed one of the largest businesses of the kind in Scotland.

The business was taken over by the House of Fraser in 1957.

DECEMBER 12TH

1715: 'The town council appoints the magistrates to write to his grace the Duke of Argyle that his grace would be pleased to give orders for removing of the 353 rebel prisoners who are lying on the town's hand, and in custody in the castle prison, and easing of the town of the burden of them and of their maintenance, in respect the militia who formerly guarded them are now gone home, which now lies upon the town; and that besides the other guards, which are very numerous, these prisoners require a guard of about one hundred men always upon them, without which they might have opportunity to escape, which very much weakens the town, and disables the town to make that opposition which otherwise the town might make in case of an attack, and also exposes the town to be attacked by the enemy in order to the relief of the prisoners.' (*Sketch of the History of Glasgow*)

———◆———

1872: This advertisement appeared in the *Glasgow Herald* this day:

> Nose Machine. A Contrivance which, applied to the Nose for an hour daily, directs the soft cartilage of which the member consists, that an ill-formed nose is quickly shaped to perfection. Anyone can use them. 10s 6d. Sent Free.

DECEMBER 13TH

1609: 'An Act of Parliament was dated this day which, among other benefits, gave the burgesses of Dumbarton the right of levying dues on all foreign vessels entering the Clyde and entitled them to demand that every vessel coming within their limits should break bulk at the quay and give the inhabitants the first offer of their merchandise. These invidious privileges were subsequently the cause of many heart-burnings and disputes between the burghers of Glasgow and Dumbarton. Ultimately the difference was settled in 1700 by a contract entered into between the contending parties by which in consideration of having received 4,500 merks Scots, the Dumbarton authorities gave up the right of levying the aforesaid dues, and the contractors mutually agreed that vessels belonging to inhabitants of Glasgow and Port Glasgow should not pay dues at the harbour of Dumbarton, and on the other hand that vessels belonging to burgesses of Dumbarton should have an equal exemption at the harbours of Glasgow and Port Glasgow. This contract was confirmed by Act of Parliament in 1701.' (*Days at the coast: a series of sketches descriptive of the Firth of Clyde – its watering-places, its scenery, and its associations* by Hugh MacDonald, 1860)

DECEMBER 14TH

1896: The *Glasgow Herald* reported on the opening of the Glasgow Subway, which took place on this day:

> For weeks previously private trials of the cars had been made with thoroughly satisfactory results. The first train left Govan Cross at 5 o'clock in the morning, running by way of Partick, a second leaving Copland Road and running by way of Kinning Park. The early cars were largely taken advantage of by workmen, and from 8 to 10 o'clock there was a great rush of all classes, the various outlying stations especially being fairly besieged. Despite this fact, the cars ran with almost perfect regularity, and the officials were beginning to congratulate themselves on the success of the inauguration. Unfortunately, however, there was a complete breakdown on the outer circle between 3 and 4 o'clock in the afternoon. Where the cars stopped in the tunnels a good deal of inconvenience was caused to passengers, who had to get out and walk along the line to the nearest station. Fortunately, as far as can be ascertained, no one sustained any injury.

December 15th

1660: 'This said day, for as much as John Wright, merchant in Edinburgh, being indebted to his sister, the sum of a hundred and six marks, because she remains within this burgh and is born therein, and a pupil, not able nor in capacity to give a discharge thereof, and that she is sick and so likely the town to be burdened with her, it was resolved that the town should take it in and delivered it to the town treasurer and the annual rent to be bestowed on the said sister, or as much of the principal as she shall stand in need of and therefore they bind and oblige them and their successors in office to warrant and relieve the said John Wright at the hands of his sister and of all cost and expenses he can incur and ordains the treasurer to be charged therewith.' (*Memorabilia of the City of Glasgow*)

DECEMBER 16TH

1831: 'Melancholy Accident. On Wednesday night, the boat which carries the workers from the cotton factory of Messrs John Sommerville & Sons to the town was stationed at the quay on the south side of the Clyde. At about a quarter to eight the people arrived and an imprudent rush was made into the boat as had been too frequently the practice before, in order to get over first. About twenty persons had got into the boat, when five others stepped on the gunwale at once, which gave a lurch to one side, and made those on board swing in the same direction, when the boat swamped, and all the passengers were thrown into the water. The cries of the sufferers at this time were loud and most pitiful, but fortunately there were three individuals on board who did not lose their presence of mind in the least, to whom most of the females clung and were got safe ashore. We are sorry to say however that three young women, two of them sisters, were drowned. We trust that this accident will have the effect of teaching the survivors to be more cautious. They had been repeatedly checked for their levity and imprudence, in going and coming in the boats.' (*Glasgow Herald*)

DECEMBER 17TH

1947: The funeral of Will Fyffe took place on this day, at St Mary's Cathedral. He had died from injuries sustained in a fall from a window in his own hotel in St Andrews. He was recuperating from an operation on his ear. Fyffe, although born in Dundee, became famous world-wide for a song about another city. He told a story that the idea behind his famous song came from an encounter at Central Station. He asked a drunk man he met if he belonged to Glasgow, to which the man replied, 'At the moment, Glasgow belongs to me.' Fyffe starred in a number of films although it is his music-hall songs and characters he is chiefly remembered for. He once entered a 'Will Fyffe'-themed talent competition at the Glasgow Empire for a bet. And came second. He made five appearances in Royal Variety Performances in London, one of which in 1937, saw him top the bill in a line-up that included George Formby, Gracie Fields and Max Miller.

DECEMBER 18TH

1866: 'A general meeting of the Glasgow Ropemakers' Society was held. A statement was then made as to the dispute now pending between the workmen and their masters. The speaker said that no body of working men were more opposed to strike than the ropemakers of Glasgow and it was only when every other alternative had failed that they resorted to such a mode of action. About the latter end of November the employers intimated to their men that the wages would be reduced from 22s to 20s per week. The men offered to compromise the matter and accept 21s per week. This offer the masters refused so the men, rather than cause a strike, agreed to accept the reduction, but as soon as the men submitted, one of the masters brought a number of female ropespinners into his work. This infringement of the right of the trade the men could not stand, they remonstrated, but could get no satisfaction, so they suspended work, for they held that after serving seven years of an apprenticeship they had claims upon the trade which no employer for a selfish end had a right to infringe. It was a notorious fact that yarn spun by women was of a most inferior quality.' (*Glasgow Herald*)

DECEMBER 19TH

1775: Regulations and fees for the Sedan Chairmen in Glasgow, as established by the magistrates and council of Glasgow, by their Act dated this day:

Every lift of a sedan chair in town, though ever so short a distance – *6d*;

From the Saracen's Head to the Wyndhead or High Church – *9d*;

From the Saracen's Head Inn to the Playhouse and Grahamston – *9d*;

From the Black Bull Inn to the Saracen's Head Inn – *6d*;

From the Trongate Street to the Wyndhead or High Church – *9d*;

From the Cross of Glasgow to any place in Gorbals – *1s*;

From any place above Bell's Wynd, and below the College, to the Calton – *9d*;

From Jamaica Street to the Cross, or the like distance – *6d*;

For every hour a chair waits (when not engaged for forenoon or afternoon) besides ordinary dues – *6d*;

For a chair attending from three to four oclock afternoon till eleven at night – *2s*;

To a chair hire for a whole day – *4s*;

To a chair hire for a week £1 *1s*.

(*Old Glasgow and its Environs*)

DECEMBER 20TH

1852: These advertisements appeared in the *Glasgow Herald*:

This day is published, small 8 vo, pp 128, cloth 1s 6d, cloth extra, gilt edges 2s: *The Theatre: Its Pernicious Tendency Addressed to Young Men*. Be not deceived: evil communications corrupt good manners by William Keddie, Esq. This work is published in the hope of providing young men with an antidote to the seductive influences with which they are plied in certain quarters, under the specious guise of Dramatic Reform, for the purpose of inducing them to frequent the Theatre. The writer has been at pains to enrich his pages with the opinions of eminent authors, both friendly and adverse to histrionic entertainments, as to the demoralizing tendency of the Stage.

Now published and on sale by the subscriber, price 2d per dozen and 1s per 100. *A Happy New Year* by the Reverend Thomas Guthrie, DD, issued by the Scottish Association for Suppressing Drunkenness. James R MacNair, 19 Glassford St.

To Be Disposed of Cheap. A first-class street lamp, 6 feet high, of a new and unique design. Apply to David Ramsay, 104 New City Road.

DECEMBER 21ST

1899: 'Yesterday Sir James King formally opened the new premises of the Glasgow School of Art which have been erected in Renfrew Street. Lord Provost Chisholm presided over a large gathering. Sir Francis Powell proposed a vote of thanks to Sir James King. Sir John Neilson Cuthbertson, in proposing a vote of thanks to the teaching staff, gave some interesting facts regarding the progress of the school during the last 10 years.' (*Glasgow Herald*)

———◆———

1908: 'A terrible murder was perpetrated in a dwelling-house at 15 Queen's Terrace, the victim being Miss Marion Gilchrist, 82 years of age, a lady of considerable wealth, who lived alone with one maid servant. The maid servant was absent from the house from five to ten minutes only, having gone to purchase an evening newspaper and from what can be gathered the lady was murdered in the interval by an unknown man, who escaped. The deceased was found with her skull battered in lying in the dining room on the hearth rug. The head was mutilated almost beyond recognition. Two men were arrested in connection with the affair.' (*Glasgow Herald*)

Oscar Slater was convicted of the murder, although doubts were expressed, expecially by Arthur Conan Doyle. Slater was eventually freed after spending nineteen years in Peterhead Prison.

DECEMBER 22ND

1794: 'On this day a soldier of the first battalion of the Breadalbane Fencible Regiment, now quartered in this city, having been confined in the guard-house upon an accusation of having been guilty of a military offence, a party of the regiment, with muskets and fixed bayonets, assembled round the guard-house, and obliged their officers to set him at liberty after committing this outrage, they behaved quietly and peaceably, though the spirit of mutiny still subsisted to such a degree, that the private soldiers would not agree to give up the soldier who had been released nor the ring-leaders in the mutiny, to be tried for their crimes.

In January 1795 the Court Martial met in the Castle of Edinburgh for the trial of the soldiers for mutiny. Four have received sentence of death and four sentenced to corporal punishment. On 27th January the four under sentence of death were taken out of the Castle and conveyed in two mourning coaches, to a field about two miles from town, where they were to be shot, but three of them were pardoned, and one who had deserted and likewise been among the mutineers was shot.'
(Broadside regarding Highland soldiers and their Mutiny in Glasgow, 1795, National Library of Scotland Rare Books Collection, shelfmark: APS.4.84.20)

DECEMBER 23RD

1902: 'The superintendent reported to the Cleansing Committee that an explosion had occurred in one of the furnaces at Kelvinhaugh through some explosive material being deposited among the city refuse and the committee, having regard to the serious nature of the occurrence and the danger to which the employees of the Department were thereby exposed, agreed to recommend that the superintendent be instructed to communicate with the Chief Constable and otherwise take steps as he might deem necessary, with the view of preventing the inhabitants in future from placing such explosives among the city refuse. Mr Brechin called attention to this and expressed the hope that in future the citzens would be careful not to put any explosive substance into the refuse as it was dangerous to the men involved. Mr O'Hare said this was confined to the West End and he hoped the people there would pay a little more attention to that. This was the third time a similar occurrence had taken place.' (*Glasgow Herald*)

DECEMBER 24TH

1660: 'This said day it being found that [illegible] Douglas was formerly appointed to remove himself off the town, which he has not obeyed, and is burnt on the cheek and is known to be an idle vagabond, without any lawful calling. He is therefore hereby ordained to remove off the town and that within ten days and not to return hereafter, under the punishment of scourging him through the town and banishing from this burgh.' (*Memorabilia of the City of Glasgow*)

———— • ◆ • ————

1660: 'This said day ordains the treasurer to have a warrant for the sum of a hundred marks Scots, paid by him to James Cors, mathematician, for his better encouragement and help, and for ten dollars paid by him to the man in Edinburgh who keeps correspondence with the town.' (*Memorabilia of the City of Glasgow*)

———— • ◆ • ————

1914: 'The new military hospital at Springburn received its first contingent of wounded soldiers early this morning. The party, which number 100, arrived at the Central Station from Southampton shortly after midnight and were taken to the hospital in motor cars provided by the Red Cross Society and the St Andrew's Ambulance Association. All the soldiers came from the region of Ypres and 25 were stretcher cases. The hospital has been provided by the North British Locomotive Company at their works in Springburn.' (*Glasgow Herald*)

DECEMBER 25TH

1745: 'The first body of Bonnie Prince Charlie's forces entered Glasgow on Christmas Day and on the following morning he himself came up with the remainder. Their clothes were in a most dilapidated condition. The length and precipitation of their late march had destroyed their brogues and many of them were not only bare footed but bare legged. Their hair hung wildly over their eyes their beards were grown to a fearful length and the exposed parts of their limbs were in the language of Dougal Graham, the poetical historian of the Rebellion and one of our own citizens, tanned quite red with the weather. Altogether they had a way worn savage appearance and looked rather like a band of outlandish vagrants than a body of efficient soldiery. Immediately upon his arrival in the city, Charles took measures for the complete refitting of his army by ordering the magistrates to provide 12,000 shirts, 6,000 cloth coats, 6,000 pair of shoes, 6,000 pair of stockings, 6,000 waistcoats, and 6,000 bonnets. The city was later compensated by Parliament for the sum of £10,000.' (*Chronicles of Saint Mungo: or, Antiquities and Traditions of Glasgow,* 1843)

DECEMBER 26TH

1583: 'Five persons were adjudged to make public repentance because they kept the superstitious day of Yule, or Christmas, and the baxters (bakers) were ordered to be inquired at when they baked Yule bread.' (*Kirk-Session records*)

1998: On this day a severe storm hit Glasgow. Winds of 93mph were recorded. The most visible structural damage was – appropriately on St Stephen's Day – St Stephen's Church in Bath Street, where a large part of the spire was sent crashing down onto the church's roof. It cost £3 million to rectify and the church reopened in 2001.

1588: 'The magistrates, considering the manifold blasphemies and evil words spoken by sundry women, direct the master of works to erect jugs, three or four steps up, that they may not be torn down. The town-council enacted that no market be kept on Sundays, and that persons blaspheming and swearing shall be punished according to law. Walter Prior of Blantyre, tacksman of the teinds of the parsonage of Glasgow, provided the elements for the communion, he was spoken to, to provide a hogshead of good wine. The time of convening on the Sundays of the communion was four o'clock in the morning.' (*The New Statistical Account of Scotland*, 1845)

DECEMBER 27TH

1790: 'The Magistrates, by an advertisement in the *Glasgow Mercury*, require all the male householders, citizens, and inhabitants, under the age of 60 and above 18, whose yearly rents are £3 sterling, to the number of 30, every night as they shall be warned by an officer, to repair to the Laigh Council Chamber at ten o'clock at night, and to continue on guard and patrol till next morning, subject to such orders as shall be given by the Magistrates.' (*Glasgow Advertiser*)

1793: 'On Tuesday morning, David Donald, smith and edge tool maker at Carmyle, was found dead within a few yards of his own door. He was a man of great natural genius and supposed to be the best temperer of iron in Scotland, perhaps in Britain, as no spades, shovels, axes, etc would sell in America from any part of England, when put in competition with his. The manner of his death is very melancholy. He was in a public house and having drank too freely, unfortunately tumbled into a hole and was unable to extricate himelf.' (*Glasgow Advertiser*)

DECEMBER 28TH

1928: 'Glasgow Man Carried Into Court. A legless man named Francis Kyle (sixty-three) was fined £30, with the alternative of sixty days imprisonment, at the Western Police Court for having conducted a shebeen at 84 Clyde Ferry Street. Kyle was carried into the dock on a chair by two constables. Superintendent McClure explained that the house was elaborately equipped as a shebeen and he characterised the accused as a "notorious shebeener".' (*Glasgow Herald*)

———— • ◆ • ————

1928: 'Theft of Sweet Machines. The prevalence of the theft of small automatic sweet machines from shop doorways was commented on at the Southern Police Court when three young men were convicted of having stolen one of these machines from premises in Govan Street early on Christmas morning. Within the past two months no fewer than 115 cases had been reported to the police. It was usually found that the culprits unscrewed the machines from the doorways and carried them into a neighbouring close where they forced open the money drawer and removed the contents, leaving the machines behind them. Commenting on the fact that the machines were small and light, Bailie Doherty suggested that it would be better if the owners placed their goods in large machines such as were in use for cigarettes.' (*Glasgow Herald*)

December 29th

1664: 'This said day, in answer to the supplication given in by Thomas Monteur, goldsmith, showing that he had served his apprenticeship in Aberdeen, and that since then he had served four years as a journeyman in Edinburgh, and that now he was attained to be a perfect craftsman, and was intentioned to transport himself to this burgh and take up one booth therein, the town making him burgess and guild brother, for his better encouragement. It was concluded that as soon as he takes up a booth, and settles himself here, he shall be made burgess without payment of any fee, and it to be held as paid, that the benefit thereof may return to him and his children and also it is promised, upon his good behaviour, he shall thereafter be admitted guild brother.' (*Memorabilia of the City of Glasgow*)

1696: 'Appoints the treasurer to pay to John Corse, late Baillie, the sum of seventy five pounds eight schilling Scots, as the price of the lamp now affixed to the corner of the Tolbooth, and cost of transportation and expenses of bringing the same from London.' (*Memorabilia of the City of Glasgow*)

1995: Glasgow's lowest-ever temperature was recorded. The temperature reached minus 20 degrees Celsius during the evening. The maximum temperature on this day was minus 12 degrees. (*Met Office*)

DECEMBER 30TH

1916: 'The New Year – The Holiday Restrictions. The equanimity with which the curtailment of the New Year holidays, which begin today in Glasgow, is being accepted may be taken as significant of the change in spirit which another year of war has brought about in the community, particularly among the Clyde workmen. When the precedent of limiting the holidays to three or four days, instead of ten days which were allowed in normal times, was introduced a year ago there was a good deal of grumbling and of criticism as to the necessity or the wisdom of imposing such a restriction. On this occasion nothing of this kind is heard. The curtailment is accepted without question and, generally speaking, the sacrifice is being faced with the best possible grace.'

1916: 'Whisky for the holidays – Queues of women purchasers. The restrictions on the liquor trade have tended to bring into prominence the eagerness of a section of the public for week-end supplies of drink. Yesterday afternoon was the last opportunity of the purchase of bottled whisky and the number who formed in queues outside the shops were even larger than on the previous day. A feature of the queues was again the large proportion of women, a number of whom were accompanied by children.' (*Glasgow Herald*)

DECEMBER 31ST

1815: 'In the Royal Infirmary on this day there were 152 patients. During the previous 12 months 1,340 people had been admitted. Records were kept and each was placed into the following categories: Cured – 779; Convalescent – 80; Relieved – 164; Advice – 46; Desire – 114; Improper – 1; Incurable – 23; Irregular – 18; Remitted – 19; Dead – 96. In the course of the year, 56 operations have been performed, many of them of a difficult and delicate nature. Since the opening of the Infirmary in 1794, 16,396 patients have been received: 11,104 of whom have been cured, and a large number of the residue relieved. During the period of 21 years, more than 40,000 out-door patients have received gratuitous advice.' (*Annals of Glasgow*)

———— • ◆ • ————

1938: 'A new plan for the public celebrations of Hogmanay has been devised by the Lord Provost. He proposes that the traditional gathering for bringing in the new year should meet not at Glasgow Cross, as has been the custom in the past, but at the more central Glasgow Square. It was his hope that the gathering at George Square would prove at once more dignified and more attractive than the celebrations of the past. The square will be brilliantly illuminated. Anti-aircraft searchlights are to be used in addition to the floodlighting at the City Chambers.' (*Glasgow Herald*)

Sources

The following are abbreviated for space in the text, others are credited where appropriate:

❧ *Sketch of the History of Glasgow* by James Pagan, 1847

❧ *Annals of Glasgow Comprising an Account of the Public Buildings, Charities, and the Rise and Progress of the City* Volume 1 and Volume 2 by James Cleland, 1816

❧ *Glasgow and its Clubs: or Glimpses of the Condition, Manners, Characters, & Oddities of the City, During the Past & Present Centuries* by John Strang, 1864

❧ *The History of Glasgow, From the Earliest Accounts to the Present with an Account of the Rise, Progress, and Present State, of the Different Branches of Commerce and Manufactures Now Carried on in the City of Glasgow* by John Gibson, 1777

❧ *The Picture of Glasgow* by Robert Chapman, 1820

❧ *Glasgow: Past and Present: Illustrated in Dean of Guild Court Reports and in the Reminiscences and Communications of Senex, Aliquis, Jb, Etc.*, 1884

❧ *Old Glasgow and its Environs, Historical and Topographical* by Senex (Robert Reid), 1864

❧ *Memorabilia of the City of Glasgow: Selected from the Minute Books of the Burgh* by James Hill and John Smith, 1835

Acknowledgements

The author would like to thank the following for their help: Moira Rankin and Claire Daniel, Duty Archivists, Archive Services, University of Glasgow; Dr Graham Hogg, Senior Curator, Rare Book Collections, National Library of Scotland; Helen Shearer, Christine McGilly, Catherine Queen from Media Resources, Herald & Times; Patricia Grant, Principal Librarian: Family History and Local History, Glasgow Life/Glasgow Libraries; Glasgow Humane Society http://www.glasgowhumanesociety.com. Thanks also go to Fran Cantillion and Emily Locke at The History Press. Very special thanks go to M-CK for her support and encouragement.